When Middle-Class Parents
Choose Urban Schools

When Middle-Class Parents Choose Urban Schools

Class, Race, and the Challenge of Equity in Public Education

LINN POSEY-MADDOX

The University of Chicago Press
Chicago and London

Linn Posey-Maddox is assistant professor of educational policy studies at the University of Wisconsin–Madison.

The University of Chicago Press, Chicago 60637
The University of Chicago Press, Ltd., London
© 2014 by The University of Chicago
All rights reserved. Published 2014.
Printed in the United States of America

23 22 21 20 19 18 17 16 15 14   1 2 3 4 5

ISBN-13: 978-0-226-12018-8 (cloth)
ISBN-13: 978-0-226-12021-8 (paper)
ISBN-13: 978-0-226-12035-5 (e-book)
DOI: 10.7208/chicago/9780226120355.001.0001

An earlier version of chapter 3 was previously published in *Teacher's College Record*. An earlier version of chapter 5 was previously published in the *American Journal of Education*.

Library of Congress Cataloging-in-Publication Data

Posey-Maddox, Linn, author.
    When middle-class parents choose urban schools : class, race, and the challenge of equity in public education / Linn Posey-Maddox.
        pages ; cm
Includes bibliographical references and index.
    ISBN 978-0-226-12018-8 (cloth : alkaline paper)—ISBN 978-0-226-12021-8 (paperback : alkaline paper)—ISBN 978-0-226-12035-5 (e-book)   1. Urban schools—Social aspects—United States.   2. Middle class—Education—United States.   3. Public schools—United States.   4. Education—Parent participation—United States.   5. School management and organization—Parent participation—United States.   6. Community and school—United States.   7. Discrimination in education—United States.   8. Segregation in education—United States.   I. Title.
    LC5131.P68 2014
    371.009173'2—dc23

                                                                    2013027589

♾ This paper meets the requirements of ANSI/NISO Z39.48-1992
(Permanence of Paper).

CONTENTS

ILLUSTRATIONS AND TABLES

FIGURES

TABLES

ACKNOWLEDGMENTS

First and foremost I owe a big thanks to all the Morningside parents, teachers, staff, and community members who shared their insights and time with me. It was truly an honor to listen to and learn from each and every one of you. Thank you also to all the Morningside students, past and present—you, as well as all the other elementary students I've worked with over the years, serve as the inspiration and motivation for this project.

I feel blessed to have had such a large community of academic support during my graduate studies at the University of California, Berkeley. Ingrid Seyer-Ochi, Daniel Perlstein, and Sandra S. Smith—my dissertation committee members—each pushed me to dig deeper and ask critical questions while providing guidance and mentorship throughout my academic journey as a PhD student. I was also incredibly fortunate to have friends who provided valuable feedback, insight, and support throughout our time together as graduate students: Becky Alexander, Liz Boner, Loan Dao, Ligaya Domingo, Erica Kohl-Arenas, Genevieve Negron-Gonzales, and Hodari Toure. Thanks also to my colleagues at the Center for Cities and Schools: Deborah McKoy, Jeff Vincent, and Ariel Bierbaum. Our many conversations and my work as part of the center's team helped to mold my thinking about the city-school nexus.

This project would not have been possible had it not been for the financial support I received from the Spencer Foundation and Ford Foundation. In addition to the financial assistance, I am grateful for the professional development opportunities that these fellowships provided, as well as the opportunity to meet so many brilliant scholars across the country. The feedback I received on the project from senior scholars at the Spencer retreat—scholars such as Bill Ayers, Pauline Lipman, Mary Pattillo, and David Stovall—was invaluable.

I am grateful for all the mentorship and support I have received in my scholarly pursuits as a faculty member at the University of Wisconsin, Madison. My colleagues in the Department of Educational Policy Studies are gems. I owe a big thanks to Bianca Baldridge, Christy Clark-Pujara, Sara Goldrick-Rab, Beth Graue, Aida Hussen, Stacey Lee, Keisha Lindsay, Mary Metz, Mike Olneck, and Erica Turner for reading and providing feedback on different parts of the book manuscript.

I've been blessed to have a number of individuals who have helped to push my thinking. Maia Cucchiara and Shelley Kimelberg, this book has been strengthened by our many conversations and collaborations. Erin Mc-Namara Horvat, I can't thank you enough for all of your helpful, detailed feedback on the manuscript. Thanks as well to several other individuals who read and offered feedback on specific chapters of the manuscript, particularly in the final hour: May Hara, Nicole Peterson, Kate Phillippo, and Aina Stunz. The two anonymous reviewers for the press, as well as my wonderful editor, Elizabeth Branch Dyson, also provided supportive and targeted feedback that helped me to strengthen the manuscript and make its contributions clearer. Thanks also to Russell Damian and the staff at the University of Chicago Press for making the submisssion and publication process so smooth.

I also want to thank all of my friends and family members who helped me to keep things in perspective throughout the book-writing process and served as great reminders that there is indeed life outside academia. A big thanks to my writing buddies for cheering me along the way and reminding me of the importance of self-care and balance on the tenure track: Leisy Abrego, Alicia Bonaparte, Roxanne Donovan, Kerry Ann Rockquemore, and Diane Yoder. Thank you also to Dawn Collins, Tanya Deryugina, Natasha Hartmann, and Kate McGinnity for the many "check-ins" and the continual support.

My family has been a constant source of support and inspiration for me. My best friend, Natasha Burrowes, has been a patient listener throughout my academic journey and has served as a great sounding board for my ideas. My mom, Mary Linn Posey, taught me what it means to be a good teacher and to persevere with undefeatable optimism when faced with challenges. To my father, Monte B. Posey, thank you for all the history lessons and words of wisdom you've given me over the years. Thanks as well to my extended family: Yvette and Ronald Weekes, and Raphael and Zenoviaf Maddox. And last but certainly not least, a big thank you to my husband and to my stepson for all the laughter, love, and great adventures. Quinton, know that our family game nights and art projects helped me to stay grounded throughout the book-writing process. Dwayne, thank you for all your patience, humor, home-cooked meals, and reminders of what's most important. I am truly blessed to have you in my life.

ONE

Middle-Class Parents and City School Transformation

Mr. Foster and I were sitting together in Morningside Elementary's court-yard, talking about the large number of people he expected to attend the Open House for prospective kindergartner families that was scheduled for that night.[1] Blooming flowers and colorful student artwork surrounded us. Mr. Foster, a veteran teacher at Morningside, described the positive atten-tion that the school had received in recent years—attention that was un-common given the historically bad press and low status associated with many schools in Woodbury Unified School District. He remarked that the district superintendent and several administrators from a neighboring district had just visited the school, and he exclaimed, "Since when does the superintendent and [neighboring] school district come to check out a Woodbury public school?" Morningside, a small public elementary school in a large urban district in Northern California, was now on the radar of many middle-class parents and community members in Woodbury and was described on one regional parent website as "an urban jewel."

Mr. Foster had witnessed considerable changes at the school over the past decade. When he started teaching at Morningside in the mid-1990s, Morn-ingside's demographics did not match those of the predominantly white middle- and upper-middle-class neighborhood surrounding the school. Many neighborhood parents sought out other schooling options or left the neighborhood altogether rather than enroll their children in the predomi-nantly African American, Title I school.[2] This was despite the fact that Morn-ingside's test scores were historically higher than those of other schools in the state with similar student demographics, and the school had a small but committed group of parents and school staff working to strengthen and ex-pand the school's academic and enrichment programs.

Yet when I spoke with Mr. Foster that day, Morningside was challenged to find space to accommodate the large number of students from both the neighborhood and other parts of the city who sought admittance. The school had a waiting list of students for its kindergarten classes, and the student demographics had steadily shifted as increased numbers of white and mixed-race middle- and upper-middle-class children enrolled in the school. Morningside's academic and enrichment programs had expanded to include integrated art and gardening programs, Spanish for all students, a salad-bar lunch program, and extensive community partnerships—all funded in large part from parent and teacher grant writing and a parent-teacher organization budget of well over $100,000. The school was high-lighted in local media and parent websites, with its recent transformation attributed in large part to Morningside's active parent community.

For those concerned with segregation and inequality in public school-ing, Morningside is an intriguing case. Here were middle- and upper-middle-class parents—and white parents in particular—voluntarily enrolling their children in a Title I city school with a majority of students of color, absent a district mandate or desegregation program. And many of these parents were not just enrolling their children in Morningside but also contributing their time and financial resources to the school. These trends run counter to dominant patterns of white and middle-class flight to more elite city or suburban schools. Given the erosion of and resistance to desegrega-tion programs in many US districts, the enrollment, organizing, and in-vestments of middle- and upper-middle-class parents at Morningside and elsewhere can be viewed as a new and promising avenue for urban school change. Indeed, laudatory accounts of the movement of the middle class into predominantly low-income or socioeconomically mixed city schools are increasingly common, with these parents praised for their volunteer-ism and efforts to integrate and improve their local public schools (see, e.g., Edelberg and Kurland 2011; Graham 2010; Petrilli 2012). As Michael Petrilli, author of *The Diverse Schools Dilemma*, remarked in an article about middle-class parents and city schools, "All we can say at this point is that this provides the best opportunity in a generation for us to integrate our urban schools" (Toppo 2012).

Yet, as I illustrate in this book, there are significant costs to relying upon middle-class parents as major drivers of urban school transformation. A school reform strategy that depends upon middle-class parents—without policies and efforts to ensure that low-income families also participate in and benefit from school change—is bad practice for two reasons. First, middle-class engagement, when unfettered, is likely to create new patterns of educational inequality and exclusion in districts and schools, often despite the best intentions of individual parents. Second, focusing on parent volunteerism and investments in urban education unfairly shifts the onus of responsibility for high-quality schooling from the government to individuals, with parents compelled to fill budgetary and resource gaps in order to ensure that things like art, music, and physical education are a part of their children's education.

To be clear, I am not saying that middle-class volunteerism and engagement are inherently bad. Indeed, as I show in the following chapters, there were middle-class parents who devoted countless hours of their time to support Morningside's collective student body and who helped to bring new and important educational resources and opportunities to the school. Rather, what I'm arguing is that the individual choices and engagement of parents (and of middle-class parents in particular) should not be treated as a substitute for the more structural reforms necessary to improve city public schools—reforms I discuss in the concluding chapter.

The arguments I make here are based upon more than two years of ethnographic research in and around Morningside Elementary, a small public school in Northern California impacted by significant demographic change. In my study of Morningside, I examine the role of middle-class parents—and particularly, but not exclusively, white middle-class parents—in urban school change efforts.[3] Specifically, I examine the following questions: What motivates middle- and upper-middle-class parents to consider the school? How do parents and teachers in the school community understand and respond to these parents' engagement?[4] What are the equity implications of middle-class parents' efforts to support and invest in urban schooling?[5]

Most studies of urban education have focused on low-income students of color, examining underresourced schools and "underperforming" students. Yet many urban areas, and urban schools, are changing due to demographic and economic shifts in cities and metropolitan regions, prompting the need for more nuanced conceptions of "urban" educational issues. Whereas changes like those occurring at Morningside were once an anomaly in the landscape of urban schooling, recent examples suggest that they are becoming increasingly common in cities across the nation as greater numbers of middle- and upper-middle-class families consider sending their children to local public elementary schools (Billingham and Kimelberg 2013; Cucchiara 2013b; Edelberg and Kurland 2011; Jan 2006; Rogers 2009; Smith 2009; Stillman 2012). Examining the role of middle-class parents in urban school change is thus both important and timely, as many civic and educational leaders seek to attract and retain middle-class families (and white families in particular) in central cities and their public schools (CEOs for Cities, n.d.; Cucchiara 2013b; Lipman 2011). For districts and schools facing dramatic budget cuts, the engagement and investments of middle-class parents are increasingly relied upon in public school reform—with funds raised by parents used for teacher salaries and academic programs in some districts (Calvert 2011; Koumpilova 2011). In-depth examinations of middle-class parental engagement in city schools are needed to uncover the consequences of using middle-class parental engagement as a reform strategy in urban education.

This book is a story about resource gaps in urban education and the limitations of relying upon middle-class parents to fill these gaps. Middle-class parents helped to garner or sustain many academic and extracurricular programs and resources at Morningside, and many of these resources benefited the collective student body. Yet these parents' fund-raising, volunteerism, and outreach to families of similar race and class backgrounds also contributed to the marginalization and exclusion of low-income and working-class families. The increased professionalization of the Morningside Parent-Teacher Organization helped to garner more funds for the school; however, the creation of positions requiring specialized skills and the expansion of fund-raising efforts changed the norms and structure of the organization in ways that privileged middle-class forms of parental engagement.

The following chapters demonstrate the limitations of relying on middle-class parents to fill the resource gaps left by state and local governments. When teacher salaries and curricular programs like Spanish and music are supported in large part by individual parent donations and fund-raising, parents who solicit or provide these funds may wield greater decision-making power within our public schools. The extant research on middle-class parental engagement in urban public schooling suggests that middle-class parents often intervene in ways that benefit their own children rather than the low-income and working-class students and their families in a particular school or classroom context (see, e.g., Cucchiara 2013b; McGhee Hassrick and Schneider 2009; Sieber 1982). This is not always the case, as some parents may have a "collective," rather than an individualistic, orientation (Cucchiara and Horvat 2009), and school staff or school policy structures may mediate parental efforts to secure advantages for their own children at the expense of others (I discuss this further in chapter 5). Yet depending upon parental fund-raising and volunteerism to support core school programs may create new avenues for middle-class parents to influence resource allocation decisions in school settings.

As I mentioned above, relying on the middle class to fill gaps in public dollars for education also unfairly positions parents as the primary drivers of school improvement. Rather than making changes in state and federal education policy that would reflect a greater commitment to public education, emphasis is placed on parents and teachers to provide the educational opportunities and material resources necessary to create and sustain high-quality educational experiences for students. This is a dangerous shift, as it works to absolve state and local governments of their responsibility to not only provide adequate funding for schools but also to ensure that educational funds and resources are distributed equitably in ways that do not disproportionately benefit the already advantaged.

Yet the story of change at Morningside is not simply about parental engagement and volunteerism: it is also a case through which to explore broader issues related to racial and economic integration and diversity in urban education. The majority of public school students in the United States attend racially and socioeconomically segregated schools, owing to a reversal of the gains in racial desegregation made after the *Brown v. Board of Education* decision (Orfield and Eaton 1996; Orfield, Kucsera, and Siegel-Hawley 2012). White students in particular are the most racially isolated group of public school students, with the typical white student attending a school in which three-quarters of his or her peers are white (Orfield, Kucsera, and Siegel-Hawley 2012). Resegregation post-*Brown* is particularly troubling, as school racial and socioeconomic demographics are commonly related to other indicators of school quality such as teacher experience and retention, facilities, and curricular materials (Orfield and Lee 2005). Creating racially and economically integrated schools is thus not simply about providing students with the opportunity to socialize and learn from peers from different racial and economic backgrounds; it is about demolishing entrenched patterns of advantage and disadvantage in public education. District desegregation policies alone do not guarantee full integration, as classes and student social groupings are often segregated *within* schools due to institutionalized systems of sorting and stratification (see, e.g., Noguera 2003; Olsen 1997; Tyson 2011). Producing fully integrated schools—rather than simply "diverse" or desegregated ones—is thus much more difficult, as racial integration requires group interactions on terms of equality and the full inclusion and participation of all races in all domains (Anderson 2010).

As I discuss in the following chapter, districts seeking to counter patterns of segregation in their local schools face significant challenges from recent legal decisions that make it difficult to use a student's race in school assignment plans. Although many districts have reverted to policies of neighborhood schooling or adopted unrestricted-choice plans, a growing number of districts concerned with the segregation of their schools have adopted economic integration plans as a more feasible strategy for school improvement in our current political and legal climate. At the time of this writing, eighty-three school districts and charter operators now employ student socioeconomic status as a factor in school assignment (Kahlenberg 2012). For many proponents of economic integration, the increased enrollment of middle-class students and the engagement of middle-class parents in city public schools are viewed as a positive turn in urban education on the basis of the assumption that middle-class parents bring with them various forms of capital that can benefit schools with low-income student populations. As Richard Kahlenberg, a prominent advocate for economic integration argues, "the economic integration strategy helps create in all schools the single most powerful predictor of a good education: the presence of a core of middle-class families who will insist upon, and get, a quality school for their children" (2001b, 1). For districts and schools pressured to raise test scores, creating middle-class schools is also seen as a way to promote student achievement and ensure school success under district, state, and federal accountability systems (Kahlenberg 2006).

I was intrigued by Morningside because it arguably represents a best-case scenario in the quest for integrated schools: it had a growing, racially mixed cadre of self-described progressive and liberal middle-class parents who not only donated their time and money to the school but also voiced commitments to diversity and to working for changes that would benefit the collective student body. Many of the white middle-class parents and teachers at the school voluntarily sought out Morningside *because* it was not a "suburban" school or one of the more elite and less socioeconomically diverse public schools in the district. Morningside was also a school that had low teacher turnover, strong administrative leadership, and a history of successfully educating African American and low-income students. Morningside thus provided an opportunity to explore a relatively new and less-studied process of economic integration: an integration driven in large part by *middle- and upper-middle-class parents* rather than district enrollment policies and practices.

Yet my data show that middle-class parents' efforts to support and improve Morningside ultimately threatened the racial and socioeconomic diversity that many of them desired in a school for their children and contributed to a process of school gentrification rather than a stable and sustainable integration. The school quickly gained in popularity among other middle-class families in the neighborhood and broader district, resulting in a boom in kindergarten enrollment. Within a span of five years, it became more and more difficult for children residing outside the largely middle-class neighborhood school attendance zone to enroll in Morningside, due to limited space and the priority that neighborhood families received in the district enrollment plan.

The demographic, social, and material changes that occurred at Morningside demonstrate some of the limitations of "diversity by choice." Economic and racial integration that occurs in the context of neighborhood schooling or unrestricted-choice models of student assignment—models that are increasingly popular in districts across the United States—may be fleeting and unsustainable over the long term in the absence of race- and class-conscious student assignment policies that work to counter patterns of residential segregation. As numerous studies have shown, unrestricted-choice student assignment plans end up privileging parents with the social, cultural, and economic capital to navigate enrollment processes and "work the system," in many cases exacerbating race- and class-based inequalities in access to high-quality public schools (Fuller, Elmore, and Orfield 1996; Roda and Wells 2013; Schneider, Teske, and Marschall 2002). This was true in the case of Morningside, as middle-class parents' social networks and various forms of capital—as well as the priority in enrollment many of them received for living in the school's neighborhood zone—made it more difficult for low-income students to enroll. Drawing from my follow-up research at Morningside two years after the original study, which showed that the school had become increasingly white and middle class, I build a case for district and school policy intervention to ensure that schools like Morningside remain accessible to low-income and working-class families of color. This book contributes to the literature on economic integration by challenging the assumption that having a core group of middle-class families—in and of itself— is the remedy for the issues facing low-income students and their school communities.

Lastly, this book is about the quest to create and sustain "good" urban public schools, and the role of middle-class parents in efforts to do so. By highlighting the voices and experiences of long-timer parents and teachers within a demographically shifting school context, the book challenges normative assumptions about quality schooling. The school characteristics that are commonly viewed by education reformers as indicators of improvement—rising test scores, competitive enrollment, and increased material resources—tell only one part of a larger story of change. A sole focus on these indicators overlooks the social contexts and histories of particular schools, often obscuring race and class-based inequalities in school change efforts. There is thus a need to understand the lived, everyday experiences of teachers and families as their school community changes; doing so can illuminate diverse perspectives and inequities that are often missed when the focus is on only dominant markers of school change.

This book discusses alternative ways of thinking about the role of middle-class parents in urban school transformation, ultimately calling for measures of progress in urban education that move beyond rising test scores and increased material resources. Rather than focusing solely on these technical and narrow indicators of progress, I demonstrate the need for urban school transformation efforts to be evaluated with respect to the goal of equitable developments in urban education (a concept I describe in greater detail later in this chapter). Doing so would require a focus not simply on outcomes like rising test scores but also on issues of access and opportunity as student populations begin to change. The case of Morningside illustrates how inequality and exclusion can occur in schools that, on the basis of rising test scores and expanded educational opportunities, appear to be improving. Yet it also highlights areas of promise in the efforts of parents and teachers to create racially and socioeconomically diverse *and* equitable public school communities.

Defining the Elusive "Middle Class"

Important to any discussion of middle-class parents is a clear understanding of what exactly is meant by "middle class." Defining social class can be complicated, however, and delineating what constitutes the middle class, in particular, is not a clear-cut task. Many Americans see themselves as middle class, despite a range of economic categories represented in this label.[6] Although there is no one agreed-on definition of class categories, most social scientists use a combination of income, occupation, and education as common markers of class status (Gilbert 2008; Thompson and Hickey 2005).

The theoretical insights of French sociologist Pierre Bourdieu provide a particularly useful framework for understanding social class and its influence on social inequalities in education. Bourdieu (1990, 1984) sees social class not simply as a position in society linked to income or occupation but as a set of relations shaped by social, cultural, and material/economic factors. Examining social class thus means taking into account not only material wealth but also the practices, dispositions, and attitudes of individuals and groups. Two individuals may have exactly the same income, for example, but have different levels of effectiveness in advocating for their children due to the extent that teachers and other institutional actors value their social and cultural resources.

Bourdieu sees class identities as constructed relationally, emerging through the mobilization of *both* material and symbolic resources. His central concern is with the stratification of social space, and he outlines multiple forms of capital—financial but also social, cultural, and symbolic—that individuals and groups utilize to maintain and enhance their position in the social order. The value attached to particular forms of capital depends on the particular institutional arena, or "field," in which an individual operates. Fields provide the "rules of the game," and individuals with a similar set of resources may differ in the skill with which they attempt to use their capital (Bourdieu 1977a; Lareau and Horvat 1999). Bourdieu's theoretical constructs are useful in examining family-school relationships because they highlight the social and cultural resources that parents may employ on behalf of their children, as well as the role of context and power in shaping which of these resources will be valued in a particular school setting.

In my analysis of the social and political dynamics occurring at Morningside, I take into consideration parents' income, education, and occupation while also examining the relational aspects of class. I treat those parents who have a college degree (BA or BS) from a US institution, regardless of income, as part of the middle class, given the connection between education and various other forms of capital (Bourdieu 1977b, 1984), as well as the link between education and social mobility. This also takes into account parents' earning potential rather than just their current income. I also make a distinction between middle-class and upper-middle-class families in my study, drawing from research that distinguishes professional and managerial workers from teachers, small-business owners, and other members of the middle class (see, e.g., Brantlinger 2003; Cucchiara 2013b). Like these scholars, I use "upper-middle class" to refer to a group in a higher social position than other members of the middle class because of their advanced educational credentials (i.e., graduate or professional degrees) and the economic, social, cultural, and symbolic capital they possess.[7] A more detailed description of the class categories used in the study is provided in appendix A.

While taking into account the material and economic basis of class in hierarchical relations, it's also important to examine how participants assess, evaluate, and debate the significance of these relations and material conditions in their narratives and participation in local settings. As Hartigan (1999, 22) writes, "However objective material conditions may appear to social analysts, their significance is usually a matter of local discussion and debate. This underscores the important recognition that class, like race, is culturally constructed; it is situational and relational rather than just an abstract variable." As is explored in chapter 3, class was a matter of "local discussion and debate" within Morningside's changing social and demographic context. When describing differences among parents within the changing school community, for example, many parents and teachers used labels that reflected both socioeconomic measures and normative judgments of lifestyles and attitudes. Several parents referred to "middle-class values" as important components of their children's education. A longtime teacher characterized other long-timers like himself as having a "blue-collar work ethic" when compared with what he saw as the more affluent and "professional" families in the school. Another parent stated a fear that the school population would become "snooty and snotty" and "uppity." Parents and teachers used geography as a marker of class as well, making distinctions between and value judgments about "urban" versus "suburban" schools and those schools in the more affluent, western part of the district versus those in the eastern portion.

Intersections with Race

> Considering class is not enough. . . . In typical American fashion, class is entwined with *and inflects* race to erect complex systems of hierarchy, domination, and disadvantage.
>
> —Pattillo 2008, 265

Race, although a social construct rather than a fixed biological marker of difference, nevertheless profoundly shapes American life and social relations. Racial categories and racial identities are contextual, dependent upon both time and place, as evidenced by the shifting systems of racial classification that mark the history of the United States and the different systems of racial classification and categorization across nations. Yet despite its fluid and constructed nature, race continues to matter in relation to life chances in the United States. As Lewis (2003, 7) writes, "Race is about who we are, what we do, how we interact. It shapes where we live, whom we interact with, how we understand ourselves and others. But it does so in specific ways depending upon our social and historical location."

Rather than treating race as secondary to class, I show how race intersects with class in shaping parents' perceptions, experiences, and engagement in public schooling. Despite post–civil rights discourses of a "color-blind" and "postracial" America, studies have shown that racial inequality persists in areas such as employment and housing (Bertrand and Mullainathan 2004; Charles 2005; Conley 2009). In the realm of education, race continues to shape the experiences of students in schools, as well as the interactions that parents have with teachers and school staff and their level of trust in educational institutions.[8] Although Lareau (2003), for example, found few differences between black and white families in what she calls "the cultural logic of child rearing," she did find that race mattered in family-school relationships. As she writes, "Among middle-class families, race played a role, not in terms of whether or how parents intervened in their children's organizational lives, but rather, in the kinds of issues that they kept their eyes on and in the number of potential problems parents and children faced. . . . Middle-class Black parents were attuned to issues of racial exclusion and insensitivity on the part of other children as well as adults" (2003, 181).

Racial inequalities are reproduced in education through institutional practices and larger structural forces, but they are also reproduced through cultural representations of difference in which race and class intersect. As Lee (2008, 312) writes, "In the dominant imagination, Whiteness and Blackness are both classed positions. Ideal Whiteness is implicitly associated with middle-class status, and Blackness is associated with poverty." Race and class were often conflated in representations of spaces, places, and individuals at Morningside, and these representations took on political significance, as they were tied to enrollment and the distribution of resources and investments in the school. Throughout the book, I explore the intersection (and often conflation) of race and class, whether in the realm of public school perceptions (chapter 3), conceptualizations of demographic change (chapter 4), parental engagement (chapter 5), or discussions of diversity (chapter 6). I show how race and class intersect in both the social constructions and the objective conditions that mark the everyday lives of parents and teachers in a community undergoing demographic change.

A Word about Gentrification and Urban Public School Change

The concept of gentrification—commonly associated with an infusion of capital, changes in the built environment, and the displacement of the poor in urban areas—deserves some discussion here. Surprisingly, middle-class enrollment and parental engagement in city public schooling have been relatively unexamined in the literature on neighborhood gentrification. In two major anthologies on the topic of gentrification, for example, none of the chapters was devoted to an analysis of families and their relationship to school and neighborhood change (see Brown-Saracino 2010; Lees, Slater, and Wyly 2008). Conversely, in the field of education, the history of white flight and urban disinvestment frames most studies of urban public schooling; rarely is gentrification used as part of an analytic framework for understanding school change. Yet as is outlined in more detail in the next chapter, "urban" America is changing in new and complex ways due to shifts in the economy, immigration/migration, and the efforts of civic leaders and developers to attract and retain the middle and upper-middle class in central cities and their public schools. As more middle-class families reside in central-city neighborhoods and consider sending their children to local public schools, frameworks for understanding the "urban" need to consider the role of these parents in processes of neighborhood and school change.

A small but growing body of scholarship examines the relationship between neighborhood contexts, the school choices and engagement of middle-class parents, and demographic shifts in city public schools.[9] Much of this work—based largely upon studies of white parents—explores the values, decision making, and engagement of middle- and upper-middle-class parents in US and European cities. Although gentrification is discussed in this extant literature on middle-class parents and urban schools, there is little conceptual clarity as to whether or not the movement of higher-income families into predominantly low-income or working-class urban schools actually represents a form of gentrification and, if so, based upon what specific criteria.[10]

Our review of the extant literature and our own research on middle-class parents in three US cities have led my colleagues and I to propose a definition of "school gentrification" that is distinct from a simple increase in the number of middle-class children in city schools that have historically served higher numbers of poor and working-class students (Posey-Maddox, Kimelberg, and Cucchiara 2012). Under the right conditions, for example, a more affluent family population may bring much-needed resources to city schools that may benefit low-income children. The enrollment of more middle-class children may also foster a socioeconomic (and potentially racial) mix as well in historically segregated city schools, offering all students the opportunity to learn from and with peers different from themselves. Indeed, most policies to promote economic integration in public education seek to bring about these outcomes.

Thus, in addition to demographic shifts, we argue that school gentrification is characterized by the following three components: (a) material/

economic upgrades in a school, such as an increase in parent-teacher organization funds; (b) the exclusion or marginalization of low-income students and families; and (c) changes in school culture and climate (Posey-Maddox, Kimelberg, and Cucchiara 2012). In contrast to those scholars who focus primarily on the potential benefits of gentrification for either neighborhoods or schools (see, e.g., Florida 2005; Stillman 2012), we argue that there are some potentially negative consequences that also merit serious attention in urban research and policy making.

My research at Morningside and research done by others show that school gentrification is a probable consequence of middle-class investment in urban public schools, suggesting that efforts to facilitate greater middle-class parental engagement in socioeconomically mixed or predominantly low-income schools may have unintended consequences that ultimately work against the goals of diversity and equity in US public education (see, e.g., Cucchiara 2013b; Kimelberg and Billingham 2013; Posey 2012; Sieber 1982). This is particularly true in the case of schools like Morningside that have neighborhood-based enrollment policies and that are located in historically middle-class communities, as well as those located in gentrified or gentrifying neighborhoods. Research in both the United States and London, for example, shows how neighborhood schools that become favored by middle-class families can become less accessible to low-income and working-class students, who cannot afford to live in the gentrifying or gentrified neighborhoods surrounding these increasingly popular schools (Butler, Hamnett, and Ramsden 2013; Cucchiara 2013b; Posey 2012). This process—whereby schools become inaccessible to new low-income students because of an oversubscription from affluent neighborhood families—is similar to the "exclusionary displacement" that Marcuse (1986) describes in his work on neighborhood gentrification. An uneven distribution of the resources garnered by middle-class parents is also likely in city schools with defined systems of sorting and tracking, such as those with separate programs for Gifted and Talented students. More equitable outcomes are possible, however, based on the unique characteristics of public schools and their local social, political, and policy contexts.

Equitable Developments in Urban School Reform

In a primer on neighborhood gentrification and policy change, Kennedy and Leonard (2001) outline the concept of equitable development in urban change processes and propose it as a goal for those seeking to mitigate the potentially negative consequences of gentrification. According to the authors, equitable development entails "the creation and maintenance of economically and socially diverse communities that are stable over the long term, through means that generate a minimum of transition costs that fall unfairly on low-income residents" (2001, 4). Whereas gentrification is often marked by an unstable and fleeting socioeconomic diversity that can result in the displacement and marginalization of the poor, equitable development is characterized by a socioeconomic mix that is sustained over time and by change that does not unfairly burden low-income residents.

Applying this concept to public education, I posit that equitable development would mean that material and demographic changes in schools would not result in the social, political, and demographic exclusion of low-income and working-class families. Rather, these families would have access to schools like Morningside that receive an infusion of resources, and they would help *shape and benefit from* investments in urban schools. Ensuring equitable developments in public schooling would require school reformers and researchers to understand the lived experiences, hopes, and desires of parents with children in schools impacted by increased middle-class parent enrollment. Whereas more scholarly and media attention has been paid in recent years to the preferences, choices, and experiences of white "professional" or "gentry" parents enrolling in urban schools, we know little about the perspectives and experiences of parents and teachers who were at these schools prior to a boom in middle-class enrollment.[11] Understanding the perspectives and lived experiences of parents and teachers experiencing school change is important, as they may illuminate alternative understandings and histories of educational reform that are not captured in dominant narratives of school improvement.

Pursuing the goal of equitable development in urban education would also require that low-income parents have a role in school change efforts. It would require attention to the *process* of school change rather than simply focusing on the *measurable outcomes* (e.g., test scores and rising enrollment) connected to demographic, material, and academic shifts in urban schools. Equitable development is a process through which to bring about full integration in public school communities rather than simply a fleeting and unstable diversity. I explore the concept of equitable development further in chapter 7.

With the goal of informing equitable-development efforts in urban public schooling, this book illustrates *processes* of school gentrification or "school gentrification-in-the-making." I studied the changes at Morningside during the 2006/7 school year—the first year in which there was a boom in kindergarten enrollment—and followed up at the school in 2007/8 and then again in 2010 (when white middle-class students became the largest racial group at the school). My initial and follow-up research illustrates processes of exclusion and marginalization linked to middle-class enrollment and parental engagement. Yet it also reveals the potential for equitable development in urban school transformation, as some parents and teachers negotiated and resisted these processes and sought to maintain a school culture based upon a "commitment to everyone." As the chapters that follow will show, school gentrification is never uniform or inevitable. Parents, educators, and policy makers can play key roles in resisting and mitigating racial and economic inequalities in urban public schooling.

Researching the Politics of Change at Morningside

During the 2006/7 school year, I engaged in intensive data collection in and around Morningside. I conducted interviews with parents, teachers, staff, and community members, attended school and community meetings and events, and volunteered in a kindergarten classroom for two hours each day and a fifth-grade classroom twice a week. Although the 2007/8 school year was largely devoted to analysis and writing, follow-up interviews and observations at school and neighborhood events continued until the spring of 2008. To explore how the changes at Morningside played out over time, I also returned to the school and conducted follow-up research in the spring of 2010 (see chapter 6).

My research findings are based upon four main sources of data: (1) over six hundred hours of participant observation in school and community meetings and events; (2) interviews with parents, teachers, and community members (seventy-one individuals in total), (3) a survey of current parents at Morningside and a survey of prospective Morningside parents; and (4) the analysis of documents related to the school's history and context and to the demographic changes occurring at Morningside and in the broader region.

Utilizing case study research methods, my aim was to gain an in-depth understanding of a process or phenomenon and to raise questions that would inform future research (Yin 2009). By focusing on Morningside Elementary as a single case, I provide a detailed examination of middle-class parental engagement in urban public schooling and the social and political dynamics that their engagement engendered within a particular school community. I use ethnographic case study methods in particular to understand and interrogate notions of "progress" and improvement in urban change efforts, as well as the role of parents in the quest for "good" public schools. A more extensive description of my methodological approach and my own role as a mixed-race (white and African American), middle-class researcher appears in appendix B.

Outline of Remaining Chapters

In chapter 2 I build a case for a more nuanced understanding of urban schools and populations, discussing changes in cities and metropolitan regions over the last two decades and the significance of these changes for scholars of urban education. First, I outline how recent social, political, economic, and demographic shifts in cities complicate conceptions of the "urban" generally found in the research literature and media. I then bring these more macrolevel realities to bear on the shifts occurring at Morningside Elementary. Using the demographic changes at Morningside as an example of changing urban spaces, this chapter highlights the need for understandings of the "urban" that include a focus on the contours and consequences of middle-class parental engagement in city neighborhoods and schools.

Chapter 3 focuses on the influence of neighborhood and community engagement in processes of urban school transformation. Specifically, I focus on the efforts of a middle-class neighborhood parent group to increase neighborhood enrollment and investment in Morningside Elementary. Through an analysis of parents' efforts to create what several described as a "critical mass" of middle-class families at the school, this chapter explores the equity implications of neighborhood parent group organizing for urban school reform. The findings suggest that middle-class parents are not simply taking advantage of urban revitalization efforts led by developers and civic leaders but may be key actors in processes of school and neighborhood change.

Chapter 4 investigates the social and political dynamics that the increased enrollment of white and mixed-race middle-class children brought about within the school community. Drawing from the experiences and perspectives of "long-timer" teachers and parents at Morningside, I show how "progress" and "improvement" were socially constructed and contested within the school community, as not all parents and teachers saw the movement of the middle class (and particularly the white middle-class) into the school as uniformly positive. The findings outlined in this chapter illustrate the limits of using test scores and student demographics as the sole markers of "good schools," since a reliance on these commonly used symbols of school success often works to devalue or ignore positive characteristics of urban schools that may not be captured in these dominant measures. The research highlights the importance of understanding the sociocultural and historical contexts of school communities in efforts to evaluate or improve public schools.

In schools like Morningside, parents—and particularly middle-class parents—are filling the gaps left by state and local governments through their fund-raising, grant writing, and volunteerism. Little is known about how these parental investments shape family-school relations and, specifically, norms and practices related to parental engagement within particular school contexts. Chapter 5 addresses this issue by examining the scope and consequences of middle-class parents' school improvement efforts at Morningside. Although parents brought new resources and educational opportunities to Morningside, I show how their engagement through the Morningside Parent-Teacher Organization and the school's reliance on their contributions engendered tensions and exacerbated existing status positions among parents. With these findings, I demonstrate the limitations of depending upon middle-class parents to sustain resources and opportunities in schools. A reliance on these parents may not only privilege middle-class norms of engagement in school settings but also relieve the government of its responsibility to provide and ensure high-quality public schooling for all children.

Chapter 6 presents follow-up research on the changes occurring at the school using district data and interviews with parents and school staff more than two years after the initial study officially ended. I discuss how the issues and changes at the school played out over time, as well as how parents and school staff interpreted and responded to the material and demographic shifts occurring at the school. My follow-up research suggests that schools like Morningside that are experiencing what I call "free-market diversity" (a concept that I outline in chapter 2) are unlikely to sustain their socioeconomic mix over time. Rather, there is a need for dedicated resources and explicit school and district policies to ensure that low-income students have access to city public schools impacted by middle-class parent investments.

In chapter 7 I highlight the need for critical and nuanced studies of urban change, as well as evaluations of progress and reform in urban education that extend beyond commonly used indicators of school success. I discuss the role of middle-class parents in school integration efforts, providing a framework that privileges the overall goal of producing equitable developments in public education. I conclude with several recommendations for policy makers, district and school staff, and parents.

TWO

Reconceptualizing the "Urban": Examining Race, Class, and Demographic Change in Cities and Their Public Schools

The urban is real insofar as it is demarcated by zones, neighborhoods, and policies. However, it is imagined to the extent that it is replete with meaning, much of which contains contradictions as to exactly what the urban signifies. . . . In light of power relations, urban may signify the hallmark of civilization and the advances it offers, or a burden and problem of progress.

—Leonardo and Hunter 2007, 779

When used in reference to issues of public schooling, the term "urban" is imbued with race and class connotations that move beyond mere geographic designations. In the media and in our popular imagination, urban schools are commonly framed as segregated, underresourced institutions with a majority of low-income black or brown students. This portrayal of urban schooling is captured in popular films such as *Waiting for Superman* and *Dangerous Minds*. It also characterizes many seminal education texts such as Jonathan Kozol's *Savage Inequalities* (1991), a book that continues to be used in teacher education classes and introductory courses in urban education.

Dominant framings of urban public schools are not entirely inaccurate, as high teacher turnover, racial segregation, concentrated poverty, and insufficient material resources are all issues that still affect many city public schools. Yet demographic shifts linked to gentrification, rising economic inequality, immigration, and residential preferences have complicated dominant conceptions of "urban" and "suburban" populations and issues, prompting the need for new ways of conceptualizing urban education.

My goal in this chapter is to push back against popular framings of the "urban" and build a case for more nuanced and contextually specific understandings of urban schools and populations. To do this, I outline changes in metropolitan regions that call into question dominant framings generally found in the media and in the academic literature. Using the demographic shifts at Morningside Elementary as an example of changing urban spaces, this chapter demonstrates the need to reconceptualize the urban to include a focus on the contours and consequences of middle-class engagement in city neighborhoods and schools. Without addressing the heterogeneity and complexity of urban spaces, policies and funding devoted to improving urban schooling may exacerbate existing patterns of inequity in city districts and schools impacted by demographic shifts.

Changing Cities, Changing Schools

Cities and their suburbs are changing. A "demographic inversion" (Ehrenhalt 2012) is taking place in many metropolitan areas, as central cities are increasingly home to a more affluent population while greater numbers of poor and working-class residents reside at the outskirts. Growing numbers of people of color and low-income individuals are being pulled (or pushed) to suburban areas and urban fringes in search of jobs, affordable housing, and alternatives to city life. Their presence challenges old conceptions of suburban areas as the exclusive, "lily-white" enclaves of the middle class. Latino and Asian American populations are spreading out from traditional metropolitan centers and many cities are experiencing a move among African Americans to urban fringes and the American South (Frey 2004, 2006, 2011). Growing numbers of students of color are enrolling in suburban districts that have traditionally been mostly or entirely white. In the 2006/7 school year, for example, suburban districts had a student population that was 41 percent nonwhite, up from 23 percent in 1993/94 (Fry 2009).[1] Latinos are the fastest-growing racial group in suburban schools, with an increase of more than 850,000 in the schools of the twenty-five largest metropolitan areas between 1999 and 2007 (Frankenberg and Orfield 2012).

Meanwhile, neighborhood gentrification, middle- and upper-middle-class families' interest in living and raising children in urban areas, and efforts to create mixed-income neighborhoods are all factors promoting the movement of middle- and upper-middle-class families into urban neighborhoods. As Barlow (2003, 94) writes, "Some downtowns—especially those of New York and San Francisco—have become urban mirrors of the White, upper middle-class suburbs." "Global cities" (Sassen 2001) such as San Francisco, New York, and Chicago have become sites of consumption for elites; issues commonly associated with urban areas, such as weak infrastructure, concentrated poverty, and "underperforming" schools, are increasingly found in suburban areas (see, e.g., Frankenberg and Orfield 2012).

Leonardo and Hunter (2007, 780, 789) argue that urban space has been traditionally conceptualized in popular culture in three central ways: (1) as a sophisticated and modern space, (2) as an authentic place of identity for people of color, and (3) as a disorganized "jungle" marked by crime and the culture of poverty. Although the latter two still hold a prominent space in the public imagination, civic and business leaders have worked to market the cosmopolitanism and "sophistication" of cities to the "creative classes" (Florida 2005), and to middle- and upper-middle-class professionals more broadly.

With the shift from a manufacturing to a service and information economy, many cities have sought to compete for workers in the global economy through revitalization efforts that draw the urban elite (Cucchiara 2013b; Ehrenhalt 2012; Lipman 2008, 2011). Through these efforts, the urban becomes a place where affluent individuals and families may enjoy the diversity and "authenticity" that the urban has to offer. Marketers pitch these areas to white professionals as diverse, chic, and cosmopolitan: offering ethnic restaurants, walkable neighborhoods, and cultural arts while also providing a critical mass of individuals reflecting their race and class background. Marketers also target middle- and upper-middle-class professionals of color, with neighborhoods such as Bronzeville on Chicago's South Side touted as unique spaces of African American arts and history (Boyd 2005; Hyra 2008). The local public schools are a key part of these revitalization efforts; attracting and retaining middle- and upper-middle-class families in urban centers depend in large part on the quality of educational options.

Although planning and redevelopment efforts have historically occurred in isolation from educational reforms, in recent years scholars, policy makers, and civic leaders have paid more attention to the link between urban revitalization efforts and public schooling. Attracting and retaining families, particularly middle-class families, are seen by many business and civic leaders as an important strategy in revitalizing urban spaces, both for the goal of economic integration and with profit and economic development in mind. As Varady and Raffel argue in *Selling Cities* (1995, 3), "The vitality of American cities depends in part on their ability to retain and attract the middle-class."

In a 2000 survey conducted by the American Planning Association and the American Institute of Certified Planners, voters in small to medium cities and suburban areas ranked schools as first among factors that would lead them to live in a more urban location (APA and AICP 2000). Indeed, middle-class parents are a key interest group in large cities such as Chicago, Philadelphia, London, and Sydney, with strategic partnerships forged among school districts, city officials, and business leaders in an effort to create "mixed-income" or largely middle- and upper-middle-class neighborhoods and schools (Cucchiara 2013b; Gulson 2011; Lipman 2008, 2011; Smith and Stovall 2008).

Middle- and upper-middle-class parents themselves are also playing a central role in urban revitalization and school change efforts. A number of middle- and upper-middle-class parent groups—in cities such as San Francisco, Philadelphia, Chicago, Boston, and New York—have formed in the last ten years with the goal of increasing the enrollment of neighborhood parents in their local schools and supporting these schools through their volunteerism and financial contributions (Campbell 2008; Cucchiara 2013b; Edelberg and Kurland 2011; Graham 2010; Jan 2006; Smith 2009; Spencer 2012; Stillman 2012). Not only are these parents (many of whom are white) enrolling their children in predominantly low-income or economically mixed schools that have a majority of students of color, but they are sharing their work with others, forming what one Bay Area newspaper article described as a "grassroots movement." As I discuss in chapter 3, these parent groups are often at the nexus of neighborhood and school change; their efforts to improve their local schools encourage parents of similar race and class backgrounds to move into the school's enrollment zone, often affecting the demographics of both city neighborhoods and their local schools.

Targeting the Middle Class as an Urban School Reform Strategy

Efforts to attract and retain the middle class in central-city areas are backed by two competing goals, creating a tension between integration and gentrification. These efforts are often motivated by a desire for a more equitable distribution of educational resources and opportunities and the social mixing of children from different racial and class backgrounds. Yet, these social goals commonly compete against the economic goals behind gentrification and economic development.

As the cases of Chicago and Philadelphia attest, the push to revitalize city spaces and schools is often motivated by a central concern with drawing capital to the city and catalyzing economic development. This often leads to neighborhood gentrification and the exclusion of the poor rather than equitable development and full integration (see, e.g., Lipman 2008, 2011). Civic and business leaders treat middle-class parents as "valued customers" (Cucchiara 2013b) in an urban marketplace because of their potential to raise property values and test scores while also supporting businesses through their purchasing power (see, e.g., CEOs for Cities, n.d.). In this historical moment, shaped by neoliberal and "postracial" policies, efforts to foster greater diversity often reinscribe, rather than disrupt, existing racial and economic inequalities.

Integration, Neoliberalism, and Educational Reform in a Post–Civil Rights Era

The quest to create socioeconomically and racially integrated schools is not a new phenomenon. Even before the courtroom debates and organizing connected to the 1896 *Plessy v. Ferguson* case, communities of color and their allies were fighting for integrated public services and institutions on the basis of the recognition that separate is indeed not equal. Overturning *Plessy*, the 1954 *Brown* decision laid the groundwork for subsequent desegregation policies in districts across the country. Facing the resistance of local and state leaders and white parents wishing to maintain the segregated status quo, the federal government pursued a more aggressive agenda of school desegregation following the passage of the 1964 Civil Rights Act, with the goal of providing a more just and equitable distribution of educational resources and opportunities. In the historic *Green v. New Kent County* decision in 1968, for example, the Supreme Court ruled that school officials had a duty to create a "unitary" system in which schools were not racially identifiable, and that choice plans that increased segregation (e.g., by allowing white parents to insulate their children from children of color in the district) were illegal (Orfield and Frankenberg 2013, 24). In the two decades that followed, districts across the country began voluntarily (or involuntarily) working to integrate their schools using methods such as inter- and intradistrict transfer programs, busing, the creation of magnet schools, and changes to school enrollment boundaries. These efforts to combat racial segregation and discrimination were coupled with federal policies aiming to counter the deleterious effects of poverty in education, marked by the passage of Title I in the Elementary and Secondary Education Act in 1965, which granted extra funds to schools with a high percentage of low-income students.

District desegregation efforts and policies were not without their faults, given that much of the burden of desegregation (e.g., switching schools, attending schools outside one's neighborhood, facing hostile school and community environments) fell on students and teachers of color (Caldas and Bankston 2005; Ladson-Billings 2004; Siddle Walker 2009). However, there were both short- and long-term social and academic benefits to integration facilitated by the intervention of the state (Orfield, Frankenberg, and Garces 2008; Wells et al. 2009). Through education law and judicial oversight, the federal government acknowledged that racial and socioeconomic disparities in education were not "natural" and that it was the duty of the government to help address them. From the late 1960s until the early 1990s the federal government acted according to the assumption that racism and discrimination in education were the norm, requiring local districts to actively work to ensure a more equitable distribution of educational resources and opportunities.

In the present historical moment, however, the *methods* used by policy makers and educational leaders to deconcentrate poverty and foster racially and socioeconomically integrated schools have changed. So too has the political and economic *context* in which these leaders are operating. Since the early 1990s, most districts across the country have been released from their original consent decrees, meaning that they no longer bear the responsibility to desegregate students, programs, and facilities (Orfield and Frankenberg 2013). In contemporary education policy, the onus for change falls largely on the choices and actions of individual parents and families.

In a post–civil rights era, the belief that race no longer matters in areas of education, housing, and employment both frames and informs contemporary educational law and policy (Bonilla-Silva and Dietrich 2011; Leonardo 2009). Not only are districts freed from the requirement to implement race-conscious student assignment policies, but they are now largely prohibited from doing so because of the Supreme Court's ruling that such practices violate the right to equal protection under the law guaranteed by the Fourteenth Amendment. In a 5–4 decision, the Supreme Court in the 2007 *Parents Involved* case agreed that school districts had a "compelling state interest" to achieve racial integration but were in disagreement as to the means to accomplish that goal. In his swing opinion, Justice Kennedy suggested alternative methods (e.g., redrawing attendance boundaries, targeted recruitment) that districts may use to promote racial mixing (Wells and Frankenberg 2007). The divided decision was confusing to many educators, however, leaving them with little guidance from the federal government about what remains legal in their voluntary integration efforts. It also narrowed their options for promoting racial integration at a time when our nation's schools were experiencing dramatic demographic changes and increased financial pressures because of declining revenues (Tefera, Siegel-Hawley, and Frankenberg 2010; Wells and Frankenberg 2007).

Since the 2007 Court decision, many districts seeking to foster racial and socioeconomic diversity have adopted economic integration plans. Socioeconomic status is not an exact proxy for race, and economic integration plans do not account for the persistent racial inequalities faced by middle-class students of color and their families. Nevertheless, given the current political and legal climate, many of the districts with economic integration plans have shown success in deconcentrating poverty and providing some racial integration (Kahlenberg 2006, 2012). Despite their relative success in providing more equitable access to high-quality schooling—and the fact that most parents get their top school choices under these plans—district integration policies continue to face political and legal attacks. "Color-blind," neighborhood-schooling policies and student assignment plans based on parent choice are increasingly common in most districts in the United States. The economic recession that began in 2008 played a role as well: faced with budget shortfalls, districts consolidated schools and cut magnet and other programming that required transportation and financial resources, which may have a large and lasting impact on racial integration efforts (Tefera, Siegel-Hawley, and Frankenberg 2010). Given deep-seated patterns of residential segregation, neighborhood schools often reflect the stratification of the larger city, with resources unevenly distributed across district schools. Studies have shown that unrestricted school choice plans end up privileging middle-class parents, as these parents have greater access to information about "good schools" and how to increase their chances of getting into them (Fuller, Elmore, and Orfield 1996; Schneider, Teske, and Marschall 2002). As Orfield and Frankenberg (2013, 12) argue in their discussion of how choice policies can exacerbate inequality:

> If the burden is put on the victims of segregation to change the situation and the involved institutions are absolved of any significant responsibility, very little will happen. This was why strict conditions about choice procedures, transportation, and related matters were put into operation in enforcing the Civil Rights Act and why mandatory desegregation orders were found to be necessary to actually integrate the schools in many communities.

The dissolution of race- and class-conscious educational laws and policies in US public schooling during the past two decades is supported by neoliberal discourse and practices. Neoliberalism—the philosophy that free markets, unrestricted flows of capital, and free trade are the best methods through which to ensure social, economic, and political prosperity—has had a profound effect on policies, forms of governance, discourse, and ideology in the United States and abroad (Harvey 2005; Lipman 2011). As Ross and Gibson (2007, 1) write, "neoliberalism is a complex of values, ideologies, and practices that affect the economic, political, and cultural aspects of a society. Neoliberal initiatives include policies such as government deregulation and privatization that privilege the market through the elimination of government restrictions limiting capital accumulation. Neoliberalism, as an ideology, also reframes concepts such as "liberty" and "democracy." These terms are used by proponents of market-based reforms to denote the empowerment of individual consumers on the basis of freedom from government control, rather than the empowerment of communities—and particularly disenfranchised communities—through government policies designed to provide social supports and a safety net (Wells, Slayton, and Scott 2002).

Numerous works address the efforts of policy makers and educational leaders to restructure education in alignment with the neoliberal, managerial tenets of "accountability," "efficiency," and individual interest and "choice" through market-based reforms in the areas of curriculum, school funding, student assignment, assessment, and evaluation (see Apple 2006; Ball 2004; Hursh 2007; Rizvi and Lingard 2009; Ross and Gibson 2007). A neoliberal framework for educational reform emphasizes competition, privatization, and meritocracy, with educational institutions and their actors encouraged to compete in a free market of options. Parents and students are treated as individual consumers and are assumed to drive education reform as schools are forced to compete for their "business." Privileging the private sector over the public, neoliberal reforms treat education as a good for individual consumption rather than as a vehicle through which to disrupt social inequalities and enhance the public good. The assumption is that all individuals are operating on an even terrain, uninhibited by structural barriers and social inequalities.

This neoliberal framing, in turn, works hand in hand with the discourse of a postracial United States, or the belief that race no longer matters in a "post–civil rights" context (Bonilla-Silva and Dietrich 2011; Wise 2010). Despite numerous studies demonstrating the persistence and perpetuation of structural racism and discrimination (see, e.g., Bonilla-Silva 2006; Feagin 2010; Leonardo 2009), a postracial neoliberal framework uses individual and cultural orientations and behaviors to explain current racial and economic inequalities. Within this broader social, political, and legal context, state and government intervention to create and foster integrated schools is met with great resistance. Rather, individual choice and competition are positioned as tools to promote greater equity. The assumption behind policies of unrestricted choice is that parents will choose the best school for their children, and those schools that cannot compete will close or dramatically transform their organizational structure (see, e.g., Burke 2009; Chubb and Moe 1990; Thernstrom and Thernstrom 2003). Advocates of these policies assume that racial and socioeconomic integration will happen naturally through policies of choice, and if not, it will be because the individual consumer (i.e., parents) did not view it as a priority. Within this framework, "diverse" and integrated schools are commonly treated as commodities available for consumers who want them rather than as vehicles through which to ensure a more equitable distribution of educational resources and opportunities.

The discourse of what I call "free-market diversity" shapes education law and policy in our current era. As I discuss in greater detail in chapter 6, this form of diversity is characterized by its flexible and individualistic nature and is distinct from the voluntary efforts of districts to integrate their local schools. For parents and policy makers subscribing to this discourse, diversity is treated as a good available for individual consumption rather than as a stepping stone toward full integration and equity in public school settings. Under a neoliberal, color-blind framework for educational reform, diverse schools should emerge from individual parent choices and demand in an unrestricted educational "market" rather than from state or district intervention or policy. The state is viewed as no longer needed to ensure that schools are racially integrated and equitable. Indeed, as recent litigation against the use of race in student assignment indicates, efforts to do so are often perceived as "reverse racism" and an infringement on the rights of individuals.[2]

Given this broader legal and political climate, many parents and local leaders concerned with racial and socioeconomic disparities in education have pursued other methods to obtain quality educational options for low-income students and students of color. Rather than rallying for district integration policies, these groups and their allies have focused instead on making the separate more equal by garnering public and private funds for schools serving students of color and low-income students. Low-income and working-class parents of color, for example, have sought out educational alternatives such as charter, nonsectarian, and parochial schools when traditional public schools have failed to provide their children with a quality education (see, e.g., Pedroni 2007; Shujaa 1992). Although there have always been examples of racially segregated schools with high levels of student achievement, these settings are not the norm and are not available to the vast number of public school students in the United States. Indeed, even high-performing charter schools that are technically public often end up being selective because of limited space and, in some cases, weed out low-performing students or those viewed as having disciplinary issues (Lacireno-Pacquet et al. 2002; Welner and Howe 2005). Thus, efforts to make the separate more equal—within neoliberal systems of "choice"—have not produced high-quality schooling options for low-income and working-class students of color that are both widely accessible and sustainable.

Filling the Gaps: Middle-Class Parents and City Public Schooling

In a post–civil rights era marked by market-based educational reforms, many civic and educational leaders have treated parent volunteerism and fund-raising as a favorable (or seemingly more viable) alternative to more structural changes (e.g., desegregation policies, changes in public funding for education). Underlying civic and educational leaders' focus on middle- and upper-middle-class parents is the assumption that these parents will not only revitalize city neighborhoods, but also improve their local public schools by both enrolling their children and engaging with the school setting. In a political and economic context in which districts and states are faced with drastic cuts to their budgets, schools are even more dependent on parents' volunteerism and financial contributions. Although parents of all class backgrounds work to help their children succeed in school (Calabrese Barton et al. 2004; Valdes 1996), middle- and upper-middle-class parents, and white middle- and upper-middle-class parents in particular, are more likely to participate in ways that are most recognized and valued by teachers and school staff (Lareau and Horvat 1999; Lareau 2000, 2003).[3] In California, for example, many schools depend on parent volunteerism and fund-raising to maintain art, music, and extracurricular programming (California Budget Project 2011; California Department of Education 2010). Rather than simply helping their children with homework or attending parent-teacher conferences, parents in urban schools and districts across the nation are called on to write grants, fund-raise, donate money, and volunteer extensively for their children's schools. Parents with economic means and access to dominant social and cultural capital are better positioned to fulfill these requests.

As I illustrate in chapter 5, relying upon middle-class parents as major drivers of school reform is bad practice, as their volunteerism and fundraising efforts may marginalize low-income and working-class families in a school community. By emphasizing the role of parental engagement and volunteerism in a school's success, the state is also effectively absolved of its responsibility to provide and sustain critical educational resources and academic programs for students. Reflecting neoliberal policy, the onus of school improvement shifts from the structural to the individual, with parents asked to fill in the gaps left by local and state governments.

At the same time that parents are expected to do more for their children's school, families face growing financial struggles, work-life balance challenges, and little state support for caregiving. In contrast to 1960, when only 20 percent of mothers worked, by 2008 70 percent of American children lived in households in which all the adults were employed (Williams and Boushey 2010). Parents and caregivers are also working longer hours, often for less pay (Bernstein and Kornbluh 2005; Williams and Boushey 2010). Not only are parents affected by a decline in the value of real wages and a lack of public regulations and support for dual earning and caregiving, they also face rising child care, food, and transportation costs ("Annual Report of the White House Task Force on the Middle Class" 2010).

Thus, efforts to create and maintain mixed-income city schools are situated within a broader context of rising economic inequality in which growing numbers of the middle class, and those with children in particular, are finding it increasingly difficult to achieve the "American dream" of homeownership and quality schooling for their children. The increased cost of living and rising economic inequality (Aron-Dine and Sherman 2007; Piketty and Saez 2003) may push more families who may have "opted out" before to consider local public schools for their children. Indeed, recent examples suggest this may be a growing trend across the country (Jan 2006; Rogers 2009; Smith 2009). As mentioned earlier, these parents may also wish to send their children to city public schools because of their stated commitments to diversity or public education (Cucchiara and Horvat 2009; Posey 2012; Reay et al. 2008).

As I illustrate throughout the book, middle-class parents are thus positioned by many civic and educational leaders as *both valued customers and agents of change*: they are encouraged to enroll their children in urban public schools and are also asked to ensure that these schools become or remain high quality. They are treated by civic and educational leaders as key drivers of urban school reform and are also asked to fill the gaps left by state and local governments. Understanding contemporary urban school change thus means examining not only the work of policy makers and educational leaders to improve schools but also the scope and consequences of middle-class parents' urban school reform efforts.

Situating Morningside: The City, the District, the Neighborhood, and the School

Morningside Elementary is located within the Northern California city of Woodbury, a large urban area with a racially and ethnically diverse population. Although whites were a racial majority prior to World War II, white flight to the suburbs in the postwar period significantly changed Woodbury's demographics. Despite rising unemployment because of a declining manufacturing base in the decades following the war, African Americans continued to migrate to Woodbury in large numbers and formed a strong political base by the 1960s. Their numbers have steadily declined since 1980, however, and the percentage of African Americans in 2010 was just slightly greater than that of whites and Latinos (2010 US census). Although the white population has declined slightly since 2000, the percentages of Asians and Latinos have risen in the last two decades (2010 US census). In the late 1990s and early 2000s, city leaders initiated redevelopment projects to bring more residents and businesses to the downtown area. Owing in part to these efforts, as well as the city's relative affordability at the time compared with other major cities in the region, Woodbury experienced a period of economic revitalization. As in many large cities across the nation, the redevelopment efforts and demographic changes have raised questions about gentrification, with nonprofit organizations and residents organizing to ensure that low-income and working-class individuals and families have a place in the city.

Woodbury as a whole is quite socioeconomically diverse, with pockets of affluence existing in close proximity to areas of poverty in some areas of the city—sometimes within shared neighborhood contexts or on the same street. Yet most neighborhoods and sections of the city are marked by patterns of racial and socioeconomic segregation. "South Woodbury" and "East Woodbury" have greater numbers of African American and Latino residents and higher levels of poverty than the western part of the city. Asian Americans are clustered in neighborhoods near the center/downtown area of the city but are also found in other parts of the city, albeit in smaller numbers. As one travels west in Woodbury, home values rise dramatically and apartment buildings are fewer in number. Businesses shift from corner stores and taquerias to trendy boutiques and cafés. The population is also more white and affluent.

Woodbury Unified School District, of which Morningside is a part, is a large urban district serving students from kindergarten through twelfth grade. In the 2006/7 school year, African American and Hispanic/Latino students each constituted roughly one-third of the district student population, with Asian students making up less than one-quarter.[4] Whites made up less than 10 percent of the district's students, although they represented almost one-third of the city's population at that time. Almost 70 percent of district students qualified for the free/reduced-price lunch program, higher than the state total of 50 percent.[5]

The district is informally bifurcated into "eastern" and "western" schools, mirroring patterns of residential segregation in the city. Similar to patterns of inequality found in many districts across the nation, the "geography of opportunity" (Briggs 2005) within the Woodbury Unified School District is linked to race, class, and residence. Elementary schools in the more affluent and predominantly white western part of the district generally have larger parent-teacher association budgets, higher test scores, and greater material resources than those in the eastern half of the district. Compared with most of the eastern schools, these schools have less teacher turnover and limited student mobility. In large part because of substantial parent-teacher organization budgets, the western elementary schools are able to provide a range of enrichment programs and have upgraded physical plants with modern equipment. Whereas many schools in the west have waiting lists of parents from both inside and outside the neighborhood seeking to enroll their children, many schools in the east had been reconstituted or threatened with closure during the period of study because of their low test scores, low enrollment, or both. Within this system it was common for middle-class parents who were dissatisfied with their neighborhood school or their public schooling options in the district to enroll their children in one of the many parochial or nonsectarian private school options in the city. Charter school enrollment had also increased substantially since 2002, with twelve charter schools serving elementary-aged children in the district.

In 2006 the district had an enrollment policy of "choice," in which parents of elementary school children were encouraged to learn about the various schools in the district and then list six schools, in order of preference, that they wanted their children to attend. The goal, according to the district description of the program, was to ensure that all families had "equitable access" to high-performing schools across the city by giving them the opportunity to select any district school rather than simply those in their immediate neighborhood. Those families living in a school's neighborhood zone had preference in enrollment, however, meaning that in cases where there were more applicants than space available, neighborhood residents received priority. In light of this, it was common for parents who could afford to do so to purposely move into the western school neighborhood zones so that their children were assured placement in their preferred school. Those parents who lived out-of-zone, who did not already have older children at a particular school, and who could not afford to move into a neighborhood with a high-performing public school thus had limited options within the "choice" enrollment system. Although, under No Child Left Behind, parents residing in neighborhoods with schools designated as "failing" could technically opt out and choose a better option, most of the high-performing schools in the district were at capacity, reflecting similar trends across the country.[6] As a participant in a district meeting on the "unintended consequences/emerging tensions" associated with the student assignment process stated, "the location of perceived 'quality schools' privileges the neighborhood families. Many neighborhoods in Woodbury are of similar race and class, consequently homogenizing school communities."[7]

Morningside Elementary is both geographically and demographically situated on the border between the educational landscapes of east and west. The school draws from two neighborhoods that are separated by a major thoroughfare and that have different demographics. The Glenbrook neighborhood, in which the school is physically located, comprises the western part of the student catchment area. Property values increase as one moves farther west in Woodbury, and Glenbrook sits at the base of an affluent region of the city. White homeowners made up the majority of neighborhood residents (64 percent according to the 2000 census), with slightly higher numbers of Asians and lower numbers of Latinos and African Americans compared with the eastern part of the school's catchment area. Although African American homeowners have historically had a solid presence in the neighborhood, their numbers have steadily declined during the last thirty years.

In the early 2000s, because of a housing boom in the broader region, housing prices rose dramatically in Glenbrook. Although the median home value for the ZIP code was $600,000 in 2006, houses in the Glenbrook neighborhood specifically were offered at prices ranging from $700,000 to close to $1 million.[8] Houses are a mixture of two- and three-bedroom bungalows and one- and two-story homes, with many front lawns lined with flowers and native California plants. The neighborhood contains mostly houses, but two- and three-story apartment buildings, duplexes, and fourplexes (some subsidized but most market rate) are scattered throughout as well. Walking through the neighborhood, it is common to see couples pushing strollers with coffee from a local café in hand and joggers and bike riders passing by on the tree-lined streets. White families and a few Asian American families, as well as immigrant nannies from Central and South America, Asia, and Africa, congregate regularly at the local park, where toddlers play with an array of toys and on play structures.

Across a major thoroughfare from Morningside lies the Frazier Park neighborhood, where African Americans and whites were the largest racial groups at the time of the 2000 census (41 and 37 percent, respectively). Home values and the median household income are lower here (in 2000, the census tract had a $41,000 median household income versus $58,000 in Glenbrook), yet homeowners comprise the majority of neighborhood residents. Located in the eastern part of the school's enrollment zone, the Frazier Park neighborhood is characterized by two- and three-bedroom bungalows; some homes boast landscaped yards and fresh coats of paint while others have standard cut grass, a few shrubs, and fading paint jobs. A large local park, once notorious for drug activity, now draws sports teams and dog walkers. Teens chatting on their way home from school or from the local gas station/convenience store routinely pass through the neighborhood, as does the occasional car blaring the latest hip-hop or R&B song. A few elderly and retired African American residents sit on their front steps for part of the day to watch passersby and chat with neighbors.

Both the western and eastern areas of the school zone were historically middle-class neighborhoods; the neighborhoods were not "blighted" or marked by the high rates of poverty and subsequent economic development that often characterize city neighborhoods undergoing gentrification. Between 1990 and 2000, however, the median incomes and percentage of college attainment increased across both neighborhoods. Housing prices in the school's ZIP code also rose more than 300 percent between 1995 and 2005.[9] During the time of the study the number of young children in Morningside's school zone was also on the rise: based on birthrates, the number of potential neighborhood students entering Morningside was expected to grow.[10] In both the eastern and western areas of the school zone, the number of African American residents has declined in the last three decades, reflecting an overall trend in the city of Woodbury. As area homeowners passed away or sold their property, a growing number of white residents were taking their place (with the number of Asian and Latino residents growing but still representing less than 10 percent of the total neighborhood population in 2000, according to the census).

Morningside Elementary is a small school located at the edge of the Glenbrook neighborhood. Although situated within a residential area, it is a brief walk from a major thoroughfare and easily accessible by public transportation. Entering the school, the emphasis on art and the intimacy of the school community are evident. The following excerpt from my field notes illustrates the physical environment that greets visitors when they first enter the school:

> There was a long banner hanging just inside the front entrance, with a sign that said, "We are Morningside Proud." On the exterior wall of a kindergarten classroom hung 3 large student-made drawings of famous dancers, one from the Alvin Ailey Dance Group. Clustered around the courtyard were big and little pots filled with flowers. Dead-center, greeting visitors, was a big "Welcome to Morningside" laminated sign. One of the courtyard tables had student handprints on it, as well as students' names and ages at the time they made the art piece. The wall to the multipurpose room was decorated with a student-made mural.
>
> Also inside the front entrance was an "Excellence 2006" bulletin board, where "attendance" and "honor roll" were posted along with corresponding student names. Around the corner, in the hallway, was a bulletin board that had pictures of all of the kindergartners on it, with the words "New Faces, New Friends" posted above them. Next to that was a bulletin board with garden volunteer sign-ups, a copy of the Morningside newsletter, and general announcements. Right by the office door was a display with information for parents: a hanging copy of the school's state testing results, a "Woodbury Unified School District Vision and Core Values" sheet, and grade-level newsletters. On the office door were two laminated articles about parents at the school, entitled "Morningside in the News." One article was about a local artist whose children went to Morningside, and the other was about environmentally friendly, "green business practices," spotlighting the business of a Morningside parent.

I wrote the following in my field notes toward the beginning of the school year: "Students really know each other here. While walking out to recess or standing in line, many of the kindergartners say hello to older students, or some of the first graders wave to them and call their names." Students of the Month get big smiles and a certificate from the principal and staff in the front office, and children who lose a tooth while in school get a special container for it as well as an award. Student work lines the walls of tidy classrooms, and teachers meet regularly within and across the grades to talk about curriculum or to collaborate on projects or programs. Parents are commonly found chatting on the school grounds before and after school or helping out in classrooms, the gardens, or the front office.

During the period of study, the school had a strong connection to the surrounding Glenbrook neighborhood and broader community. The building was regularly used for meetings with local elected officials and neighborhood residents, and it was not uncommon to see neighbors (particularly those with young children) volunteering at Morningside or attending a school event. School activities and successes were highlighted in neighborhood newsletters, and several local businesses had contributed to school fund-raisers.

This strong connection to the surrounding community was only a recent phenomenon. In 2000, six years prior to the time of the study, Morningside was both socially and demographically disconnected from most residents of the predominantly white, middle- and upper-middle-class Glenbrook neighborhood. Many Morningside students resided in the Frazier Park neighborhood, adjacent catchment areas, or other parts of the city. Although the percentage of white students at Morningside was higher than the percentage of whites in the school district as a whole in 2000 (14 versus 6 percent), the percentage was still much lower than that reflected in the neighborhood. Seventy-eight percent of the student body was African American, compared with only 17 percent of residents in the Glenbrook neighborhood, in which the school is situated (see table 1). Although majority-minority schools are commonly associated with high levels of poverty (Orfield and Lee 2005), less than half of Morningside

Table 1 Demographic profile of school and student catchment area (2000)

	Morningside student demographics (%)	Western catchment area (Glenbrook) (%)	Eastern catchment area (%)
African American	78	17	41
White	14	64	37
Hispanic/Latino	5	7	11
Asian	2	7	5
Multiple/no response[a]	1	5	5
Poverty rate	44[b]	10	14

Source: 2000 US census and California Department of Education.
Note: American Indians comprised less than 1 percent of the neighborhood and school populations. Percentages do not add up to 100 because of rounding.
[a]"Multiple/no response" refers to those individuals who marked "some other race" or "two or more races" on the census.
[b]Received free or reduced-price lunches.

students were enrolled in the free/reduced-price lunch program in 2000, compared with a district percentage of 54 percent.

From 2000 to 2008, however, Morningside Elementary experienced considerable shifts in its student demographics, and the relationship between the school and the surrounding neighborhood began to change as greater numbers of middle-class families from both within and outside the Glenbrook neighborhood began to consider the school for their children. In the next chapter, I focus on the development and actions of the Glenbrook neighborhood parent group, a place-based group that played an influential role in the demographic and material shifts occurring at Morningside. The chapter steps back in time and focuses specifically on how members of the Glenbrook Parents' Group understood the disconnect with their local school and the actions several parents took to catalyze neighborhood support for Morningside.

THREE

Building a "Critical Mass":
Neighborhood Parent Group
Action for School Change

As parents of young toddlers and neighbors committed to public education, Emily Thompson and Lori Veloso were concerned in 2001 with the
social and demographic disconnect between their neighborhood and their
local public school. Morningside Elementary, at the time a small, predominantly African American school with many students from outside the immediate neighborhood, faced annual challenges in keeping enrollment
up and staying open because of the lack of neighborhood support. After
several conversations with each other and with other parents in the local
park, the two women (one white, one Asian American, both with graduate
degrees) decided to organize a parents' group to galvanize neighborhood
support for their local public school.

Emily and Lori delivered flyers advertising the first neighborhood parents' group meeting to every house in Morningside's enrollment zone. Reflecting on the history of the group in an interview, Emily described the
contents of the flyer as follows:

> It essentially said, "Do you have kids that are preschool age? Do you not
> want to drive your kids across town or pay private school tuition or move to
> the suburbs? Would you like to have a neighborhood school that educated
> the whole child, et cetera, et cetera? Let's explore the possibilities."

They also spoke with other parents in local parks and in neighborhood
social settings about their interest in Morningside. According to Emily and
Lori, more than fifty people showed up at the first meeting. That initial
meeting was the start of a campaign led by a small group of white and
Asian American middle-class parents to pursue what Emily described as
the following two goals: "One is to increase the sense of community in

our neighborhood, and the other is to support our neighborhood public elementary school. And I see those as totally linked."

Through their activities and outreach, the Glenbrook Parents' Group (GPG) helped to put Morningside on the radar of families in the school's western catchment area as well as those in other parts of the city. By 2006, when I first began my research, a greater number of parents from the predominantly white, middle- and upper-middle-class neighborhood were investing in their local public school rather than fleeing to private schools or more elite public schools in the district. Prospective Morningside parents in the neighborhood attended school tours and events, and children of GPG members were enrolled at the school, with most clustered in the kindergarten class. The GPG was at the forefront of what one local paper called "a grassroots movement" of middle-class parents in the city. Indeed, I spoke with and interviewed several parents in other neighborhoods who had turned to GPG leaders for advice and lessons learned when seeking to organize their own neighborhood groups.

In 2006, five years after their initial meeting, the GPG held monthly brunches, organized regular playgroups for neighborhood children, held an annual fund-raiser whose proceeds went to Morningside, and cosponsored the school's annual Spring Carnival. Through their activities and outreach, the group created what one parent described as a "buzz" about Morningside, among families in the largely middle-class neighborhood as well as in the city as a whole. In large part because of the GPG's efforts, the number of neighborhood families both interested in and enrolled at Morningside greatly increased. In the 2006/7 school year, for example, there was such an interest in the school from neighborhood families that nonneighborhood children who had no siblings already enrolled would have been denied a spot if the principal had not created a third kindergarten class to accommodate the growing demand for enrollment.

By many accounts, a larger number of parents from the surrounding middle- and upper-middle-class neighborhood began to invest in Morningside. These parents, mostly white and a few Asian American, were not stereotypical "yuppies" driving luxury cars and living in trendy lofts. In my conversations and interviews with neighborhood parents I met artists, teachers, directors of nonprofit organizations, and civil rights advocates with stated commitments to diversity, civic participation, and social justice. Indeed, these parents were in many ways similar to the "ardent integrationists" (Cashin 2004) or "Innovator and Early Adopter Parents" (Stillman 2012) described in other studies of the white middle and upper-middle class. The appeal of not having to juggle private school tuition and high mortgage payments, as well as the desire to contribute to a public institution in their community, led a growing number of these neighborhood families to seriously consider their local public school.

Much of the GPG's work was focused on increasing the enrollment of the middle- and upper-middle-class families residing in Morningside's immediate neighborhood; but it is important to note that there were African American (and small numbers of white) parents from a range of class backgrounds residing in the school's enrollment zone or outside it who had strong historical connections to the school. Some of these parents were alumni themselves or had older children or family members who had attended the school. As I discuss in greater detail in the following chapter, the school had a reputation among many African American parents (and a small group of middle-class white parents) in the district for being a good school long before its GPG-driven popularity. Historically, parents had been easily able to enroll their children in Morningside, even if they lived outside the enrollment zone. As more families from the neighborhood surrounding the school sought to enroll their children, however, the school's demographics and accessibility began to shift.

In this chapter I focus on the GPG, examining (1) the historic relationship between middle-class parents in the neighborhood and their local school, (2) the strategies the GPG used to increase the enrollment of neighborhood families in the school, and (3) the implications of the group's efforts in relation to issues of enrollment and equity in public education. Most of the extant research on parental engagement focuses on parents' goals and orientations and the consequences of parental involvement in classroom and school settings. A small but growing body of literature, however, explores the influence of parental social networks and neighborhood-based engagement in school change efforts in cities such as Chicago, Philadelphia, and New York (Cucchiara and Horvat 2009; Edelberg and Kurland 2011; Stillman 2012). The research described in this chapter contributes to this literature by focusing on middle- and upper-middle-class parents' collective, "out-of-school," neighborhood-based engagement. Focusing specifically on the place-based organizing of the GPG, the research highlights the significant influence that parents' work outside classrooms and parent-teacher association meetings can have on a local school. Despite many parents' best intentions, the GPG's efforts to support and improve its local public school ultimately worked against the racial and socioeconomic diversity that so many parents cited as a school asset. Middle-class parents' actions, combined with a district assignment policy that gave preference to neighborhood families, rendered the school less accessible to low-income students in the district. Ultimately, the findings outlined in this chapter suggest that middle-class parents are not simply taking advantage of a re-structuring of the "urban" driven by developers and civic leaders but can be key actors in processes of school and neighborhood change.

The GPG: Countering the "Revolving Door"
of Families in the Neighborhood

According to longtime residents and a local realtor, in the 1990s many parents with school-age children chose to move, transfer their children to another public school, or enroll their children in a private school. When asked for examples of why people moved out of the Glenbrook neighborhood, a local realtor stated that in addition to the "three D's" (death, divorce, and disemployment), the local schools played a significant role:

> And one of the other reasons that people were moving out of these areas that directly relates to Morningside was we had a revolving door for young couples. . . . I used to tell people if I was starting my real estate business anew, if I was a new real estate agent at the time, this was in the midnineties, my whole business plan would be to get close to every young couple I could find that was having kids, because eventually they'd be selling their house and moving out because they would not be putting their kids in the public schools in Woodbury.

Interviews with GPG members, school staff, and non-GPG parents suggest that this migration away from Morningside Elementary was in large part tied to race, class, and residence. In contrast to many middle- and upper-middle-class families in the Glenbrook neighborhood, parents residing in the less affluent areas to the east of the school enrollment zone and in other areas of the city actually sought out Morningside in the late 1990s and early 2000s as a promising alternative to their own low-performing neighborhood schools. Many African American parents who could not afford to move or pay private school tuition, or who were alums or had family members who went to the school, saw Morningside as a favorable option. Although there were also some white middle-class parents residing both in and outside the school zone who had enrolled their children at Morningside, these parents were few in number and were scattered across the grades rather than enrolling as cohorts connected to a particular neighborhood or group. I explore the experiences and perspectives of parents

who had children at the school prior to the enrollment of GPG children—
parents whom I call "long-timers"—in more detail in chapter 4.

Race, Class, and Perceptions of Public Schools

Studies of race and school choice have shown that although parents of
all races express support for integrated schools, white middle- and upper-
income parents tend to choose schools that are whiter and wealthier
(Holme 2002; Johnson and Shapiro 2003; Saporito 2003; Saporito and
Lareau 1999). Race, in particular, plays a salient role in school choice, as
studies have indicated that white families tend to avoid schools with higher
percentages of nonwhite students even when these schools have substantial numbers of affluent, academically successful students (Saporito 2003;
Saporito and Lareau 1999).

The findings in this study suggest that the racial demographics of Morningside's population played a role in the low enrollment of white middle-
and upper-middle-class families from the neighborhood surrounding the
school. In 2001, when the GPG was formed, Morningside's African American population scored higher than African American students in many
other schools in the district, and the small school was socioeconomically
mixed.[1] Yet, as described later in this section, some parents formed what
Emily, a white founding member of the GPG, called "drive-by" impressions of the school based on the race of the students on the playground
and the school's physical appearance. When asked why neighborhood parents weren't sending their kids to Morningside, she explained:

> It was race issues. I mean, people would drive by and see that it was mostly
> black kids in the yard, and they made assumptions about the school. And
> I have to say that, being fair, it's not surprising that people did that based
> partly on the news you read in the media about public schools but also
> about what statistics will tell you is, you know, schools with mostly African
> American populations tend to be the low-income schools that tend to have
> less-qualified teachers. And so they looked at African American kids in the
> yard and they had those assumptions that "oh, they must not have qualified
> teachers, et cetera, et cetera." So I think that was a large part of it.

As Emily suggested, race, class, and school quality were conflated in the
minds of many neighborhood parents. A school with a predominantly
African American population was associated with poverty, which, in turn,

was connected to a less rigorous academic program. Neighborhood parents saw a majority of black students and, as one parent said, a school building with "weeds growing out of the asphalt" and assumed that their children would not be challenged academically at Morningside.

In addition to the conflation of race, class, and school quality, several white parents in the neighborhood described in interviews their misgivings about Morningside's social climate, linking race and class to issues of peer and family influence. Claire Hansen, a white upper-middle-class parent in the neighborhood who chose to send her child to a private school, shared that she wanted her son "to be sheltered" from the negative experiences she herself had had in public schools. After visiting a classroom at Morningside, she said that she was concerned about behavior issues and negative peer influences on her child. Later in the conversation, when she spoke about the reported incidents of crime on her block that had occurred that year, she confided, "This is how I'm putting it together in my head, but I start to think that maybe those people who are committing the crimes are the dads of the kids who would be going to school with my son if he went [to Morningside]."

She mentioned that she knew it sounded bad, but she stated, "It's a subtext for a lot of people. . . . They don't talk about it, but it's there." Claire went on to clarify her comment, however, saying that "it isn't the color of people's skin, but people do make these generalizations." She emphasized that "it's the socioeconomics, and our culture has created it. . . . It goes back to the one-in-three African American men in prison." When I asked her how the socioeconomic background of students affects dynamics at the school, she stated that "it shows up with discipline and behavior issues."

Although Claire emphasized that it was purely a matter of socioeconomics, the association she made among African American men, crime, and students' behavior issues highlights the ways in which race and class were conflated in her judgments of the school culture. Claire was concerned that her child would be negatively affected by students with discipline issues, students whose parents were, in her mind, potentially responsible for the increased crime in her neighborhood.

For Christina Johnson, a white upper-middle-class parent who was living in the neighborhood and had attended several GPG functions when her son was a toddler, race also played a role in her decision to send her child to a private school rather than to Morningside. When I interviewed her in 2006, she felt that that year's kindergarten class was "a nice mix" compared with previous years, yet she was concerned with what she saw as a lack of diversity in the upper grades and the fact that whites were in the minority:

C: When we moved in, he would have been one of the only white kids at the school. If I had a rough-and-tumble, outgoing kid, then I might put him in a situation where he was the minority because I would feel like he could handle it. But just to be totally frank, I walk by Morningside . . . and I feel like the way the kids talk to each other would be totally foreign to him. And it would be something that, you know, maybe if he was a really adaptable out-there kid he would just sort of get in there and figure it out, but I think he would be very intimidated.

I: *By the nonwhite kids?*

C: Yeah, the nonwhite kids. It's very different than how we talk at home, and I think that would be very hard for him. But I mean, I see the changes [in demographics], but I don't know if they're going to continue up the upper grades as well.

In interviews, both Claire and Christina stated their support for public schooling, but they felt that Morningside was not a good fit for their own children. As upper-middle-class professionals, they were ultimately able to exercise their power of choice and send their children to private schools, with Morningside's student population playing a significant part in their decision.

Building a Bridge between Neighborhood and School

Seeking to allay parents' fears and build a network of parents interested in Morningside, the founders of the GPG brought neighborhood parents with young children together to talk about their local public school. In interviews, several GPG members described the group's first meeting at a local community center, a neutral space where parents could talk openly about their concerns and perceptions of the school. Here neighborhood parents discussed their fears and hopes related to Morningside. Following the initial meeting, a group of parents from the GPG met with Woodbury Unified School District's superintendent to get more information about district reforms as well as to voice their concerns about the large urban district. They also met with Morningside's principal, seeking to learn more about the school and identify areas where they could lend support.

In their reflections on the history of the GPG's involvement in the school, both Emily and Lori were careful to point out what they saw as Morning-side's strengths prior to the GPG's involvement. As Lori explained:

L: Because I think that was what we found—once we looked at Morningside, once we got in the door, it's a really great place on the face of it. And so you feel the energy. I mean you still have all these concerns—the district curriculum, funding, all these issues—but a lot of those stereotypes of public schools break down when you walk in the door of Morningside. So that was major I think.

I: *What things made you break down those stereotypes?*

L: The environment. I think the facilities were different than the mental image I had of California public schools, which is toilet paper on the ceiling and leaky bathrooms and asbestos everywhere. And you walk into Morningside and there's art everywhere, there's gardens everywhere, and I think that is so important. And so building our neighborhood community and finding ways to bring the neighborhood into the school was key.

Although the garden and art programs were less developed in 2001 when Lori and Emily first visited the school as parents of prospective students, in interviews both parents spoke of the positive aspects of the school that they recognized at that time. Emily described how impressed she was by the principal's leadership and connection to students during her first visit to the school. Lori spoke of what she saw as a group of "dedicated parents" at the school who were "willing to work towards a vision of what they wanted for their children," as well as the school's rising test scores. Both women sought to spotlight and build upon the work that was already being done at the school and make the school's strengths more visible to families in the neighborhood.

To counter negative perceptions of the school, Emily and Lori created opportunities to get neighborhood parents on school grounds. About a year before her children were enrolled at Morningside, for example, Emily became involved in the planning for the school's annual Spring Carnival; the event was eventually cosponsored by the neighborhood group. In an interview Emily shared that she had visited another school in the district that had an event cosponsored by a community group, and she wanted to "amp up" Morningside's Spring Carnival so that it could serve as an opportunity to bring the community into the school. After presenting her ideas at a Morningside Parent-Teacher Organization (MPTO) meeting, she and a few other GPG members worked with a few MPTO parents to plan the event. GPG leaders also planned an annual Book Drive sponsored by the organization, where neighborhood parents could both donate and buy books and come to the school grounds to volunteer at the event. The proceeds of the Book Drive went directly to the school. As Emily described, the purpose of these events in the eyes of GPG leaders was not simply to raise money but also to raise Morningside's visibility by getting prospective parents and community members to the school:

> And then whenever the school had fund-raisers, we were very clear that they have dual roles as PR [public relations]. The Book Drive would probably make more money if it wasn't located on the school yard because the school yard isn't very visible to passing traffic, but the whole idea is that when people come to buy things, they're going to come to the school yard and say, "Oh, what a cute school." And the Spring Carnival has also always had a dual role as a PR thing. And a lot of people have said that one of those two events was one of their very first experiences at the school.

In addition to planning activities aimed at supporting the school directly, GPG leaders also created social activities to build a sense of connection among families with young children in the neighborhood. In interviews, parents who were a part of that early group stated that the GPG's age-specific playgroups were key in fostering these connections, as both children who would be entering kindergarten and their parents were able to develop friendships. Holiday activities for children in the local park and monthly neighborhood brunches held at members' houses were other ways in which the group built community.

The GPG also sought to facilitate greater communication among neighborhood families through the creation of an online listserv. Parents could post or receive information about community events, playgroups, and Morningside Elementary, as well as local resources such as nannies and plumbers. By 2007 the listserv had more than 350 subscribers, including families living outside the immediate neighborhood but who nevertheless sought to access the information the electronic mailing list provided. Members of the GPG cited this listserv as a key component of their efforts to increase connections among neighborhood families and build support for Morningside. During the 2006/7 school year, for example, GPG parents who had children at Morningside often solicited neighborhood support for the school through the listserv. In addition to disseminating information about upcoming school events and volunteer opportunities, parents used the listserv to share "insider information" on topics such as how to best navigate the district enrollment process.

In interviews, several teachers and non-GPG parents with children at the school recounted their initial skepticism regarding the group and their fear that, as Hannah Sorenson, a white, upper-middle-class, longtime member of the MPTO, stated, "the yuppies were going to come in and take over the school." As Hannah and other long-timers recalled, several parents with children already enrolled questioned the need for a group that was separate from the MPTO. The founding members of the GPG, however, felt that a separate group would enable neighborhood parents to feel comfortable talking about their educational choices and would build a sense of community among neighborhood families. Emily explained:

> The neighbors weren't ready to come to the MPTO meetings because if you come to the MPTO meetings, then it looks like "I'm sure I'm going to go to this school." Or you're afraid people are going to look at you like you're a hypocrite if—and that's one of the things I think we did that was smart, too—there was not going to be any casting of blame or there's no signing on the dotted line, or if you don't go to the school you're a bad guy. So part of the attitude was trying to be "oh, if you don't go to this school, then all the more reason why you should be involved in your neighborhood, so you know people."

Although the GPG was to remain a separate entity, the founding GPG members hoped that, with time, members of the Morningside community would see that their intentions were to support, rather than fundamentally change, the work that teachers and parents were already doing to make the school great.

Despite their initial reservations, parents and teachers in the MPTO remained open to the possibility that the GPG's efforts could benefit the collective student body. Hannah recognized that the group could bolster student enrollment and bring much-needed material resources to the school: "I realized that OK, this is a good thing, basically, and we just gotta find a way to make it work." The administration, teachers, and a small, multiracial group of parents were already working to develop the school's academic and extracurricular programs and saw an opportunity for the GPG to support their efforts.

While their children were still toddlers, several GPG parents worked with Hannah and a few other parents from the MPTO in the early 2000s to develop school-based activities, such as tours for prospective parents, and to expand the Spring Carnival. These collaborations were not free from tensions; both GPG and MPTO members described some initial conflicts. Lori, for example, spoke in an interview about how several of the long-timer parents who were active in the MPTO were skeptical of the motives of GPG members. Reflecting on some of the tensions she experienced in her first few years of volunteering at Morningside, she stated:

> So actually one of my favorite stories is that the second year I was in charge of food. And I started calling around and asking for food donations, and [a local bakery and pastry shop] answered the call and they donated all of the bread donations. And a parent who was in the MPTO leadership made the comment that the fact that we had bread from there and not Wonder Bread could be construed as being elitist and middle class and not respectful of the community, Morningside's existing community.

Lori went on to note that it was the long-timer white middle-class parents in the MPTO—parents who were few in number at the school but active in planning school events and activities—who were commonly the ones encouraging GPG members to be sensitive to class issues in their event planning. Indeed, in interviews, several white middle-class parents who had been active in the MPTO in the early 2000s recalled their discomfort with some of the initial changes proposed by GPG leaders, particularly related to the Spring Carnival. Molly Clausen, a white middle-class parent who lived outside the neighborhood but had been a Morningside parent since the late nineties, expressed her concern about the expansion of the Spring Carnival:

> So the Spring Carnivals just get more and more elaborate. You know, like we've got the juggler—it's just too much. Before we just would have a party; we'd have like a band playing and food. And that was it, and it was fun. And we didn't need to have a carnival. We didn't need to have it like this [affluent] school or that school.

Molly went on to describe her discomfort with the selling of tickets for food and activities at the event because she thought it might "alienate" kids whose parents were unable to buy them a lot of tickets. In their interviews on the history of the organization, GPG leaders spoke freely about these difficult conversations and tensions and stressed that their intentions were to support, rather than "take over," the school. For Lori, the opportunity to "be challenged" and to work with different kinds of people was a positive aspect of the school:

I don't know, I think Morningside is a really wonderful place, and it's rare that we get challenged in areas like that. I think we all kind of walk around in our own little work [and] social circle areas, but Morningside, you know, it's a lot of really different kinds of people. And that's hard, but it's also really great.

Tensions related to the volunteerism and fund-raising of parents were present throughout the almost two years I conducted research at the school, and I discuss them in more detail in chapter 5.

Whereas activities like the Book Drive and Spring Carnival brought the community onto school grounds, during the time of my study the relationship between the GPG and the school was not a reciprocal one. Although technically any parent could attend GPG events, few parents from outside the school's immediate neighborhood did so. Indeed, in my interviews and conversations with low-income and working-class Morningside parents who lived just outside the school's enrollment zone, I found that many had not even heard of the group, let alone subscribed to the listserv. From the time of its inception, middle- and upper-middle-class neighborhood families had been the primary focus of the group's outreach efforts, with the majority of GPG activities held in parents' homes or the local park and advertised through word of mouth, neighborhood flyers, and the GPG listserv.

Forging a Community in Support of Public Schooling

The GPG's strategies created a web of social connections rooted in a particular spatial location. Neighborhood parents with young children were attracted to the prospect of building a neighborhood community, and the GPG organizers gently steered their neighbors in the direction of the local public school. Two themes emerged out of interviews with GPG members: (1) the desire for a "critical mass" of "like-minded" parents in relation to schooling, and (2) the desire for diversity and the embracing of civic responsibility in relation to public spaces and institutions.

Achieving a Critical Mass

The desire to connect with other parents and families with similar education and values, two markers commonly associated with social class, was a common theme in interviews with GPG members. Many of the mothers (and some of the fathers) in the Glenbrook neighborhood stayed at home or worked part-time while their children were young. For first-time parents, in particular, the neighborhood parent group provided an opportunity to get out of the house and interact with other parents in a social setting as well as to share child-rearing information. Parents often met for playdates in the local park or met socially with their families at monthly brunches or weekend social gatherings. Parents had the opportunity to, as one mother stated, "see what was in the realm of normal" for children the same age as their own children, as well as to socialize with other parents who were similar to themselves. Natasha Jacobson, a white upper-middle-class parent, stated, "It was nice to see what other babies were doing. And everybody seemed very well educated and with a great sense of humor. It was a really nice camaraderie and community."

The GPG not only provided social opportunities for children in the neighborhood but also allowed parents to meet other families with whom they had a great deal in common and who were of a similar class. Jackie Turner, a white upper-middle-class parent who had participated in the group since its inception, described her connection to it:

J: It is kind of remarkable that I feel like I like the families and the people in our neighborhood so much. I just kind of feel like we all have similar values. . . . And I don't think that I'd feel that way particularly if I lived in a fancier neighborhood. I don't think I'd like the people as much.

I: *What kind of value system? How does that differ from a fancier neighborhood?*

J: I don't know. I mean, I hear myself talking and it's just getting so stereotypical or whatever. I don't know. . . . Well, I mean, there's definitely people in general who are liberal, and that's just around here but probably more so in the neighborhood. And people seem to be highly educated but not necessarily pursuing careers that are big moneymaker careers. More people involved in, not necessarily nonprofits, but just kind of lifestyle choices that aren't focused on money, money, money. I think a commitment to diversity, although when I think about that initial group of people [in the GPG], it's not a particularly diverse group of people in terms of race and ethnicity.

There was a sense of camaraderie among many neighborhood parents that was based on a shared educational background and economic position, desire for community, and a perceived set of values (e.g., being a "liberal") that were distinct in their minds from the values of those living in more affluent and suburban areas. Parents were also attracted to the group because of the peer group it provided for their children. The age-specific playgroups created through the GPG fostered cohorts of students that gave parents some assurance that their children would enter the school already knowing some of their classmates and their families.

The fear of their child being "the only one" from the neighborhood was often expressed in interviews with parents in the GPG as well as with other white and Asian American middle-class parents whose local school was predominantly African American. In interviews with these parents, "neighborhood" was commonly used as a signifier for "middle class." For example, Nancy Park, an Asian American middle-class parent and organizer of another Woodbury neighborhood parent group seeking to increase neighborhood enrollment in its local school, said that she no longer wanted to enroll her child in the school, given that all the other neighborhood parents had backed out when it came time to enroll. She explained, "If there was, like, one other family who wanted to get into it with me, I would feel so much more hopeful. I would be like, 'OK, let's do what we can do. Let's go to kindergarten and try to recruit all the other parents and try to make some changes.'" When I asked Nancy to describe how the neighborhood families were different from those at the school, she stated: "We're talking about parents who were professionals with a college education, which is generally not the makeup of the population at Jamestown. And I didn't think that that would be such a big issue, but I'm finding that it is an issue for me as well when I'm really face-to-face with it." Nancy sought out and was ultimately able to enroll her child at Morningside, explaining that the school population seemed "much more aligned with [my] values" and that Morningside had "a very active community; the parents are very involved."

Similarly, a GPG member stated that she was "OK with sending [her] kids to school with another middle-class kid, whatever that background is, but I'm not so comfortable sending my child to a school with too many poor children." As found in other studies of white middle- and upper-middle-class parents and urban schooling, having the assurance that there would be families with class backgrounds similar to their own at the school was key (see, e.g., Cucchiara 2013a, 2013b; Kimelberg and Billingham 2013; Stillman 2012).

Sarah Anderson, a white upper-middle-class GPG parent who ultimately chose to send her child to a school outside the neighborhood, believed that the GPG's strategy of "critical mass" was essential to its success in increasing the enrollment of neighborhood families at Morningside:

> There have always been people from the neighborhood who have gone and insisted that their kid has gotten a great education at Morningside. And they're probably right. But I think the sentiment I perceived was that people

didn't want to be the only one sending their kid. . . . And the school worked with the neighborhood to give the parents a sense of a critical mass so they would have some control over the peer group and that sort of thing. I think that was critical.

For many GPG parents with young children, this critical mass was not simply about class but also about race. In interviews, for example, white GPG parents expressed concerns that their child would be "the only one" of his or her race. As Sarah stated, "I don't think I'd want my son to be the only white kid, just talking about race. And I wouldn't want to be the only black kid going to an all-white school." Parents of Asian American children, although fewer in number in the GPG, also worried about their child being "the only one" of their race in a classroom setting. Judy Chu, for example, shared how her own experiences growing up in a predominantly white school and region informed her desire to have her daughter attend a more racially mixed school. She explained that people used to always ask, "What are you?" and it gave her an outsider status that has shaped how she looks at things. She said that she hasn't left Woodbury because she doesn't want her daughter "to have that outsider experience" in a predominantly white setting.

For Natasha Jacobson, a white upper-middle-class parent who had participated in some of the early GPG events when her daughter was a baby, the GPG helped increase her familiarity and comfort with the school. She described her early impressions of Morningside:

In 2001, I hadn't heard anything. I had walked by Morningside. And— umm—it was mostly a lot of black children at the time, African American. And so I had this feeling like it wasn't the neighborhood school because it didn't match the demographic of the neighborhood, and so it didn't even occur to me that it was a neighborhood school. You know, we had some, but—there were three children across the street—none of them went to Morningside.

Despite these early impressions, however, she ended up enrolling her child at Morningside because of the connections she developed with neighborhood families in the GPG and the comfort she had in knowing other parents who were enrolling their children. In interviews, parents commonly "co-mingled race and class explanations" (Horvat 2003, 15) in their narratives about the historic disconnect between Glenbrook parents and their local school. As the examples I have given suggest, race and class were intimately connected in GPG parents' desire to have a "critical mass" of "neighborhood" parents at Morningside.

Parents' use of the term "critical mass" to describe a cohort of largely white middle-class students enrolling at Morningside stands in stark contrast to the meaning attached to the term in most academic and policy discussions of diversity and public education. In the landmark Supreme Court case *Grutter v. Bollinger* (2003), the University of Michigan's Law School argued that there was a compelling state interest to ensure that a "critical mass" of students from minority groups, particularly African American and Latino, was reflected in the student body. The aim in creating this critical mass (through the use of race as one factor among many in admissions) was to provide more opportunity for students to interact with peers from different backgrounds *as well as* to ensure that students of color did not feel isolated or like spokespersons for their race. The building of a critical mass thus referred to efforts to provide access and support to students who were historically denied access to and were currently underrepresented in many predominantly white institutions of higher learning in the United States.

Although white students enrolling at Morningside were indeed racial minorities within the school context, they were not in fact racial minorities within the broader context of the United States and were not a group historically denied access to quality public education in the city. In addition, the principal and the majority of teachers at Morningside were white, as was the majority of the school's neighborhood population. Thus, white parents' reappropriation of the term "critical mass"—a term commonly used in reference to historically marginalized groups—obscures broader racial hierarchies in the United States and the privileges and resources that white students may enjoy despite being a racial minority in a particular school context. Indeed, as I discuss later in the chapter, the building of a critical mass of largely white middle- and upper-middle-class families can ultimately result in *less access* to high-quality schooling for low-income students and students of color.

Seeking Diversity and Embracing Civic Responsibility

At the same time that GPG parents wanted a critical mass of families from similar race and class backgrounds at Morningside, they also wanted their children to attend a "diverse" public school. Many parents shared stories of their own educational experiences, stating that they wanted their children to attend a racially and socioeconomically diverse school either because they were denied this experience themselves as students or because their own experiences in diverse learning environments were seen as an asset. GPG parents liked that the school was increasingly multiracial, with higher numbers of Asian American and Latino students in recent years in contrast to the predominantly African American student population of years past. The growing racial diversity at Morningside was seen as an asset, as their children could attend a school that "looks like [the city of] Woodbury" and that provided their children with what several parents described as a "social education." Yet as Reay et al. (2007, 1053) have argued, white middle-class parents' desire for racial diversity in their children's school may be simply "another, if slightly risky, exciting way of resourcing the middle-class self." Having exposure to and familiarity with students from other cultural, linguistic, and racial backgrounds may enable middle-class children to "get ahead" later in life, providing them with cultural competencies that they can draw on in future employment and in higher education. In this sense, attending a "diverse school" can serve as a form of capital for white middle-class students. And by creating a critical mass of neighborhood kids who were attending the school together, parents were able to expose their children to students from different racial, socioeconomic, and cultural backgrounds while also ensuring that there was a cohort of families like their own at the school.

My interviews suggest that middle-class parents' desire to enroll their children at Morningside was not purely instrumental, however, as parents also wanted to "give back" to their local public school. Many parents mentioned their commitments to public education and their desire to contribute their energy and resources to their local school rather than fleeing to the suburbs or private schools. Matthew Turner, a white upper-middle-class member of the GPG and father of a Morningside student, shared his experiences in a public school during the time of busing, school strikes, and school closures. He compared that with the work of the GPG, stating that "one of the things that was going on was that parents had an implicit or explicit pact to stick it out for a while . . . and I feel like that's what we have going on in this neighborhood." Emily Thompson, one of the founding members of the GPG, expressed her motivations in sending her children to Morningside despite other schooling options:

> Morningside's not the right place if you think your kid is the center of the universe. You know, I always feel like I chose public education because I'd rather choose what's good for lots of people over what's necessarily the very best for my kids. But then, on the other hand, I see that what's good for everybody is part of what's good for my kids.

For GPG parents like Matthew and Emily, sending their children to Morningside and getting involved at the school were part of their civic responsibility, or their desire to contribute to a larger collective rather than being responsive only to the needs of their children. At the same time, they described the school's academics as strong enough that they did not feel they were sacrificing their children's education. As Lori, a self-described "left-of-center progressive," stated, "[Morningside] actually spoke to me in a way that made me decide to put my money where my mouth was and live my values." Like Lori, those GPG parents who ultimately enrolled their children at Morningside took pride in the fact that they had not opted out of the public schools, and they felt a need to contribute based on their values and political orientations.

Parents' desire for diversity, however, ultimately competed with their desire for a community of "like-minded" parents. As information about Morningside spread both within the neighborhood and across the city via playground talk, social networks, and online postings, greater numbers of middle- and upper-middle-class parents became interested in the school as an option for their children. This threatened the socioeconomic diversity of the school that many parents said they valued: although existing low-income students at the school were not "pushed out" or forced to give up their spots, the socioeconomic mix of students in the lower grades began to shift as greater numbers of middle-class parents sought to enroll their young children in the school.

Outreach, Marketing, and Public Relations

In this day and age, sort-of nonprofits like schools and colleges have very much taken on the language of marketing and business and competitiveness and all of that stuff, which may be crap, but it is reality. . . . I just feel like there's nothing wrong with spending our money and our time marketing against private schools.

—Matthew Turner, GPG parent

In the first few years of the organization several GPG members, in combination with a few Morningside parents and teachers who also sought to increase enrollment at the school, captured the attention of middle- and upper-middle-class parents in the neighborhood and across the city through school beautification efforts, marketing, and parent-to-parent outreach. They deliberately tried to create what Mr. Foster described as "curb appeal" by creating gardens and murals that parents would notice when driving or walking by. In an interview, he explained:

I mean, what a shift. And the irony is that the school's always been good. The academics have always been good. The school is prettier now than it's ever been. I mean, I remember sitting with parents nine years ago, deliberately talking about curb appeal. How do we get people to stop driving by? How do we get them to stop and maybe walk in? Once we got them to walk in, they were amazed. They wanted their kid there.

In addition to those who lived or frequently drove by the small elementary school, families across the city began to hear about Morningside through newspaper articles, listservs and websites, social networks, and parent forums that were largely spearheaded by GPG leaders. Several members of the GPG and a few other Morningside parents posted favorable reviews about the school on a popular website for regional parents and on a national website that provided school information to parents. In interviews about the school choice and enrollment process, middle- and upper-middle-class parents commonly cited these two websites as key sources they used to obtain information about the local schools. One GPG member wrote numerous articles about Morningside for the neighborhood newsletter, highlighting the school's assets as well as announcing upcoming school events. Another created a website for the school. In addition, GPG organizers and a few MPTO leaders set up information booths about the school at local street fairs and regional events for parents. By 2006 when I first began my research, Morningside had gained a favorable reputation among a growing number of parents in the city based on its expanding academic and enrichment programs, as well as the fact that it was relatively easy to get into compared with the more affluent public schools that were oversubscribed by neighborhood families clamoring for a spot.

Many of the parents from outside the immediate enrollment zone who were interested in Morningside were college-educated, middle- and upper-middle-class parents who were dissatisfied with their neighborhood schools, and most were considering the more elite public schools as well as private and charter schools in the area.[2] In my survey of and interviews with prospective parents, Morningside's small size, emphasis on the arts, dedicated principal and staff, and level of parent involvement were commonly cited as attractive features. In the late 1990s and early 2000s Morningside would not have been on the radar of most parents able to afford private schools; however, by 2006 a growing number were considering Morningside among other highly sought-out schools in the city.

GPG parent leaders knew the influential role that public perceptions can play in school choice. They knew they were working against all the negative associations that many parents had with the local public schools. The school district had attempted to counter these negative perceptions through information campaigns, public forums, and fairs. This aligned with the district's newly adopted enrollment process, a more centralized process aimed at making enrollment more equitable by giving principals less power and discretion over enrollment decisions and by increasing the information that all parents had about district schools. Given their busy schedules and work demands, few teachers or staff members at Morningside had the time to focus on marketing and outreach. In reflecting on the changes at the school, the principal stated, "I've never been good with PR stuff. It's not my thing. So [Emily Thompson] and that group were essential to bring community folks back to the school. There's no doubt about that."

Parents talking to other parents was a key strategy used by the GPG to get the word out about Morningside. GPG leaders created opportunities for parent-to-parent conversations about the school through tours, a Parent-to-Parent Forum, and booths at local and district events. Although some Morningside parents and teachers expressed in interviews that "marketing" work was not of interest to them, Hannah and a few other parents in the MPTO attended some of these events with GPG leaders in order to represent the school and share their experiences as Morningside parents.

The following excerpts from my field notes taken at a district-wide School Fair illustrate the efforts of some parents and a teacher at the school to generate prospective-parent interest in the school:

> I went over to Morningside's table at the fair, where Mark Fisher [an MPTO leader], Emily Thompson, and Mr. Foster [a teacher] were sitting. There was a book called "Our Families Are Special" put together by kindergartners, as well as a fifth-grade digestive system project and a cell project. There was a slideshow of the school on a laptop and a glossy display about the school with descriptions of the school's stated strengths: "strong academic growth; supportive neighborhood and friends; creative, hardworking teachers; a visionary principal; a unique learning environment; academics enriched by arts; an active community of parents." I also recognized the binder full of newspaper articles and flyers about the history of the school that Emily had created. There was also a Spanish student-made book and a calendar of events.

> I heard Emily talking to another white woman about the school, saying, "We have a neighborhood listserv to try to get neighborhood residents

to go to the school." I also heard Mr. Foster inviting a white female with twins to the Garden Work Day this Saturday. The white woman who was talking to Emily said, "When I did the tour, I saw that there was a broad range of diversity represented, but what other aspects of diversity are there?" I later heard her follow up by saying, "What's the racial demographics in the kindergarten classes this year?" Emily responded, "There's not a true majority." The woman explained the reason for her question by saying that "one of my children is biracial and the other one is white, and I want something that's diverse for both of them." The woman told Emily that she lives outside the school enrollment zone. She said, "Just by walking on campus [at Morningside], I thought this was the place for them."

An African American woman approached the table and said that she had called the school and heard that there was no space for first graders. She said that she was looking for a school with an after-school program, since she works until six and her husband works at night. Emily encouraged her to keep checking back with the school, because spots open up. She asked the woman if she had visited the school, and the woman said no. She said that her coworker had just enrolled her kid at Morningside for next year and she had heard about the after-school program. Mark said, "Morningside's a great school, we love it," and told her that she should definitely come to the Open House if she could.

An Asian American woman who said she lived in the school enrollment zone adjacent to that of Morningside asked Mr. Foster how long he's been at the school, and the parent commented that the school seems like "it's nice and diverse." Mr. Foster said, "It's diverse racially and socioeconomically—we have kids coming from all over."

Later, in a conversation I had with Michelle Warner [a white neighborhood parent] about her reasons for enrolling her child at Morningside, she explained that Emily had led her tour of the school. She said Emily was really positive and had only good things to say about Morningside. Michelle said the school is "all great, it's everything I like." She said, "It seemed to me that there would be compromises for every school, but this one has everything." She said, "Did I mention that it was free?"

GPG leaders and MPTO parent organizers wanted to maintain a racially and socioeconomically diverse student body, and they attempted to reach out to a wide range of parents. Targeting middle- and upper-middle-class families, GPG leaders organized a parent-led annual event for prospective parents that was purposefully held in the fall to get Morningside on the radar before private school enrollment deadlines. At the same time, flyers about the school were sent to a long list of preschools that included Head Start and to others that served low-income students, and all current Morningside families were encouraged to pass out flyers to friends and fellow church members. As reflected in the field notes above, parents also spoke with prospective parents at district-sponsored events.

Parents' efforts to reach working-class and low-income families were not enough to counter the broader forces that were causing more middle-class families to move into the school. Whereas parents' outreach to Head Starts or other predominantly low-income preschools took the form of flyers or one-time presentations, GPG organizers had created numerous social opportunities to connect with families in the largely middle- and upper-middle-class neighborhood surrounding the school, attracting many parents based on the fact that they saw (and got to know) "people like them" in the school community. Similarly, middle-class parents from outside the neighborhood who had access to extensive information about the enrollment process (e.g., through listservs and their social networks) were in a privileged position when it came to gaining a spot for their children at the school. And finally, the district's preference for neighborhood families and the high cost of housing in the student catchment area meant that as the school increased in popularity among middle-class neighborhood families, low-income and working-class parents were less likely to be able to enroll their children at Morningside.

Sheila Hill, a working-class African American long-timer parent, spoke about the need for different methods of outreach. She had been asked by MPTO parents to share her experiences as a Morningside parent at several events for prospective families, and in reflecting on her outreach experiences she noted that most of the information about the school was sent through e-mail, the GPG listserv, a regional parent listserv, or flyers at local preschools. She noted:

> So the outreach that's been done is mainly electronic and in ways that are not really advertised unless you know already. And I think that just precludes a lot of underrepresented minorities from even knowing about the school. And even knowing about the deadlines and when to enroll with the district and all that stuff. I mean all that stuff needs to be like—which makes me think I should have gone to my old preschool and done some outreach. . . .

Because my son and daughter went to an all-black preschool in Woodlawn.
And I've been meaning to do some outreach there for Morningside.

According to Sheila, there was a need to personally visit local preschools
serving low-income students and students of color and to talk with parents
who may not have access to the information passed along through online
listservs and middle-class social networks.

As Mr. Foster reflected, the school was now receiving attention not
just from prospective parents but from local universities and foundations
as well:

> That started to shift here and I think there is a political core of the people
> who did come in and they liked what they saw, and that was enough to
> like crack that door, and then gradually their conversation grew and grew
> and grew, and now I mean, they even laugh. Like, we are the darling of the
> [region]. Everybody wants, even grant people, even universities, everybody
> wants to get their photograph with us.

By 2007, the Parent-Teacher Organization budget had risen from $15,000
to $129,000, as a result of grants, fund-raising events, and increases in in-
dividual parent donations. As I discuss in greater detail in chapter 5, there
was a concern among school staff and parent leaders that the need for parent fund-raising would be even greater in the future if the school lost the
over $50,000 it received in Title I funds on the basis of the demographics
of its student population. In the 2008 enrollment period, there were no
longer spots available for children who did not have siblings already at the
school and who lived outside the neighborhood enrollment area.[3]

In addition to the socioeconomic profile of its families, the racial demographics of the student population also significantly changed (see table 2).
The percentage of white students at Morningside increased from 14 percent in the 2000/2001 school year to 24 percent in 2007/8, significantly
higher than the percentage of white students in the district at that time
(6 percent). The percentage of African American students declined during
the same period, and in 2007/8, African American students composed only
38 percent of the student body (compared to 78 percent in 2000/2001).
Most of the African American students were concentrated in the upper
grades. The first-grade class in 2006/7, for example, was 33 percent African American, whereas the fifth-grade class was 79 percent. In the 2006/7
school year (the year of the study), there was a large jump in the number

Table 2 Demographic changes at Morningside

	2000/2001	2007/8
African American	78%	38%
White	14%	24%
Hispanic/Latino	5%	4%
Asian	2%	3%
Multiple/no response	1%	30%
Free/reduced-price lunch	44%	41%
Parent-Teacher Organization budget	$15,000	$129,000

Source: California Department of Education.
Note: American Indian students represented less than 1 percent of the student population. Percentages do not equal 100 because of rounding.

of students marking "multiple/no response" when asked their race. Kindergartners were overrepresented in this group, with 91 percent of kindergarten students classified as "multiple/no response."[4] The percentage of Latino and Asian students changed little from 2000/2001 to 2007/8. In contrast to the student population, the administrative and teaching staff were predominantly white and female, reflecting trends in many schools across the nation. The majority of Morningside's support staff, however (e.g., teachers' aides, custodians, office staff), were African American.

Table 2 shows the demographic shifts. It does not, however, fully capture the complexities of the changes occurring at the school or how parents and teachers experienced those changes. Although district and school data did not account for the unique racial backgrounds of the large number of kindergartners self-classified as "multiple/no response," for example, my observations at the school and discussions with teachers and parents suggest that by 2006/7 there were more children from mixed-race families (Asian-white, Latino-white) and transracial adoptees in the lower grades than in years past. There were also fewer kindergarten students who were racially identifiable as African American, particularly in contrast to students in the upper grades at the school. For example, Marisa Collins, a white parent of a fourth grader, described what she saw as a noticeable decline in the number of black families at the school and a rise in the number of mixed-race (Asian-white) families:

I mean now you look at the kindergartens and they're probably half-white and, you know, a lot more Asian. I mean there were very few Latinos and very few Asians at the school in my child's cohort. And there are many more

Asians and Asian-white mixtures now than there were then. Now that said, you can't tell by looking at somebody what their ethnic background is.

Like the reported racial demographics of the school, the number of students enrolled in the free/reduced-price lunch program is only a rough marker of the socioeconomic makeup of the school: it doesn't account for the range of class backgrounds at the school or the ways in which class is "lived" within the school context.[5] Even a slight increase in the number of middle-class and upper-middle-class families can have a significant impact on a school community because of the capital these parents bring to a school and their particular forms of engagement. Although the aggregate percentage of enrollment in the free/reduced-price lunch program showed only a slight decline, interviews with long-timer teachers and parents and data on financial contributions to the school suggest that there were more affluent parents in the lower grades than in years past. The fund that the MPTO established for individual family donations rose from less than $1,000 in 2001/2 to $37,000 in 2006/7, for example. As a member of the MPTO budget committee stated in an interview:

> The budget has probably at least doubled, if not tripled in the five years I've been there. And that is due to better organization and a much higher—a layer of higher socioeconomic level in a greater proportion of the people. You know, there's just a lot more people now who can give more. So some of it is just organizing. I mean, the Morningside Fund was launched in, I think, my second year here. And the expectation that everybody would give monthly or a one-year donation was made, and that first year, you know, we got a lot of checks for $25 and $100. Now we get checks for $5,000. There were two people this year who gave a check for $5,000. These are the folks that probably could have spent $12,000 or $15,000 sending their child to a private school, and did not because Morningside is their neighborhood school and they wanted to politically—or, you know, or they thought, "Oh, we're saving $15,000." But they're in a position to be giving $5,000.

The school, traditionally much smaller than other schools in the district, faced increasing pressure in 2006/7 to find space to accommodate its growing student population. The increased demand for enrollment at Morningside and the growing popularity of the school among middle-class families in the city affected not only the school but other elementary schools in the district as well. A growing number of middle-class families from adjacent neighborhoods also enrolled their children in Morningside and contributed time and economic resources to the school that they may have otherwise invested in their own neighborhood school had they considered it a viable option.

GPG Outreach: A "Double-Edged Sword"

By 2006, the first year of the study, it was common for families to intentionally stay or move into the neighborhood so they could send their children to Morningside. A local realtor commented that "as the school has become more and more desirable, people now move into that area, and their thought is not to sell. [They're thinking,] 'Gosh, can we get a bigger house in the neighborhood, can we remodel our house, how can we stay here?'"

Reflecting their initial goals, GPG leaders had fostered a greater sense of community among Glenbrook parents and increased the level of neighborhood support for Morningside. During the period of study, for example, it was common to see groups of neighborhood families walking their young children to school together, and GPG children often participated in playdates with each other. In addition to a greater number of middle- and upper-middle-class neighborhood parents choosing to enroll their children, other young professional parents from across the city began to take an interest in the school. Neighborhood residents (including several GPG families who ultimately chose private schools for their children) donated money to Morningside and volunteered their time and resources for school events.

Yet Morningside's transition to more of a "neighborhood school" engendered tensions within the school community. The GPG's efforts to increase community support for their local school ended up attracting those of similar racial and socioeconomic backgrounds both within and outside the school's enrollment zone, ultimately threatening the diversity of Morningside's student population, which many parents cited as an important asset. As described in further detail in the following chapter, this was a point of concern for many teachers, staff, and parents. Although they liked the resources and support the group offered to the school, many long-timer parents and teachers voiced concerns that Morningside would ultimately become more like the predominantly white and affluent schools in the western part of the district.

Several GPG parents recognized that their efforts to build a critical mass of neighborhood families at Morningside may have had unintended consequences. In an interview, Jackie described what she characterized as the "double-edged sword" related to their outreach efforts:

So in a way it's sort of a double-edged sword. Because if you market so well to the neighborhood and no one went to private school, then you would lose a lot of your diversity, and I think that would be a problem for the school. Or not a problem, but it would be a different kind of a school. Which in a way, then, it is [a problem] because we all like it just as it is.

As alluded to in this quotation, GPG parents did not see themselves as gentrifiers seeking to "take over" the school community; they took pride in the fact that they lived in the city and sent their children to a racially and socioeconomically diverse public school.

They lived in a residential area with comparatively high property values, however, and many actively sought to foster place-based and school-related bonds with "like-minded" parents of similar social class—those they saw as sharing their values and lifestyles. Although they wanted their children exposed to children from different racial and socioeconomic backgrounds, many also desired a "critical mass" of families like themselves in their local school. In developing this critical mass of middle-class (and predominantly white) parents, however, the GPG helped to facilitate the demographic shifts at Morningside. Given the demographic shifts occurring in the broader region, the power of middle-class social networks in school "choice" processes, and the district's student assignment policies that privileged neighborhood schooling, the socioeconomic diversity that characterized the Morningside school community was thus unstable and unlikely to be sustained.

The case of the GPG illustrates the power of middle-class social networks and outreach in urban school change efforts, as well as the potentially negative (and perhaps unintended) consequences of middle-class parents' school improvement endeavors. Studies of school choice have shown that social networks are highly influential in the school decision making of middle-class parents; parents often rely upon the judgments of other middle-class parents in their evaluations of school quality and appropriateness for their children—more so than test scores or official informational materials from schools and districts (Ball and Vincent 1998; Dougherty et al. 2009; Holme 2002). This was certainly true in my research. The case of the GPG shows *how* middle-class parents influence other parents from similar race and class backgrounds by illustrating the methods and processes through which neighborhood parent support for urban public schools is built and mobilized.

The enrollment of the children of GPG parents (and the resulting demographic shifts in the lower grades at the school) can be seen as a form of voluntary integration, a promising trend in light of a national political and legal climate that has made it increasingly difficult for local districts to foster school racial and socioeconomic diversity through student assignment plans. Yet as the demographic shifts outlined above suggest, it is unlikely that Morningside will be able to sustain a socioeconomic mix of students in the long run without explicit and intentional efforts to ensure that the school remains accessible to low-income and working-class students who do not reside in the largely middle-class neighborhood enrollment zone. Indeed, my follow-up research at Morningside two years after the original study (see chapter 6) illustrates the growing competition to get into Morningside and the increased affluence of the school community. Thus, voluntary, parent-led efforts to integrate urban public schools, despite the best intentions of these parent groups, may ultimately result in school gentrification rather than full, sustainable economic integration. The promises of economic integration—the social benefits for all students and the access to high-quality schooling that it can facilitate for low-income students—are not likely to be realized if only a small percentage of low-income students are able to access and benefit from the investments brought by middle-class parents.

In the aggregate and the short term, the Morningside student population had become more racially and socioeconomically diverse: there were growing numbers of mixed-race and white students attending the school. However, with this came a decline in the number of African American students and low-income students enrolling in the lower grades, which changed the social and political dynamics and engendered tensions within the school community. As I discuss in the following chapter, Morningside Elementary was not a blank slate: it was viewed as a positive option for many families long before middle-class families in the neighborhood and district deemed it so.

FOUR

The (Re)Making of a Good Public School: Parent and Teacher Views of a Changing School Community

I think [Morningside has] improved in these last two years. . . . I think because more neighborhood parents are involved and they have the same values around education.

—Claire Hansen, neighborhood private school parent

I think that there is this perception in the community now that "wow, Morningside is a great school." And I think there was a perception before that because the test scores weren't in the ninetieth percentile and it was predominantly African American, it wasn't a good school. And it always was. It always was. So that bothers me a bit. I find that just disturbing a little bit.

—Molly Clausen, long-timer Morningside parent

As Morningside Elementary received greater attention in the local media, and as a growing number of middle- and upper-middle-class families in the neighborhood and across the school district enrolled their children in the school, long-timer parents and teachers wanted to ensure that the school's history and culture were honored and preserved. They sought to counter the view, like that alluded to above by Claire Hansen, that the school had suddenly become "good" because of the enrollment and investments of a greater number of middle- and upper-middle-class families. In a local newspaper article exploring the growing number of white middle-class families in the city of Woodbury who were considering public, rather than private, schools for their children, Ms. D'Anza, the school's principal for almost a decade, pointed out that the school had "stood on its own" before more neighborhood families began to consider it as an option for their children. Likewise, Marcus Weeks, an African American longtime

Morningside staff member and parent, stated in an interview that the small public school had been Woodbury's "best-kept secret." For many parents and teachers who had been at Morningside before the changes, attributing the school's success solely to the efforts of the Glenbrook Parents' Group (GPG), or to the new middle- and upper-middle-class families in general, rendered invisible the historic and current contributions of many parents and teachers at the school.

In this chapter, I use Morningside as a case study to question normative assumptions about how to identify and create "good" public schools. In an era of educational reform in which accountability and choice are emphasized, urban schools seen as improving are commonly framed as those with rising test scores and increased consumer (i.e., parental) demand for enrollment. Indeed, the fate of most urban public schools rests almost entirely upon the extent to which they are able to raise (or maintain) student test scores and enrollment: those schools failing to raise scores, experiencing declining enrollment, or both are commonly threatened with closure or reconstitution under No Child Left Behind's system of accountability (de la Torre and Gwynne 2009; Kirshner, Gaertner, and Pozzoboni 2010). Attracting and retaining middle-class families—influential consumers or "customers" in a broader educational marketplace—are commonly key components of district and city leaders' efforts to remake or improve urban schools (see, e.g., Cucchiara 2013b).

More scholarly and media attention has been paid in recent years to the preferences, choices, and experiences of white middle-class parents who are considering city public schools for their children; yet we know little about the perspectives and experiences of long-timer parents and teachers who chose these schools prior to a boom in middle-class enrollment.[1] What led parents and teachers to these schools, and why did they stay? How do they interpret and understand the changes affecting their school community? How do their perceptions of the changes and of the school community compare with those of "newcomer" middle- and upper-middle-class parents? Investigating the perspectives and lived experiences of parents and teachers experiencing school change is important, as they may illuminate alternative understandings and histories of educational reform that are not captured in dominant narratives of middle-class parent school improvement.

My aim here is not to valorize all traditional urban public schools as inherently "good schools." There are numerous examples—both historically and contemporarily—that demonstrate the ways in which traditional public school settings have failed to serve children of color and low-income students. However, I want to stress that there are different "urbans" in urban education—schools and communities with different contexts, histories, and records of success and "failure." Indeed, as this chapter will show, Morningside was not simply an urban institution in need of middle-class renewal: the school had a history, culture, and context that made it a "school of choice" for parents and teachers prior to the boom in middle-class enrollment. The findings outlined in this chapter demonstrate the limitations of using test scores and percentages of middle-class students as the sole markers of "good schools." A reliance on these commonly used symbols of school success often works to devalue or ignore positive characteristics of urban schools that may not be captured in these measures alone. Rather, the perspectives of parents and teachers presented in this chapter highlight the need for educational leaders and scholars to understand the social and historical contexts of school communities in their efforts to evaluate or improve urban public schools.

The Makings of a "Good School"

Proponents of economically integrated schools see the presence of middle-class students and their parents as a key ingredient in school success. As Richard Kahlenberg (2001a, 62), a leading advocate for economic integration, argues, "Educated middle-class parents are more likely to be involved in their children's schools, to insist on high standards, to rid the school of bad teachers, and to ensure adequate resources (both public and private)—in effect to promote effective schools for their children." He claims that the work of middle-class parents benefits not only their own children but the entire student population, as they "raise the average achievement of all children in the school" (2001a, 63). This view of middle-class parents as critical to the success of urban schools is also reflected in popular and political discourse. In an *Edutopia* article highlighting the work of middle-class parents at one Philadelphia elementary school, for example, the school district's former CEO, Paul Vallas, stated that two affluent parent leaders at the school "improved the school climate and made it more academically rigorous," adding that "these improvements were good for everybody, including those who didn't have the option to send their kids anywhere else" (Smith 2009).

Race is at play here as well. As discussed in the previous chapter, studies have shown that white parents tend to avoid schools with predominantly African American student populations, even when one controls for other factors such as poverty rate and test scores. Whiteness serves as a symbolic resource (Lewis 2003) in school choice: "white" schools—with white parents—are often assumed to be better than "black" schools. This means that predominantly black schools typically have to work harder to counter parents' negative perceptions and to prove their worth and success in the public eye.

Many long-timer parents and teachers regarded Morningside as a good school prior to the increased interest from middle- and upper-middle-class and white parents, suggesting alternative systems of valuation beyond student demographics. In contrast to framings of school choice that position parents as individual actors making choices based almost entirely on test scores or other quantifiable data, many parents from outside the enrollment zone had sought out the school on the basis of their historical and social connections to the Morningside community. These long-timer parents—who had children enrolled at Morningside in the late 1990s and early 2000s—saw it as a positive alternative to their neighborhood schools: it was small, had low teacher turnover compared with most schools within the district, and had a favorable reputation among families they knew. Although the school's test scores and its parent-teacher organization budget were not as high as those of the more affluent schools in the district, there were other aspects that made it a good school in the eyes of long-timer teachers and families.

I first met Laneisha Jackson, a working-class African American parent, in 2007, when her child was in the fourth grade at Morningside. Her mother lived in one of the few affordable-housing apartment buildings in the neighborhood, and her older siblings had attended Morningside. In an interview, Laneisha compared Morningside to her neighborhood school, a school that was located in a predominantly African American area of the city with high rates of concentrated poverty and that was designated as "underperforming." She described the school as "more rough, more hard-core" than Morningside. When describing her motivation for enrolling her child at Morningside, she talked about what she saw as more positive peer influences for her child and a chance for social and economic mobility. She said, "I want my kid to have the best. I didn't graduate on time from high school, but I picked it up later on. . . . I just picked it up in the last three or four years, though, but I did go back. I just don't want them to make the same mistakes I did. That's all—I'm just overprotective." Laneisha's desire to send her son to Morningside was also linked to child care and safety, as she had a long commute to a suburban job and she felt better knowing that her mother was nearby if anything happened at the school during the day.

Hannah Sorenson, a white upper-middle-class parent of a fifth grader and former member of the leadership of the Morningside Parent-Teacher Organization (MPTO), had been a parent at Morningside since the late 1990s, when her oldest child first enrolled. Both she and her husband had a history of activism in district and community politics. They lived just outside Morningside's enrollment boundary and were concerned about sending their child to the neighborhood school because of the school's large size and what Hannah described as a weak academic program. Although she and her husband could have afforded private school, in an interview Hannah described her commitment to public education and desire for her children to attend a racially and socioeconomically diverse school:

> I felt like we could provide a lot of support for academics for our children, but what I felt we could not provide was an experience of working with and being—working and playing with a diverse group of kids—a socioeconomically and racially diverse group of kids. And so I felt like if there were any weakness in the public schools related to academics, we could make up for those. But there was no way we could replace the opportunity that my kids would get in a public school socially.

When Hannah enrolled her oldest child at Morningside, her daughter was one of a few white students in her grade (white students were less than 15 percent of the student population). Long-timer whites like Hannah were almost all middle-class homeowners with college educations. Most lived in the racially mixed or predominantly African American neighborhoods just outside Morningside's enrollment zone. In interviews, these parents described how they had sought out Morningside based on their strong commitments to public education and the favorable reputation of the school's leadership and staff. Like some of the white GPG parents I interviewed, several mentioned that they were a bit nervous about their child being the only white child or one of a few in their class. Yet unlike other white neighborhood parents, who were hoping for a critical mass of neighborhood families to enroll their children, long-timer whites entered the school knowing few if any other families at Morningside.

In interviews most white long-timers cited the quality of teaching, administrative leadership, and opportunities for social mixing across lines of race and class as important factors they considered when choosing a school for their children. Suzie Miller, a white middle-class parent of a fifth grader at Morningside whose older child was a Morningside alum, had had the option of enrolling her older child in a school with higher test scores and greater numbers of white middle-class families. She stated in an interview, however, that she came to Morningside "because of the staff," having heard good things from a friend about the school's teachers. In addition, she talked about how she liked the fact that the racial demographics of the student body were similar to the demographics of her predominantly black neighborhood. When asked why she didn't consider sending her child to Manchester, a public school in an affluent part of Glenbrook that had higher test scores than Morningside, she replied, "I hate to say it, but it's really white. And we live in Woodbury. . . . My husband and I thought that that was really important for our son to go to a school that looked like our neighborhood."

In contrast to most long-timer whites, who had heard about the teaching staff but had no prior relationship with the school's families, many long-timer African Americans spoke of the social, geographic, or familial connections that drew them to the school. Many knew friends or family members who had attended Morningside or were connected to a child care provider near the school. Dawn Traylor, for example, lived in the house where she grew up, just a few blocks away from the school. She had attended Morningside, her older children had graduated from the school, and many of her friends' children attended as well. In an interview, she said she hadn't even considered private schools for her children, given her economic situation, and was pleased that her children were able to attend Morningside. In describing her visit to Frazier, another elementary school close to her home, she said, "It was like horse races when the bell rang in the hallway at Frazier, and I was like, no, he can't go here. And I immediately went to Morningside." Reflecting the findings from other studies of the school choices of African American low-income and working-class parents, these parents considered a range of factors beyond test scores in their evaluations of schools for their children (e.g., safety, proximity to home or child care, familiarity) (Deluca and Rosenblatt 2010; Schneider, Teske, and Marschall 2002). Likewise, their choices were relational, shaped by both the social contexts within which they were embedded and the broader constraints (e.g., transportation, child care, enrollment policies, economic capital) they faced (Cooper 2009).

Most Morningside teachers and staff were long-timers as well and spoke favorably about the school in relation to other schools in the district. In 2006, all but two of the teachers, for example, had worked at the school for at least three years, and most were veteran teachers with more than eight years of teaching experience. A few of the teachers and staff members had older children who had attended Morningside, with their historical connection to the school dating back to the 1980s. When asked what brought them to Morningside, teachers commonly spoke of the school's small size, "safe environment," "active" group of parents, and administrative leadership. In comparing Morningside with other schools in which they had worked, for example, many spoke of the principal's prior experience as a veteran teacher and what one teacher described as her "pedagogical priorities." As Ms. Harper, an upper-grade teacher stated, "I think Marilyn [the principal] has really good priorities, and she sort of figured out what she needs to do. We probably spend a huge, huge amount on buying really beautiful books. I think the budget reflects values, and I think the values of our leadership are in the right place." Mr. Stein, a kindergarten teacher, described how the principal gave teachers "pedagogical license" to modify their curriculum beyond the scripted program adopted by the district. Under the principal's leadership, many teachers participated in professional-development training related to literacy and arts education, and most teachers regularly collaborated with their grade-level colleagues in planning lessons and units.

Long-timer parents and teachers acknowledged that the school had had its share of challenges; in interviews, several described incidents dating back to the 1970s in which racial tensions flared between African American and white parents, as well as periods of administrative turnover that had affected enrollment. A white veteran teacher at the school and in the district described Morningside as having "gone through cycles" in the 1980s and early 1990s in terms of academic rigor and quality, with things really turning around once Ms. D'Anza became principal in 1997. Yet many long-timer teachers and parents were careful to stress that Morningside was a good school prior to the establishment of the GPG and the recent boom in enrollment. In an interview, Ms. Brown, an African American staff member who had been at the school for over a decade, asserted:

> It's always been a good school. I was here under two great principals. The first was great at writing grants and getting money. Under her leadership Morningside had money coming in from alternate sources—not necessarily fund-raisers but from grants. Mrs. D'Anza [the current principal] brought in a new group of parents, and the MPTO has taken off. Parent involvement is up. Parents have been involved since preschool, and once they get into the school, their expectation is here [*raises hand to represent a high bar*].

For these parents and teachers, the school had many positive aspects that had gone unnoticed by the broader community and that simply needed to be built upon and more fully supported.

During the last three decades, for example, a small and interracial group of working- and middle-class parents from both within and outside the neighborhood had been advocates for the school. According to long-timer Morningside parents and teachers and parents of Morningside alums, parents and staff had fought and won a battle against the district in the early 1970s when the school was slated for closure because of low enrollment. Several leaders of Morningside's parent group were later elected to positions in city government and education.

In the late 1990s and early 2000s, under Ms. D'Anza's leadership as principal, a small but active group of teachers and parents worked to enhance the school's curriculum and bring in more resources. Art was more fully integrated into the curriculum, and teachers received extensive training in balanced literacy. Because of the number of students qualifying for the free/reduced-price lunch program at the school, long-timer teachers and parent leaders were able to secure several large grants for enrichment programs and an after-school sports program. Although the MPTO budget at that time was much smaller than it was during the period of my research, the school used funds from the organization to help offset the costs of the school librarian, field trips and educational materials for students, and some of the school's enrichment programs. Parents and staff also worked together to develop a fee-based after-school program for families whose income exceeded the requirements for the school's subsidized program, creating a seamless, economically mixed after-school program for students. These resources and opportunities were uncommon in many of the district's schools, particularly those with large numbers of low-income students. Although the school was not one of the top-ranked schools in the district in terms of academics, student test scores were steadily improving in the early 2000s, and the school consistently met its growth targets for students of color and economically disadvantaged students.[2]

Thus, a number of factors—beyond simply test scores and student demographic data—shaped long-timer parents' and teachers' conceptions of Morningside as a "good" school. These factors, particularly the historical and social connections that individuals have to schools and the realities of their daily lives, are often overlooked in discourses of school choice that position parents and students as individual actors who make decisions based largely on measurable and quantifiable data (Fuller, Elmore, and Orfield 1996; Kirshner and Pozzoboni 2011; Schneider, Teske, and Marschall 2002). Long-timers' choices and systems of valuation demonstrate the need to understand the social and historical contexts within which both schools and parents are embedded, as these broader contexts shape parents' choices and conceptions of value. Those parents who chose Morningside in the late 1990s and early 2000s—both middle class and low income—were not simply uninformed. Rather, they decided to invest in Morningside on the basis of a set of criteria in which test scores and the percentage of white students were not primary.

Long-Timer Views of a Changing School Population

In large part due to parents' outreach efforts, the school in 2007 was quite different from that of the late 1990s and early 2000s, when many long-timer parents had first enrolled their children. As shown in table 2 in chapter 3, the percentage of African American students and students qualifying for free or reduced-price lunches had significantly declined, particularly in the lower grades. The school had also received increased interest from white, multiracial, and middle-class families in the neighborhood and broader district. In a survey of prospective parents who attended Morningside's Kindergarten Open House in 2007, for example, twenty-seven out of the twenty-nine respondents stated that they had a bachelor's degree or higher, with twelve holding a master's or professional degree. The majority of respondents were white and had family incomes that topped $100,000 (with eighteen out of twenty-nine respondents selecting $100,001 or above).[3] Ms. Porter, a kindergarten teacher, described the changes as follows:

> But it's changing. I think Mr. Stein [another kindergarten teacher] has a larger group of white students this year. If you look at the entire kindergarten body, then it's definitely become more white. If you look at my class alone, there was a good deal of diversity there. But it's definitely becoming more upper-middle class.

Indeed, in working as a volunteer in both a kindergarten class and a fifth-grade class during the 2006/7 school year, I observed kindergarten classes that, when compared with fifth-grade classes, were whiter and more biracial (white-Asian, white-Latino) and had a greater number of parents in professional positions (e.g., business owner, lawyer, researcher). The three kindergarten classes included the first major "cohort" of neighborhood families connected to the GPG—a group of about seven children—as well as a large number of middle-class children whose parents resided just outside the school's enrollment boundary and who were on the GPG's listserv. Not all prospective parents and kindergarten parents were affluent, however, as there were several low-income and working-class students who were siblings of upper-grade students or who were children of staff members at the school. "Kindergarten parents" and "neighborhood parents," however, became euphemisms in many long-timer descriptions for what was seen as a group of largely white, affluent, and professional families.

For long-timer teachers and parents, it wasn't simply the socioeconomic differences that stood out: in fact, a few of the long-timer white parents who voiced concerns about the shifting demographics had occupational statuses, household incomes, and educational backgrounds that were similar to those of many of the newcomers.[4] What was different in their eyes was that there were a greater number of professionals with potentially different forms of engagement and values. The new mix was seen by many long-timers as a potential threat not only to the school's racial and socio-economic mix of students but also to the school culture as well. Those parents who had volunteered regularly and devoted many hours to supporting the school over the years were the most vocal in their concern about the changing family population. They voiced concerns that the critical mass of middle- and upper-middle-class families would quickly become a wave of change that would not serve the collective school population. These parent leaders talked about kindergarten parents as having different values, focused less on communalism and "hands-on" volunteerism and more on test scores and resources that would benefit their children specifically. The following statement from Suzie Miller captures this sentiment:

> And I haven't witnessed this, but I've heard there's a big drive, and they want to have their own kindergarten fund-raising for a playground, and very group-oriented rather than school-oriented is what I feel is going on. That there's a definite dividing line between . . . and I'm not sure that when they came to Morningside, I'm not sure that they realized that Morningside isn't just high test scores. There's a lot of kids there that need a lot more help than their kids need, and that's part of the deal that you come here and you're not going to be just exposed to people like you. But I could be pretty harsh in saying that, because I actually don't know any of these people. That's my impression.

Long-timer middle-class parents like Suzie Miller who had volunteered many hours for the school and who were what one veteran teacher described as "pioneers" worried that the new middle-class parents were more concerned with benefiting their own children and that they wouldn't contribute to the collective school community.

This concern about a change in school culture was voiced by several teachers as well. In interviews, when asked what brought them to Morningside, most mentioned that they were committed to working in an urban school and wanted to teach underserved students. They feared that the demographic changes would eventually transform the ethos of the school into more of a "private" or "suburban" school where, in their minds, parent volunteerism was more focused on fund-raising rather than, as one teacher said, "hands-on" work within the school. Ms. Hawkins, a white veteran teacher at Morningside, stated the following when asked how the school has changed over the past five years:

> There has always been a sense at Morningside that we are working towards making this a great school, and I don't get the feeling with these new kindergarten parents that they are willing to work. They would rather pay for things, and that worries me. As a teacher, I don't want to just be teaching at a suburban school. If it starts to be that there are no more kids of color or socioeconomic diversity, I don't know if I'll stay here.

For many Morningside teachers, part of what made Morningside a good school was having "kids of color" and a socioeconomically mixed student population. Linking geography to student demographics and forms of parental engagement, Ms. Hawkins voiced a fear that the school would become more like a "suburban" school with a more white and affluent population.

White middle-class long-timers' orientations toward and visions of school change in many ways mirror what Brown-Saracino (2010, 261) describes as "social preservation": "the culturally motivated choice of certain people, who tend to be highly educated and residentially mobile, to live in . . . authentic social space, embodied by the sustained presence of 'original' residents." Whereas gentrifiers seek to invest in the future of a space or institution, social preservationists desire to preserve both the past and the present attributes of a particular place. In her research on urban and rural communities affected by gentrification, Brown-Saracino (2010, 261) found that social preservationists' desire for a sustained presence of old-timers was "rooted in a combination of altruistic concern for those threatened by displacement and taste for an 'authentic' version of community predicated on the struggle of marginalized old-timers." Like the white social preservationists in Brown-Saracino's study, white middle-class long-timer parents and teachers at Morningside had been attracted to the school largely because of what it already was rather than what it could be if a critical mass of families like themselves were to enroll.

Although critiques of the new group of parents were usually framed in relation to white middle- and upper-middle-class parents, the concerns voiced by long-timers were not simply about race and class—for both white and black parents and staff members who had been at the school for several years, it was not the mere fact that greater numbers of middle-class families were considering Morningside that bothered long-timers. For them, it was the *kind* of white and middle-class family and their forms of engagement with the school. In an interview, an African American staff member described the differences she saw between the upper-grade parents and the new parents, whom she called "a different breed":

I: *When you say "different breed," how are they a different breed? Can you describe some examples?*

SM: Like go-getters. Like "Well, we should take the excess from our budget and invest it and get interest." And you know, just really, having them empowered—it's like the empowered, privileged class. I don't know. That's something I don't know much about.

I: *And that's different than the [upper-grade] parents?*

SM: I think the [upper-grade] parents I work with are—there's a different tone. They're like "We know this job's hard enough. What can we do to help?"

I: *A different way of working with teachers and staff?*

SM: They [upper-grade parents] want to just like kick back and help you. You know like kind of kick back with you and say, "We appreciate you, here's some flowers." As opposed to "Well, how do I get my kindergartner prepared for exams?"

Similarly, Ms. Porter, a kindergarten teacher, described how some of the prospective parents she has encountered were "so demanding and their expectations are so high I feel like I am in Maple Grove [an affluent, predominantly white suburb of Woodbury]." When I asked her to explain, she offered the following example:

I had this one who has written me three letters, three e-mails, about how she is not sure if her child is ready for kindergarten. She said that everyone is telling her that she is not. That is a very popular question: is my kid ready? The next question is how are you going to be challenging my child?

Sheila Hill, a working-class African American parent of a fourth grader, described the positive association she had with the white parents and teachers who had been a part of the school community since the early 2000s, when she first enrolled her child:

> There are several families that are white families that have been a part of the Morningside community with no regard to how many other white people were there with them. And they were very much in the minority and have just hung in there and are very much committed to that school. And the staff is the same way; you know, there's kind of this universalist approach. But they're very committed to everybody. Not once have I come up against anything that had me feeling like "This is some racist bullshit." Not once have I felt like they're trying to pull one on me.

Sheila went on to describe the changes she saw in Morningside's family population, changes that she described as starting when the first cohort of kids from the GPG entered the school:

> I could see that the school got more white families, more middle-class families interested in it and attending. That's the biggest thing. . . . You know, it's brought some really good things, like more parent participation, more resources at the school. We've never raised this kind of money at the annual giving drive. We've never seen these numbers at MPTO meetings. And all those things are good things, you know, but we also like the fact that the school is really diverse and was really small and had a heart for the people who went there. And a sense of caring and respect. And I think when you're in an environment that's mostly people of color, you kind of take for granted that people really care about you or really—you know, when you bring in people that are different, you start to question if that's really true. I think it's true for the most part, but do we want—I guess people don't want Morningside to become an elite place. They want it to be accessible to people—for people who live, say, in South Woodbury, they want those people to have access to what's good about Morningside.[5] What's good about Morningside is not just for the people that can bang on the door the loudest.

In interviews and in my conversations with them at the school, Sheila and several other African American long-timer parents spoke favorably of Emily and Lori, the GPG's founders. They were concerned, however, that the parents the GPG was attracting would not show the same "commitment to everybody" that they felt many long-timer white parents had shown in their years at Morningside. Although their own children would not lose a spot at the school as a result of the demographic shifts occurring in the lower grades, they were concerned that school traditions, values, and forms of parental engagement would be displaced as more middle-class and white parents enrolled their children. As Lynda Washington, a working-class African American parent, stated in an interview, "The one challenge that we have is keeping Morningside Morningside. Not making it a snooty, snotty, uppity, upper-class school, but keeping it an eastern, diverse, everybody-have-a-good-time school." Lynda, like other long-timer parents, described Morningside as a great school in large part on the basis of what, in her mind, it was *not*: a selective, white, and affluent public school that did not represent the racial and socioeconomic diversity of the city.

The views and concerns described above highlight those aspects of the school that long-timers felt played a significant role in making it a "good" public school. The school was accessible: low-income and working-class parents like Laneisha Jackson who lived in neighborhoods with low-performing schools were able to enroll their children at Morningside. Parents in the neighborhood who waited until right before school began in the fall were able to do so as well. The school was not a predominantly white or affluent school associated with the western part of the district, and although the parent community was not immune to race and class issues and tensions, there was a sense among some of the long-timer African American parents that long-timer whites had what Cucchiara and Horvat (2009) describe as a "collective orientation" in their engagement with the school. There was also a small but active group of parents and teachers who, as several parents and teachers commented, "did the work" to develop and sustain programs and secure resources such as the integrated after-school program that benefited the entire school community. A "commitment to everybody," as Sheila described, was a core value shared by school and parent leaders. Long-timer teachers' and parents' views of what constituted a good school, as well as their views on the changing school community, were thus influenced by their social position, their historical and current relationship to the school, and their engagement within the school community. Although they valued having a racially and socioeconomically diverse school population and more resources, they were concerned about the processes through which the school was becoming more "diverse" and the implications the changes might have for the school community.

Long-timers' views of the demographic and material shifts at the school illuminate a key tension associated with the movement of middle-class parents into urban public schools: how to take advantage of the benefits that greater numbers of middle- and upper-middle-class families might offer schools while also ensuring that school improvement efforts reflect a "commitment to everybody." Ensuring this commitment to the collective—and particularly to low-income and working-class students—is no easy task. It runs counter to dominant educational reform discourses and policies that implicitly privilege middle-class parents through a focus on individual "choice" and neighborhood schooling. Like many school districts in the United States, Woodbury Unified gave first preference in enrollment to neighborhood families, meaning that as Morningside became popular among these families—and received an infusion of material resources—it was increasingly difficult for parents who could not afford to live within the school's enrollment boundaries to enroll their children.

Having "a Mix": Racial and Socioeconomic Diversity as a School Asset

Throughout the period of my research, "diversity" was commonly cited by parents across the race and class spectrum as a key part of what made Morningside a good public school. The school's diversity was highlighted in informational brochures, on the website, and in Morningside parents' and teachers' conversations with prospective parents. Although almost all Morningside parents—both newcomers and long-timers—stated that diversity was an important aspect of the school, there was no uniform understanding of just what constituted diversity. Commonly used to denote race, class, or both, diversity was also sometimes used by parents and teachers in reference to sexual orientation or family structure. Just as parents' conceptions of diversity varied, so too did parents' motivations and explanations for seeking out a "diverse" school. In this section I discuss the different "diversity discourses" (Berrey 2005) at Morningside, describing how parents conceptualized diversity in relation to good schooling and demonstrating how diversity was connected to both their individual and their collective goals.

Diversity for Social Exposure and Learning

White parents commonly spoke of diversity in terms of their children's exposure to those of different racial or cultural backgrounds and the learning that could result from this exposure. In a conversation about school choice options, for example, a white parent who was also an educator said that he intentionally chose Morningside for his first grader rather than his more affluent and highly sought-out neighborhood school in the west: "I appreciate the diversity, and how heterogeneous it is. . . . My kids will learn how to deal with the world." Carrie Hendrickson, a white middle-class parent of a kindergartner who also lived outside the school's enrollment zone, described her reasoning for choosing Morningside over several public schools in the more affluent western area of the city:

> We chose Morningside because we live in a neighborhood that's probably 70 percent of color. I love Woodbury. I love that you can get any type of food—and I wanted [my daughter]'s world to reflect that. I did not want her to go somewhere and it's like you live in Woodbury but you're going to plop someone out [by enrolling in a predominantly white school].

Parents like Carrie took pride in the fact that their children attended not only a Woodbury public school but a school that was racially and socioeconomically diverse. In an interview, Carrie said that she could have used the address of a relative to get a spot in a public school in the western area of the city but chose instead to send her child to Morningside because of the diversity and social environment it would provide her child. Although the "diversity" that attracted Carrie to Morningside was based upon a different demographic mix than in the early 2000s when long-timer parents first enrolled their children, the desire of parents like Carrie to enroll their children in a school that was not affluent and predominantly white was similar to the sentiments expressed by long-timer whites.

In interviews, most parents of color also spoke of social dimensions and the benefits of diversity. Charles Allen, a low-income African American parent who lived in the eastern half of the school's enrollment zone, said that Morningside was teaching his second grader "to be versatile, to deal with different races and nationalities." In an interview, he compared Morningside to the predominantly African American and Latino school his son had attended in Los Angeles, stating that "later on in life, being that he's African American, if he were to stay down there [in his former school] it would be difficult for him to step outside the circle, so to speak, and socialize with other races, you know, on different levels."

Morningside's racial and socioeconomic diversity was also valued by parents of color and white parents of interracial or transracially adopted children. Many of these parents felt that a diverse student population would allow their children to develop a positive sense of self in an environment in which a range of identities were represented. In a meeting of the school's Diversity Committee, for example, a small and racially mixed group of parents talked about their children's experiences with race at Morningside. Paula Mattison, a white parent whose adopted daughter was Latino, said, "I chose Morningside because I thought this [school] is a rainbow world and she's going to be safe." Claudia Harris, an African American parent who had family members of other races, responded by saying that her daughter loves the school, and that in her family they "have a mixture, so she's used to a mixture." Paula responded that it's different for her and her husband, since their home and work settings are not racially diverse. She explained to the group that "the school and the park are the only places where [she and her daughter] can get it."

In interviews, several parents of color stated that they did not want their child to be in a predominantly white setting or "the only one" of his or her race and color in the school. At the same time, the socioeconomic mix of students at Morningside provided an opportunity for children of color to be around, as an upper-middle-class African American parent of a kindergartner stated, "both the middle-class families of color and the low-income families . . . so that there's not some association made with one or the other specifically." Similar to Noguera (2008), who wrote about his efforts to support his son's process of identity formation as a black middle-class youth, this African American parent wanted his child to be in an environment in which a range of "blackness" was represented.

Diversity for Educational Resources and Opportunities

For all parents, the ability to find a socioeconomically mixed *and* academically successful school in the district was exceptional, because most of the high-performing schools in the district were predominantly middle and upper-middle class. As Mark Fisher, a white middle-class Morningside parent, stated, "Morningside is a very successful, inner-city, eastern public school, whereas any other examples you find of that are in the west." To many parents of color in particular, a diverse school meant that their children could be around other students of similar racial backgrounds while also benefiting from a community that had many resources and educational opportunities—resources that were uncommon in many of the predominantly black, Latino, and Asian public schools in the district. Although the student population was not as racially diverse in the late 1990s and early 2000s, when many long-timer parents enrolled their children (e.g., it was more than 75 percent black), the school was nevertheless more socioeconomically diverse than most of the predominantly black schools in the district (44 percent of Morningside students qualified for the free/reduced-price lunch program in 2000/2001).

Middle-class parents of color spoke about the connection between diversity and school resources such as teacher quality. Many of these parents lived outside Morningside's school zone and described their own neighborhood schools as unacceptable options due to negative peer influences, safety concerns, and poor academics. In an interview, James Hall, an African American middle-class parent of a first grader, explained his and his wife's desire to send their child to a school outside the predominantly working-class Latino neighborhood where they owned their home. As an alumnus of Woodbury public schools, he described his local school by saying, "I already knew that it was a school where I didn't want my son to go." When asked what attracted him to Morningside, he said that it was probably "the ideal school" because of its diversity:

> I wanted [my child] to definitely get a good education. . . . And I felt like with certain schools in my neighborhood he wouldn't have the opportunity to gain as much as he possibly could, whether it be peer pressure or the teachers, you know, taking a real interest in their kids, . . . so those are the two main factors. Education, and being in a diverse situation. I think it's really important for kids to see a lot more than what they actually do in some of the just inner-city schools.

Similarly, Dorothy Washington, an African American middle-class parent of a fifth grader, saw opportunities and resources as following white students in particular, given the multiple forms of capital that many white parents at Morningside possessed:

D: And I think that at a school such as Morningside, with white parents who make demands on the school district or the school board, there's a different weight given to that than, I think, to folks of color.

I: *And so how does that play out at Morningside?*

D: I think that it's because you have that dynamic going on, then all the children will benefit. You know, even those children whose parents may not come up to the school or whatever. But everyone gets to benefit.

I: *In what way?*

D: Resources, the level of education that you're able to get. When you raise the bar, when you raise expectations, by and large I think that the children, anybody, can come up to the level of those expectations. Especially if they're supported.

Dorothy's daughter had been assigned to Morningside the previous year when the district closed the predominantly African American school closer to her house because of its low enrollment and test scores. In an interview, she described her preference for Morningside:

> We were happy they had shut down. Because my daughter then had an opportunity to go to another school. I couldn't afford for her to go to some kind of private school, so that was not an option for me. So when they closed Frazier, Morningside opened up to her. Because I think they just assigned children to certain schools, and the universe was kind to us.

For Dorothy, the fact that there were white parents at Morningside who advocated for the school at the district level meant that all children at the school would benefit. According to Dorothy, these white parents—when working on behalf of the collective student body—could use their racial privilege and various forms of capital to secure and sustain educational resources and opportunities for Morningside students. Thus, for her, the racial and socioeconomic mix of the student population wasn't simply about the social education her child might receive but the resources that her child might benefit from as well.

In contrast, when most white parents spoke of the association between diversity and material resources, it was often in relation to the things their children were *not* able to get out of their Morningside experience. Some parents, and particularly prospective white parents, expressed concerns that their children would not be academically challenged at Morningside because of the socioeconomic diversity, and in interviews, they shared that they were considering private schools and keeping Morningside as a "backup" option. Even those white parents for whom Morningside was their first choice—and who shared that private schools were not an option—commonly described the ways they supplemented their children's education through after-school enrichment programs and their own one-on-one academic work with their offspring. Many of these parents, working through the GPG, the MPTO, or both, sought to expand Morningside's academic and enrichment offerings to include resources and programs similar to those found in many of the more affluent western schools. In doing so these parents engaged in what Lareau (2003) calls the "concerted cultivation" of middle-class parents: customizing and intervening in order to ensure that their children's education is on par with (or better than) that of their similarly situated peers.

Diversity for Equity and Collective Benefits

In addition to diversity discourses that centered on social and material benefits for individual students, diversity was also talked about in relation to equity and efforts to support a broader "public." Many parents, like the GPG leaders quoted in chapter 3, saw their decision to enroll their children in a "diverse" school like Morningside as connected to a desire to support public education and to provide opportunities to the collective student body. Erica Zimmerman, a white middle-class parent of a kindergartner, linked diversity to her commitment to public education. She stated that she "liked the idea of our children being educated in the context of the public—versus the, you know, the elite or some very small subsection." Parents like Erica devoted countless hours to the school to bring resources, such as a mental health counselor and a salad bar, that were not simply for the benefit of their own children.

Members of the school's Diversity Committee also described diversity in relation to collective, rather than individualistic, benefits. During the period of my research, this racially mixed group of largely middle-class parents was working to promote a vision of diversity that moved beyond simply food and fellowship and confronted hard issues related to race, class, and gender head on. Whereas in previous years the work of the committee had largely focused on planning and hosting the school's annual Diversity Dinner, during the time of my research the small committee organized a film viewing and discussion on white privilege and had numerous conversations in their meetings about the race-related experiences of families at the school and the demographic shifts. Parents talked about issues such as the small number of teachers of color at the school, as well as the decline in African American students. In Diversity Committee meetings (which were separate from the MPTO meetings and often took place in parents' homes), parents spoke about diversity not simply in regard to social and material benefits but in relation to issues of power, identity, and access.

Defining Diversity in the Context of Demographic Change

Morningside was described by many parents and staff as a diverse school, but there was a sense that its socioeconomic and racial diversity was fragile and fleeting because of the increased interest of middle-class families and white families from the neighborhood and across the city. As one white long-timer parent commented in the parent survey I administered:

I have loved Morningside for a long time, but it is definitely changing. I came to Morningside because it had wonderful teaching and had kids that looked like Woodbury—every color, lots of economic diversity. People came from outside the neighborhood because they wanted to become part of Morningside. Morningside has changed into more of a neighborhood school. This is not a bad thing, but it is a different school than the one I chose many years ago.

Cherene Clark, an African American middle-class parent of a third grader at Morningside, had tried for two years to get her child a spot at Morningside. She expressed similar sentiments when we spoke at the school's annual Jump-A-Thon fund-raiser:

While we sat on the grass and watched the kids jump, I asked Cherene what led her to enroll her child at the school. She said Morningside is really "your ideal neighborhood school. . . . Who wouldn't want their child to attend, especially when you look at the school's diversity and parent participation?" She mentioned that they have eighty parents who attend MPTO meetings, and that "you have parents who really care about their child's education, public education." She then mentioned that people from the neighborhood were really wanting to send their kids here. She said, "I think the concern now is just making sure that the school remains diverse." She went on to explain that "I would like, as we get parents—how can I say this, those who have higher income levels—I'd like them to be concerned about contributing to the community." When I asked her what she meant by this, she said that she would be concerned if there were parents saying that we should have separate after-school programs or that fee-based [activities] should be separate.

This concern that Morningside was losing its students of color and low-income students (and changing into more of a "neighborhood school") was not limited to long-timer parents. There was a sense among several parents of color with children in the lower grades that Morningside did not have as many students of color as they had envisioned. For example, Araceli Aguirre, an upper-middle-class parent whose son was mixed race (Latino and African American), said she did not want him to attend her neighborhood school because of its low test scores and what she saw as an unchallenging curriculum. She explained that she was first attracted to Morningside after looking at the school's aggregate student demographics online but was disappointed when she learned that her child's class had fewer African American students than she had expected. Whereas the school as a whole was 66 percent African American in 2005 when she first researched the school, only 39 percent of the students in her son's class were of African descent (African American or mixed race) the following year. She stated, "We chose this school specifically because of what we thought the diversity was, but when you get into kindergarten, you realize it's a lot more white than you thought, and that's the trend the school is moving in."

As the school population began to change, parents and teachers struggled with how to describe the changes as well as the meaning they had for the school community. Like Araceli, some parents saw the school as increasingly "less diverse" because of the decline in African American students and low-income students, whereas others (and sometimes the very same individuals) described it as "more diverse" because more Latino, Asian, multiracial, and gay and lesbian families were enrolling their children. Mark saw the increased diversity as connected to processes of gentrification in the school community:

> The more our school gentrifies, the more, you know—Morningside's more diverse than it's ever been. I mean, in the last ten years, fifteen years, whatever, in urban America, "diverse" has been a code word for African American. And so—using those terms, you know—Morningside used to be *very* diverse. And, you know, when in fact, Morningside is much more diverse than it's ever been. There are more Latino families, there are more Asian families, there are more Middle Eastern families, there are more gay and lesbian families—and, you know, people with other alternative family structures than there have ever been before. I mean, the only way that Morningside is less diverse now is, of course, socioeconomically. And I don't even know if that's necessarily true. I just think there's probably a wider gap between the haves and the have-nots than there used to be.

Thus, although "diversity" was a shared symbol that many Morningside parents used to describe the school, it was used to signify different things, given one's point of reference and purpose in choosing a "diverse" school.

(Re)Claiming Narratives of Change

The different diversity discourses at Morningside and how the changes at the school were described were not simply about semantics. Public images and narratives of change shape not only who is attracted to particular schools but also the extent to which existing members of a school community feel valued for their contributions and "seen" in processes of school change. Several Asian American parents, for example, critiqued what they saw as simplistic and binary media portrayals of the changes at Morningside. When a local news article came out about greater numbers of middle-class parents considering public schools in Woodbury, two Asian American parents at Morningside voiced their frustrations with the portrayal of the changes as simply a decrease in African American families and a corresponding increase in affluent white families, who were seen as improving the school. In a conversation about the article after an MPTO meeting, for example, Judy Chu, an Asian American middle-class parent of a kindergartner, stated that even though she and several other Asian American parents were in the newspaper photos of the school, "[the author] only talked about all the white parents chatting on the playground before school." Similarly, Lori Veloso—an Asian American parent who had volunteered countless hours in support of the school through her work in the GPG and MPTO—argued that solely attributing the positive changes at Morningside to white families "completely ignores and marginalizes Morningside's families of color and their contributions to the school."

Dominant framings of urban public schools often fail to capture all the elements and people that make for a "good" school and the ways in which student and community identities are tied to the educational institutions of which they are a part. In Kirshner and Pozzoboni's (2011) study of a school closure in a large urban district in the United States, students cited trusting relationships with adults, connection to place, and sense of belonging as features of their school that they felt were devalued in the district's decision to close their school. Similarly, the working-class youth in Reay's (2007) study of schooling in inner-city London viewed the demonization of their schools as an affront to their own sense of self and identity. Rather than internalizing the portrayals of their schools as "unruly places," however, these youth struggled "to preserve a sense of themselves and their schools as 'good enough'" (2007, 1195).

Like the youth in Reay's study, many long-timer Morningside parents and teachers tried to deflect the popular images and discourses that portrayed schools in the urban district as dysfunctional, "bad," and in need of "saving." They were well aware of the implications of this imagery for student enrollment and resources. As Emily Thompson stated, "Personally, I feel like the newspapers are just full of bad news about public schools, and people are fascinated with them in the same way that people are fascinated with articles about train wrecks. And just trying to get good news out through that filter has been part of what we've been trying to do." In addition to concerns about student enrollment, the desire to shape the images and discourse surrounding school change was driven by concerns about representation and power. The portrayal of a school revitalization led by white middle-class parents, for example, marginalized the historical and current contributions of parents of color. For many parents, and long-timer parents in particular, representations of school change at Morningside were deeply personal, highlighting the intricate relationship among space, identity, representation, and power.

Although the school had a higher MPTO budget in 2006/7, several Morningside parents and teachers described what they saw as the potential downsides of the demographic shifts at the school. Beyond a shift in norms and forms of parental engagement, there were also concrete programs and resources that the school could lose if more middle-class families were to enroll their children—programs that many parents and teachers described as key components of what made Morningside a "good" school when compared with others in the district.

The school, for example, was in danger of losing the thousands of Title I dollars it received on the basis of the number of students who qualified for the free/reduced-price lunch program. This was money that helped to pay for the school's parent liaison and support staff as well as several enrichment programs. Losing the Title I designation would have huge implications for the school's ability to secure grants for things like the sports program. As the MPTO treasurer stated in a budget meeting, "If and when we lose this Title I funding, MPTO may have to step in to fill the financial gap." Programs like the subsidized after-school program that served low-income and working-class students would be shut down if the school lost its Title I status. As one staff member commented, "Then the parents would have to fund [the after-school programs] themselves, and then the squeeze would be on the poor folks who couldn't afford to pay." Those elements of the school that were so attractive to many parents, both "new" and "old"— the blended after-school enrichment programs and the racial and socioeconomic mix, for example—were the very things that parents and teachers feared would be lost as more middle-class families enrolled their children. In describing the enrollment and space issues the school now faced, Marisa Collins, a white long-timer parent, stated: "In a sense we're victims of our own success."

The Politics of Progress in Urban Education

Rather than focusing directly on structural issues (e.g., disparities in academic offerings across schools in the district), the media and other public figures commonly position middle-class families as the driving force in helping urban public schools to improve. Yet the tensions caused by demographic changes at Morningside, as well as teachers' and parents' perspectives on the changes, complicate the assumption that an increase in the number of middle- and upper-middle-class parents in urban schools, and white parents in particular, will be uniformly beneficial and positively received by teachers and parents. As explored in both this chapter and the next, a central focus on the potential benefits of creating middle-class schools may render invisible the historic contributions that parents and teachers make to a school, devaluing the engagement, perspectives, and lived experiences of those parents who are not middle class or white.

At the same time that Morningside parents and teachers sought to manage the perceptions of others outside the school community, their own views of the changes were mixed. Long-timer parents and teachers liked the increased material resources flowing into the school as a result of the presence of a more affluent group of parents: teachers had more money for field trips, they were able to hire a school counselor, and the MPTO budget was at an all-time high due in large part to the financial contributions and fund-raising efforts of the lower-grade parents. Yet they were fearful that the school would become an affluent and predominantly white "western" school and lose the diversity and "commitment to everyone" that had attracted many parents and teachers in the first place. Questions of parental engagement were key, as parents were central actors in struggles between "the new" and "the old" and over issues of race and class.

FIVE

Professionalizing the MPTO: Race, Class, and Shifting Norms for "Active" Parents

In an economic climate in which a number of school districts face drastic cuts in local and state funding, parent volunteerism and involvement are increasingly employed by educators and policy makers as key interventions in contemporary urban school reform efforts. Many parents—and particularly middle-class parents—are helping to fill the gaps left by state and local governments through their fund-raising, grant writing, and volunteerism in urban public schools. City public elementary schools with art, music, and academic enrichment programs, for example, are in many instances those with large parent-teacher organization funds and parents who are able to volunteer their time to ensure that these programs are sustained through grants and fund-raising.

Parent groups across the nation are raising thousands of dollars to fund teacher salaries, curricular materials, and academic programs for their children's schools, thereby playing a key economic role in the sustainability of school programs (Calvert 2011; Koumpilova 2011). Bake sales and car washes are a thing of the past in a growing number of city public schools, as parent-led fund-raising efforts now include online donor campaigns, strategic marketing, and silent auctions. This level and type of parent fund-raising and volunteerism in public education have commonly been associated with affluent suburban schools and school districts, particularly in California, where Proposition 13 severely limited the amount of funding that schools were able to receive from property taxes.[1] This move toward a more professionalized form of parental engagement in urban public education, led by the middle and upper-middle class, stands in sharp contrast to historical patterns of middle-class flight and disinvestment from city public schools.[2] Yet little is known about how these parental investments shape family-school relations and specifically norms and practices related to parental engagement within particular school contexts.

In this chapter I demonstrate the negative consequences of positioning parents, and middle-class parents in particular, as key components of urban public school success. Although parents brought new resources and educational opportunities to Morningside Elementary, their engagement through the Morningside Parent-Teacher Organization (MPTO), and the school's reliance on their contributions, engendered tensions and exacerbated existing status positions among parents. On the basis of these findings, I ultimately argue that relying on middle-class parent volunteerism and fund-raising in urban school reform is a dangerous move: it not only privileges middle-class norms of engagement but also absolves the government of its responsibility to provide and ensure high-quality public schooling for all children.

Middle-Class Parental Engagement in Urban Public Schooling

Middle-class parents are positioned by many civic and education leaders as a central element of public school success because of the assumption that their involvement will bring about changes in the school that are beneficial not just to their own children but to the collective student body (CEOs for Cities, n.d.; Kahlenberg 2001a; Varady and Raffel 1995). Middle-class parents can employ their social, cultural, and economic capital to secure much-needed resources for public schools, increasing the quality of academic programs in ways that benefit low-income students as well. While this perspective is indeed plausible, research has shown middle-class parental involvement to reinscribe, rather than counter, class-based inequities in public schooling through support of policies that favor their children at the expense of others (Brantlinger 2003; McGrath and Kuriloff 1999; Wells and Serna 1996). Research on middle- and upper-middle-class parents' engagement in urban public schooling suggests that their efforts are not uniformly beneficial to all students within a school setting. This emergent research on middle-class parents' involvement in socioeconomically mixed or predominantly low-income city public schools in the United States demonstrates that the engagement of these parents may ultimately reinscribe or create new patterns of inequality in local school and district contexts (Cucchiara 2013b; Lewis 2003; McGhee Hassrick and Schneider 2009; Posey 2012).

Parent-teacher organizations can serve as a useful window through which to examine issues of exclusivity, power, and access in public school settings. Although parents across the race and class spectrum work in ways to support their children's educations (Calabrese Barton et al. 2004; Graue and Oen 2009), research on the intersection between race, social class, and parental engagement suggests that white middle-class parents are more likely to participate and take leadership positions in school-based groups such as parent-teacher organizations, which are commonly recognized as acceptable forms of parental engagement in schools (Cucchiara 2013b; McGrath and Kuriloff 1999). The idea that most parent-teacher organizations do not fully reflect the demographics nor represent the issues of their collective school communities is not new. Few studies, however, have examined processes of professionalization in public parent-teacher organizations and the implications of having middle- and upper-middle-class parents play a major role in urban public schooling through their extensive volunteerism and financial support. Whereas previous studies highlight conflicts between educators and active parents in affluent suburban schools (Lareau and Muñoz 2012; Lewis and Forman 2002), less is known about how educators and other parents understand and respond to the collective engagement of middle- and upper-middle-class parents in underresourced urban schools. What are the consequences of relying on parent organizations for the acquisition and sustenance of academic programs and opportunities for students? As parents are called upon to give more and do more, how does this shape school dynamics? What are the implications of this in relation to equity and access in public schooling? Understanding shifts in parents' school improvement efforts and how these shifts impact the social and material contexts of public schools is both important and timely, given the sharp cuts in local and state education budgets and increased calls for parental contributions in public education.

Questions of Value and Advantage in Family-School Relationships

As discussed briefly in chapter 1, French sociologist Pierre Bourdieu's concepts of capital and field are useful theoretical tools for examining middle- and upper-middle-class parental engagement in urban public schooling. Previous research has examined the ways in which parents' cultural capital (e.g., their ability to comply with educators' expectations, their knowledge of schooling and the curriculum) relates to their children's success in school (see Lareau and Weininger 2003 for an extensive review of relevant research). Similarly, studies have shown how middle-class parents' social capital enables them to secure advantages for their children (Horvat et al.

2003; McGrath and Kuriloff 1999). Social capital, as defined by Bourdieu (1985, 248), is "the aggregate of the actual or potential resources which are linked to possession of a durable network of more or less institutionalized relationships of mutual acquaintance or recognition."

As several scholars have rightly pointed out, notions of social and cultural capital must not be employed as stand-alone concepts. Rather, it is important for researchers to position them in relation to the other major concepts in Bourdieu's theoretical project, namely, habitus and field (Emirbayer and Johnson 2008; Horvat 2003; Lareau and Horvat 1999; Lareau 2003). Habitus, according to Bourdieu, refers to the internalized dispositions toward culture, society, and one's future that one generally learns at home from family. Bourdieu argues that schools place differential value on the social and cultural resources of students and their families, since certain ways of speaking and acting are privileged over others. He contends that families from higher social classes have an advantage in home-school relations, as their home-based experiences and dispositions (i.e., habitus) often more closely match those valued by most institutional actors in schools (Bourdieu 1977a, 1977b, 1990; Bourdieu and Passeron 1977).

According to Bourdieu, the mere possession of a particular social or cultural resource does not guarantee that it will translate into advantages. Much depends on the particular "field" of interaction, or structured space of dominant and subordinate positions based on types and amounts of capital (Swartz 1997). Fields of interaction ("rules of the game") structure what constitutes acceptable and valued behavior and goals in a particular context. It is not guaranteed that the school improvement efforts of middle-class parents will be well received in all contexts, for example, because social-class differences between parents and teachers and norms at a particular school shape parent-teacher relationships (Lewis and Forman 2002). In other words, the power afforded any one form of capital is based on its perceived value in a given field. Fields are sites of struggle and are never completely stable; they shift over time and vary on the basis of social, historical, political, and economic contexts.

Attention to fields of interaction is critical in examining middle- and upper-middle-class parental engagement in urban public schooling. Notions of what constitutes an active and "involved" parent are socially constructed; they are both culturally and historically dynamic and context specific. The particular expectations that educators have for parents, for example, have shifted over time (Lareau 1987). Although school actors calling upon parents (especially mothers) to support their children's schools is not a new phenomenon, neoliberal education policies have shifted the role of the state in the provision of public education. In most states across the nation and in California in particular, cuts to public education budgets were widespread and deep between 2007 and 2010 (Johnson, Oliff, and Williams 2010; California Department of Education 2010). These massive budget cuts have paved the way for a greater involvement of private actors in public education, with private foundations, nongovernmental education reform organizations, and individual parent donors playing an increasingly influential role in urban public schools (Fabricant and Fine 2012; Lipman 2011; Watkins 2012).

Within this context of shrinking education budgets and limited resources, forms of parental engagement that support *all* students in a school are highly valued. Parental help with homework or volunteering in a classroom may be seen by teachers as legitimate forms of involvement, but parents' work to bring grants and initiate new programs may be afforded an even greater value by institutional actors in underresourced schools faced with few other forms of support. Political, economic, and social changes in the United States have promoted shifts in the "rules of the game," potentially shaping the value, scope, and methods of parental engagement in particular school contexts.

In the remainder of this chapter, three key findings related to the norms and consequences of parental engagement at Morningside are outlined. First, the volunteerism and engagement of middle- and upper-middle-class parents in the MPTO were afforded greater visibility, and implicitly greater value, than other forms of engagement within the school context. Second, the demographic shifts occurring at the school and the sociocultural context mediated the collective benefits of the resources brought by these "active" MPTO parents. Finally, the increased professionalization of the MPTO led to a redefinition of norms for parental engagement within the school context, ultimately exacerbating race and class tensions and status positions among parents.

"Ask What You Can Do for the School": The Active Morningside Parent

In newspaper articles, my interviews with teachers and parents, school promotional materials, and my conversations with parents at local parks and community events, Morningside Elementary was lauded for what one school brochure described as its "active community of parents." At the school's annual Spring Carnival, for example, Molly Clausen (a long-timer parent) introduced me to a newly hired, upper-level district administrator who had met Morningside's MPTO cochairs at a school board meeting. This man, a Latino who looked to be in his midthirties and who had grown up in Woodbury, said that he "came here to check it out and learn how they do things here." He said that out of the eighteen schools in the section of the district that he was responsible for in his position, sixteen did not have active parent-teacher associations. He said that Morningside "had the diversity" and "had the parents who were really active in getting things for the school."

The parental body also served as a key point of attraction for many prospective parents, and teachers and staff cited it as an important component of the school's success. Although many parents supported their children's schooling through home-based activities and encouragement, their school-based involvement (e.g., volunteerism and fund-raising to support staff positions and programs) was what was most visible and discussed by teachers, staff, and other parents. Parental engagement was both lauded and emphasized at the school, with Mr. Foster characterizing the school's philosophy as "don't ask what the school can do for your child, ask what you can do for the school." Mr. Foster explained that new parents at Morningside needed to understand that Morningside's success was largely dependent upon parent volunteerism and fund-raising. He stated that

> it's not going to happen if you don't roll up your sleeves and come in here and work or raise money or something. The state is not going to help—and I think that's always the worry. This place, it does go through cycles. I think in another ten years, Lord only knows what it's going to be.

For Mr. Foster, Morningside's success was fragile and dependent upon parents' and teachers' willingness to "roll up their sleeves" and work to make up for the gaps left by the state.

Morningside parents were in fact very engaged with the school community; in my interviews, parent/caregiver survey, and observations, I found that most parents, across the race and class spectrum, were or had been engaged in some form of school-based involvement. Although not all parents participated in the MPTO, most Morningside parents were or had been involved in efforts to support both the school and their children's education. I commonly observed parents tending the school gardens, volunteering in classrooms, chaperoning on field trips, and organizing events and fund-raising activities. In a survey I conducted of Morningside parents and caregivers, for example, more than 90 percent of parents within each racial group had attended a school event during the 2006/7 school year, and more than 60 percent in each group had helped a teacher (e.g., chaperoned, worked with kids, or served as a room parent).[3]

The MPTO was a central and visible hub of parent volunteerism at the school. Led by two elected parent cochairs in 2006/7 (one white middle-class male and one African American working-class female), the organization played a major role in supporting academic and enrichment programs at the school. Meetings commonly consisted of budget updates, announcements of volunteer opportunities, committee reports, and special presentations by community members (e.g., district staff, nonprofits). Although the principal gave a brief report on school activities during the monthly meetings, few teachers or staff attended the evening meetings on a regular basis (to do so would mean staying at the school until after 8:00 p.m. after a full day of teaching). Attendance at the monthly meetings sometimes surpassed forty parents (and the first meeting of the year was much larger than subsequent meetings), but a core group of approximately fifteen to twenty parents regularly attended MPTO meetings and actively participated in the work of various MPTO committees.

Race- and class-based patterns shaped parents' school-based forms of engagement. White middle- and upper-middle-class parents were disproportionately represented in MPTO meetings (when compared with their representation in the total school population) and were more likely to engage in activities at the school and district levels, such as doing committee work or attending school board meetings. Interviews with long-timers suggest that this pattern was not a new one at Morningside; what was different, however, was the fact that these families now made up a much larger proportion at the school and were clustered in the lower grades. Middle- and upper-middle-class parents from the neighborhood (most of whom were early members of the Glenbrook Parents' Group [GPG]) were particularly active in the MPTO; now that their children were enrolled in the school (and now that there was a "critical mass" of neighborhood families in the lower grades), many of them chose to focus their energies on school-based, rather than neighborhood-based, forms of engagement. Although GPG members still organized the annual Book Drive and participated in neighborhood-based social events, much of their volunteerism was now channeled through the MPTO.

In contrast, parents of color and low-income and working-class parents were more likely to volunteer in their children's classroom or attend child-related meetings and events such as performances and classroom meetings. My parent/caregiver survey, conducted at the end of the school year, revealed that families whose household income was less than $35,000 had a greater percentage of parents who had helped a teacher than those in the $35,000–$50,000 and $50,001–$75,000 household income ranges. Although a handful of African American parents (almost all middle class) consistently attended MPTO meetings and were involved in committee work, the number of African Americans in the MPTO did not reflect their numerical presence in the school. Asian American and Latino parents were also few in number within the MPTO; however, their numbers were not as disproportionate, as each group represented less than 6 percent of the school's student population. MPTO members were aware of the demographics of the organization and spoke of their efforts to make the organization more representative of the student population through targeted outreach to parents of color and the provision of child care and food at meetings.

As in many schools across the country, a gender imbalance in forms of parental engagement also existed at Morningside. Although some fathers attended MPTO meetings and were involved in a number of activities at the school, mothers made up the majority of classroom volunteers and MPTO meeting attendees. Whereas mothers commonly took the lead in social activities at the school, fathers were leaders in a number of select areas (e.g., chairing the Disaster Preparedness Committee and the Technology Committee, helping teachers with manual-labor tasks).

Not all forms of school-based parental engagement were viewed equally within the school context, as certain forms were granted more visibility and value than others. In an interview, Ms. Harper, an upper-grade teacher, noted the association made in the school between parental participation and the MPTO. She offered a more expansive definition of parental participation:

H: What is parent participation? If I have a potluck and everybody brings a dish, that's 100 percent participation. But if those, a few of the same parents who brought lasagna, which would have maybe taken just as long as an MPTO meeting to make, but if they don't go to the MPTO, they're counted as a nonparticipant.

I: *By whom?*

H: Sometimes people say there aren't enough people of color at the MPTO meetings. And so I think we need to redefine that word because there's a lot of people who do a lot of stuff. And we have to broaden that definition to include people and value what they do.

In school meetings, in interviews with parents and teachers, and at events for prospective parents, descriptions of Morningside's "active" parents rarely focused on individual child-centered activities such as homework help. Nor did they focus on parent donations of food for an event. Rather, many parents, teachers, community members, and the media praised parents for the resources and educational opportunities they provided for the school through their involvement in the MPTO.

When asked to describe Morningside's strengths, for example, a third-grade teacher saw parental support as a key asset of the school and one that made it stand out in comparison to other district schools. As Ms. Halverson stated, Morningside had "a parent group that will do just about anything for these kids and for the teachers. . . . The support we get from the parents is probably our biggest strength." When asked in interviews to describe parental engagement at the school, most teachers focused on the financial and volunteer support they received from the MPTO and the material resources individual parents provided for their classrooms. In the context of a school faced with declining district and state funding, it is perhaps no surprise that teachers and other parents lauded the efforts of MPTO parents to bring prized resources to the school. Indeed, thanks in large part to the fund-raising and organizational work of the MPTO, the school was able to fund a music teacher and a Spanish teacher, and teachers had a substantial budget for field trips. The work of MPTO parents was afforded great visibility and value, as most teachers' and parents' descriptions of active parents commonly referred to those who were visible in the school and involved with the organization.

Working for the Collective

Although parents and teachers lauded many of the resources that MPTO parents helped bring to the school, not all middle-class parents' forms of involvement were legitimated within the school's institutional culture. Many middle-class parents possessed resources that could benefit the school community as a whole, yet within the particular field of interaction, the extent to which parents were able to activate their capital largely depended on the methods through which they sought to support or improve the school. Long-timers valued parents who had a "collective orientation" (Cucchiara and Horvat 2009), or who engaged in efforts that appeared to serve the broader student population, over those who appeared to have largely self-interested motives for their engagement. Many teachers and long-timer parents spoke with pride about their work to create the school's economically integrated after-school program, for example, describing the efforts of teachers and parents to ensure that the fee-based program for middle-class families was seamlessly integrated with the district's subsidized program for low-income families. As described in the previous chapter, teachers, parents, and members of the administration had devoted countless hours to make Morningside a "good" city public school, and their expectation was that new parents would carry on the tradition of working on behalf of not only their own children but the broader school community.

Indeed, many MPTO parents had volunteered numerous hours to bring resources to the school that would support all children rather than simply their own. The mental-health counselor, the salad-bar lunch program, the fund-raising to support art, music, and enrichment programs—all were framed as serving the collective. In the period in which this study was conducted, the district's finances were controlled by the state because of prior mismanagement, and the budget for the 2007/8 school year was approved with a deficit of more than $1 million.[4] The debt-strapped district was also situated in a state that ranked below the national average in per-pupil expenditures. Woodbury Unified schools without substantial parent-teacher organization budgets and private financial contributions were, as one parent stated, "functioning at a bare minimum." With the changing demographics and declining number of students qualifying for free or reduced-price lunches at Morningside, the school stood to lose the more than $50,000 in Title I funds that historically had been used to help offset the cost of staff positions and academic-support programs for students. Thus, within the institutional context, a valued active parent was one who not only possessed multiple forms of capital but sought to activate this capital in ways that would benefit the collective student body.

Engagement in Context: Issues of Access and Equity

Despite the collective orientation expressed by many MPTO members, the organization's school improvement efforts did not benefit all students equally. First, the changing demographics of the school meant that fewer numbers of low-income students stood to benefit from the resources and opportunities that middle- and upper-middle-class parents were bringing to the school. Not only were low-income students fewer in number, but the fact that they were in decline in the lower grades was significant. Reflecting a trend common in most schools, parents of students in the lower grades were traditionally overrepresented among those parents taking on leadership positions in the MPTO and serving on committees, while many parents of students in the upper grades felt as if they had paid their dues in previous years. As the number of low-income students began to decline in the kindergarten and first-grade classes, fewer low-income students stood to benefit from the new programs and resources that were flowing into the school. A small group of kindergarten and first-grade parents raised over $16,000 for a new kindergarten play structure, for example, convincing the district to tear up and remove the old asphalt and provide an in-kind donation for the project. Based on the social connections of one of the parents, the group also secured a landscape architect who agreed to work pro bono. The design included a dry creek bed, a small amphitheater, a playhouse, a raised garden bed, and a climbing rock/wall. This new play structure was destined to serve a more affluent group of students if the demographic trends that the school was experiencing continued. The kindergarten aides that were proposed for part of the following year's MPTO budget would do so as well.

Although middle-class parents had historically predominated in the MPTO, in the past they were scattered throughout the grades and did not have, as one parent described, a "critical mass" at the school. Their efforts to bring resources to their children's classrooms or grades were more likely to benefit low-income students and working-class students, given that students were in a shared classroom setting. Although many of the middle-class parents of fifth graders socialized with each other, they were a numerical minority in the sole fifth-grade class in the school and had numerous opportunities to interact with low-income and working-class students and their families through their classroom volunteerism and participation in fifth-grade events. In contrast, low-income students were few in number in the kindergarten classes, and upper-grade families—many of whom did not regularly attend MPTO meetings or other school-wide committees—had little interaction with the new kindergarten families.

Second, as the MPTO created more formal systems for budget allocations, middle- and upper-middle-class parents in the lower grades had a greater advantage in constructing proposals that would be passed. Many of these parents had experience writing grants (or knew friends or colleagues with experience) and were able to draw on these professional skills and connections in their efforts to secure resources for the school. Several parents presented opportunities for grants or programs that they knew about as a result of their professional work or their connections to other parents in private or more affluent public schools in the area.

Few upper-grade parents possessed these professional skills or had access to these forms of social capital, and those few that did expressed that they had already "paid their dues" and chose instead to focus their volunteerism on their children's class rather than on MPTO committee work.

Similarly, upper-grade teachers, who knew the particular needs of their students, had full teaching loads and limited time to develop, write, and present budget proposals. As a result, the needs of students in the upper grades, who were predominantly working-class and low-income students of color, were less likely to receive attention in MPTO decision making and budget allocation. Ms. Harper, for example, heard that the MPTO had a budget surplus and asked if they could fund a tutoring and intervention program for fifth-grade students who needed extra academic support before middle school. The MPTO had implemented a policy that required individuals to submit formal budget proposals by a specific deadline, however, so that they could review and vote on requests for funds. In an interview, a member of the budget committee described why the group ultimately decided against the program proposed by Ms. Harper:

> Everybody really respected her desire to help those kids before they were gone from Morningside, but ultimately the group decided this wasn't a carefully thought-out plan. There was no clear sense of how the money could be spent or how effectively it would be implemented. So the idea was shelved, and we said let's work rather toward, you know, budgeting for something when we have a real plan.

The motivation behind the MPTO's budgeting process was well intended. Members sought to increase discussion and deliberation about how funds were spent and ensure that specific grades wouldn't fund-raise to support their children only. Indeed, the prior year the group had approved funding for a mental-health program at the school that was intended in part to serve students who may not have the economic resources to see a counselor outside the school day. But, given the limited representation of fifth-grade families in the group, as well as the time, knowledge, and comfort required to construct a formal budget proposal, the needs and issues of low-income students in the upper grades were less likely to be addressed in MPTO meetings.

The extent to which low-income and working-class students benefited from the work of MPTO parents was shaped not only by the broader demographic changes that the school was experiencing but also by MPTO parents, who played a role in these demographic shifts. As discussed in chapters 3 and 4, the work of GPG and MPTO parents attracted many middle- and upper-middle-class parents within the neighborhood and across the city. The numerous enrichment programs that the organizations funded and the visible presence of Morningside parents at district and community events were commonly mentioned as points of attraction in my interviews and conversations with prospective middle- and upper-middle-class families. The marketing and outreach efforts of GPG members who were now involved in the MPTO played a role as well, as their postings about the school on parent listservs and in neighborhood newsletters and the information passed through their social networks targeted prospective middle- and upper-middle-class parents residing in the surrounding neighborhood and other parts of the city. The engagement of MPTO parents both shaped and was shaped by the demographic changes impacting the school community.

Thus, although the MPTO brought many new resources to Morningside, the extent to which these resources benefited the collective student body was mediated by the particular sociocultural and demographic context of the school. Middle- and upper-middle-class parents were overrepresented in the MPTO and in most cases determined what resources would be brought to the school and how they would be distributed. Some of these resources served the entire student body; however, many of the decisions about how to allocate funding (e.g., hiring kindergarten aides, building a kindergarten playground) benefited only students in the lower grades, who as a whole were of higher socioeconomic status than upper-grade students owing to the demographic shifts occurring at the school.

Shifting Norms of Engagement

Interviews and conversations with long-timer parents and teachers (as well as parents of alumni) indicated a shift in norms and practices associated with parental engagement during the period of my research. Although in the late 1990s and early 2000s, the MPTO was disproportionately white and middle class compared with the school's demographics, long-timers described the organization as much smaller (both in number and in scope of activities) than the current MPTO. While a few MPTO leaders had worked with the principal and school staff to bring in grants, most of the organization's activities had been social rather than economic. Suzie Miller, a long-timer parent who had been a regular member of the organization when her children were younger, stated that "we had like six people who were active in the MPTO in the late 1990s and it was really hands on. . . . We didn't have gigantic projects like we do now, just small, simple stuff."

By 2007, parents were working with an MPTO budget of $129,000, owing to increases in individual family donations, parent fund-raising efforts (donations from individuals and businesses), and grant writing. This substantial budget prompted changes in the organization: new systems of financial management were implemented, and new volunteer roles were created. In previous years, doing the work of an active parent meant organizing school social events such as the annual school barbecue or small-scale fund-raisers, but now the roles of MPTO members were expanded to include a greater number of positions that required specialized skills such as a financial analyst, a webmaster, and a large-donor campaign coordinator.

New fund-raising events and systems were established as well: after visiting the auctions of several more affluent public and private schools in the area, for example, parents decided to implement a school auction at Morningside to bring in funds for the school. The event, free and open to the public, was held in the school cafeteria/auditorium and raised thousands of dollars. In the auction I attended in 2006, parents bid on items such as a hand-crafted cookie jar made by a Morningside teacher, horseback-riding lessons, four tickets to a local aquarium, and a two-night stay at a beachside hotel. Several Latino and African American parents attended the student band performance held at the beginning of the event, but most left with their children immediately afterward. The rest of the evening was attended primarily by white and Asian American parents at the school.

Marisa Collins, an MPTO parent who had managed parent donations for the past three years, described the shift in parent giving at the school:

M: Oh, and this year for instance at the auction—the auction organizers had credit card payments. And we've never had credit card payments before. We got over half of the payments on credit card. I mean people bought like 500 bucks worth of stuff at the auction. . . . So the kind of socioeconomic slice that has a credit card that can put $500 on it and wants to do it so that they can go on vacation with the miles is completely different from people who—I mean I have people walk up and give me a $5 bill for their donations. And I know that they're choosing to do that instead of buying groceries. And there's people who send from one of those check-cashing services; they send me $20 a month. And there's people who give me twelve checks for $10; they postdate them and I put them in each month. So there's every kind of ability to donate, but over time in the three years I've done it, there's just been so much more of the institutionalization of the expectation of giving and of the ability. And of all the convenience.

I: *Is there a particular grade that stands out in being able to do that?*

M: Always—the kindergarten and first grade always give more time and money than any other grade, and it goes down over time. There is no question.

Although in Marisa's experience the parents of lower-grade students had always given more of their money and time, she described how the amount of parent giving had greatly expanded in the last two to three years. She also described how the organization had received more employer matches from parents who worked at major corporations in the area.

In addition to an increased emphasis on parent fund-raising at the school, parents and teachers described a shift in commonly used forms of communication among parents at the school. When I asked Ms. Brown if the MPTO had changed since she first arrived as a staff member at the school in the late 1990s, she responded that the organization was "getting more parents with degrees." Ms. Brown, who worked closely with low-income Morningside students and their families, said that "people with less education become reluctant based upon fear, embarrassment, or the feeling that they can't contribute." When I asked her to explain, she talked about how the MPTO now relies upon e-mail as a major form of communication among parents:

> The MPTO really relies on e-mail and not all parents have e-mail and so they miss them that way. They get information later but as it happens they miss out. I'd love to figure out a way to reach all parents. Not all parents are readers and so it makes it more difficult and that parent should not be disinclined. Learn to make our information not as long.

Felicia Martinez, a low-income parent of a kindergartner, talked about being the only, as she described, "Spanish parent" at an MPTO meeting and the difficulty she had, as an English-language learner, getting to know other parents at the school. Like Ms. Brown, she also spoke about the MPTO's reliance on e-mail as a form of communication and social connection:

> Well, at the beginning I think it was more just like people just talking to themselves because they know each other better. And they also communicate on the Internet, and I have no computer. I don't have nothing of that, so they don't really, it's hard to know me.

Email was indeed a major form of information sharing among middle-class parents at the school. In addition to the school information shared by parents on the GPG listserv, the MPTO had a listserv that included information about district initiatives and policies, calls for parent volunteerism, updates about MPTO projects, and information about upcoming school events. The school had a newsletter about school events and activities that was sent home with students, but there was a great deal of information that was passed along via the listservs that was not included in the newsletter. The listserv also provided an opportunity for parents to connect with other parents within the school community, as they read and often responded to each other's postings and the information provided.

In contrast, long-timers described how most of the information sharing and relationship building that occurred among Morningside parents in the early 2000s was through personal, face-to-face interactions or phone calls. Dolores King, an African American long-timer parent, talked about how MPTO members would "go to kids' birthday parties, build trust with the parents, talk and get to know each other, find their strengths and weaknesses." She explained how, in her mind, these personal connections were essential because they allowed MPTO members to get to know parents' individual situations as well as the strengths of many of the low-income families of color at the school: "We knew what we had to know so that when the time came when we needed their services, we knew that 90 percent of the time that person would be able to do it. Because we knew what that person would and wouldn't be able to do." A few of the low-income parents of color whom I interviewed and spoke with talked about how both of the current MPTO cochairs had reached out to them personally and invited them to participate in MPTO events. Most, however, did not come into regular contact with MPTO members or their families. Even Felicia, whose daughter shared a class with several of the regular MPTO members, did not feel that parents in the organization knew her.

Between 2003 and 2007, school events were expanded and highly publicized in the local community. Fliers for events such as the school's annual Spring Carnival had been drawn by hand in the past; most were now produced by a professional graphic designer who was a parent at the school and were posted in the windows of local businesses. The event—broadened to include numerous booths and activities (such as a rock-climbing wall) for kids—also became a fund-raiser, as students and families were asked to buy tickets for food and games. MPTO parents had also modified the annual Jump-A-Thon, an event that had always been a fund-raiser at the school, in an effort to increase participation and funds raised. Getting a "Super-Jumper" medal was now more closely tied to fund-raising, as students were asked to get fifteen pledges of any amount *or* $100 worth of pledges as well as jump for a designated number of minutes according to their grade.

The shift in requirements for the Jump-A-Thon illustrates the tensions that some of the changes in the MPTO evoked at the school. The event organizers—part of a subcommittee of the MPTO—sought to raise more funds for school programs by requiring a minimum number of donations in order to receive the Super-Jumper medal. Just before and during the event, however, several parents who were not regular attendees at MPTO meetings expressed their frustrations with the new fund-raising requirement for the medal. The following is an excerpt from my field notes at the event:

> A white woman with a toddler was watching her son jump, and I said hello. I asked her how the jumping system worked, and she said that she was upset because this year the students had to get pledges from at least 15 people to get a medal, or raise $100. She said she didn't think it was really fair for people like them who didn't have big families they could count on for donations. She said she ended up just donating money herself. She said, "It teaches you how to work the system though," saying that you just make up names and assign them 15 cents each. She said she didn't come up with $100, but she did get the pledges so that her son could get a medal. She said she told a few MPTO members that the system wasn't fair.

Several parents, like the one described above, simply wrote down a bunch of names so their child could get the medal but also expressed their discontent to MPTO leaders. Others sought to circumvent the new fund-raising requirement altogether. I observed the grandmother of a first grader, for example, respond to her granddaughter's pleas for a medal by asking the parent working the registration desk if she could have one anyway without having donated money. This elderly African American woman—who had contributed to the school in other ways through her work in the school garden—was eventually able to secure a medal for her granddaughter. Other students, however—many of whom were African American students in the upper grades participating with their peers rather than their parents—did not get a medal but nonetheless joined in the jumping.

The Jump-A-Thon planning committee had not intended for the event to be exclusive; one member described how students could simply give "fifteen pennies and write down the names of all of their aunties and uncles and cousins on the pledge form." Creating an incentive to donate more money was a major motivation for the changes in medal requirements, however. One MPTO member stated: "I don't deny that a Super-Jumper Medal is a coveted prize, but the whole point of the organizing committee's decision was that by making that such a coveted prize, you're stimulating that extra effort to fund-raise to a certain goal." Indeed, the event brought in a record $13,500 that year. There was a key tension between social processes and material outcomes in the time I spent at Morningside: parents within the MPTO sought to bring a greater number of programs and resources to the school and to sustain the programs they had; yet their emphasis on the economic functions of the organization often competed with and detracted from a focus on issues of inclusivity, equity, and access within the changing school context.

Needing "a Résumé to Participate"

Despite MPTO leaders' stated desire for the organization to be more racially and socioeconomically diverse, parents who did not regularly attend MPTO meetings pointed to the structure, culture, and content of meetings as deterrents. Mariah Brown, a mixed-race African American and white working-class parent, described feeling "inadequate" as a single mother with limited time. Although she occasionally chaperoned on field trips, attended school events that involved her child, and helped her child's teacher, she was not a regular attendee at MPTO meetings. Reflecting a common sentiment expressed by many parents interviewed, she described feeling "overwhelmed" by the MPTO leadership's calls for volunteerism:

> The first year was like "we need this, do that, raise this money." It just seemed like, for parents who don't have time nor the money to do it, you start feeling inadequate because you can't be this PTA mom, and doing all this stuff for the kids. And sometimes that's just not in their personality, period. Even if they had the time, you know, they're not into that. So that was one thing. And I still feel slightly inadequate. Or not inadequate, but maybe that I should just do a little more or give a little more. But, you know, when you're a single mom, your time is precious and your money is short.

Mariah said that when she voiced her concern to the MPTO leadership the previous year about the pressure to volunteer, they were receptive, and "they haven't been so 'donate, donate, do do do' since then because it was really, really strong." Yet the feelings of inadequacy she expressed for not being able to "do more or give a little more" suggest that some parents received implicit messages that certain forms of parental engagement were valued more than others within the school community despite the efforts of many MPTO members to make the organization more representative of the broader school community. One could argue that Mariah was an active parent, given that she worked full-time, raised a daughter as a single mom, and helped out in her child's classroom when she could, but even she did not see these efforts as "adequate" forms of engagement. Highlighting the often invisible and pernicious ways in which exclusion occurs, Mariah critiqued the MPTO for what she saw as undue pressure placed on parents to donate time and money, yet she internalized a feeling of inadequacy on the basis of the ways she did, or didn't, participate at the school.

Time and schedule were not the only factors contributing to the underrepresentation of low-income and working-class parents of color in the MPTO; elements relating to the MPTO's culture and structure were cited as well. In a conversation about possible changes to the MPTO's structure, Jessica Rodriguez, a Latino and white working-class parent whose daughter was in the fourth grade, described the intimidation she felt, "especially as a young mom." She explained that she didn't have experience working with a budget and felt like she needed "a résumé to participate" in meetings. Although Jessica had leadership experience in community organizations, the sense of intimidation she felt in MPTO meetings underlines the disconnect she perceived between her own background and the specific skills, knowledge, and types of competence emphasized within the organization.

The feeling that one needed professional credentials in order to participate, compounded by the fact that the MPTO did not reflect the full diversity of the school's families, deterred some low-income and working-class parents from participating in the organization. Dawn Traylor, an African American working-class parent, rejected the MPTO's calls for parent donations, seeing parent fund-raising as beyond the scope of her responsibility as a public school parent:

When [the fliers about fund-raising] come home, I just throw them away, because I know that I'm a parent and I'm doing enough. I'm sending her there—what more do you want from me? Now if she was in a private school, it would be different. I would expect to have to pay for certain things at certain times and maybe contribute to the PTA or whatever like that. But a public school? I don't remember my parents ever having to do that. I remember going with my dad to the PTA a couple times, and they talked about issues, things they wanted to do for the kids and what they wanted to have. They wanted to build a new playground, they wanted to paint—OK. But all this other stuff, I don't get it. It's like it's more political now. The more money we raise, they compare us to [name of a more affluent school in the district]. Now you know that school's predominantly white. And our MPTO's talking about how they raised over $100,000 last year. OK, so. But that's the difference; I think that's what's going on.

Dawn saw her decision to send her child to Morningside—rather than the less academically successful school near her house—as "enough" participation as a public school parent. She saw MPTO meetings as "more political now," choosing instead to focus her energies on activities like helping her child with homework. Indeed, as other studies have found, low-income and working-class parents often support their children's education through participation in more informal spaces that offer them a voice and a sense of purpose, whether it be in the home, their children's classroom, or in parent groups in which their particular social, linguistic, and cultural resources are valued and built upon (Dyrness 2011; Perez Carreon, Drake, and Calabrese Barton 2005).

Many long-timer parents described MPTO meetings as "more bureaucratic" than they had been in the past, with a great deal of time spent talking about budgetary and programmatic issues. During the period of research, a large part of the agenda of MPTO meetings was devoted to discussions about how to sustain or expand the number of programs at the school. The organization's budget was a key part of these discussions, with members strategizing over how to save and more efficiently manage the organization's growing funds. In one meeting, for example, a parent who had experience leading financial-training sessions at nongovernmental organizations helped to facilitate a discussion of the MPTO budget:

The presenter passed out a handout that showed last year's expenses compared with this year's and stated, "So if you look at our income, we're actually doing well, but that's also because we're only five months into the school year." He explained to the group that "we're getting to the point in this organization where we're starting to have some extra money—we're at the point where we're not spending down." Mark Fisher [an MPTO member who played an active role in helping to bring in grants for the school] said that they just received a $5,000 grant for the gardening program, and they were hoping to get $12,000 again this year for the sports program. He said that they have to reapply for those funds each year, so it's always somewhat up in the air. Jackie Turner, a kindergarten parent, added, "There's also a number of funds that will be coming in for the kindergarten playground—hopefully $15,000." The parent/presenter said, "So it looks like we have about $25,000 in grant requests out there right now."

Mark said that they're "waiting to hear back on the grant that funds the art teacher." Mr. Foster added that "they always give you slightly less than what you ask for, and last year we asked for $20,000 and got $16,000." One parent spoke up and said, "I thought I heard the principal say that if we lose Title I, we'll lose a big chunk of our money." Mark responded by saying that the $70,000 to $75,000 in Title I funds currently pays for the Parent Outreach position and part of the librarian's position. He said, "We'd have to come up with those funds [if we lose the Title I money]." Lynda Washington chimed in and said, "We're sitting pretty well right now, but I hear what you're saying. That's been one of Marilyn's [the principal's] big concerns."

Much of the budgetary discussions centered on a desire to plan for a potential loss of Title I funds the following year, as the school would be even more dependent upon the MPTO to fund and sustain staff positions.

Dolores, who had been a regular and very involved member of the organization in the early 2000s, expressed in an interview her frustrations with what she saw as a shift in the MPTO's focus:

> Wait a minute. The money is just there for fund-raising. We're not trying to be no company! They're trying to make the school into a company. Now you're getting into starting to talk about taxes and all that other stuff. Who's going to do that? Why handle more paperwork? That's taking away from the kids, see what I mean? You're turning the school into a corporation. Let's go look at small fund-raisers. But when you talk about putting all this money away and getting interest off of it, now you're starting to talk about paperwork. Are you going to find a parent that's willing to do that type of accounting? And if you do find a parent willing to do that, you're taking that parent away from that child now. Because that's more work that the parent has to do.

For Dolores, the shift in the MPTO—which had become what she described as more like a "corporation"—created more work for parents and took away from the time they had to focus on their children. MPTO members, however, were now working with a budget of over $100,000, and the programs and activities the organization funded were constantly expanding. MPTO leaders did spend a great deal of time in meetings and in planning, with a few describing their work as equivalent to a "part-time job." These parents felt this was necessary, however, in order to sustain many of the programs, such as art and music, that parents and teachers valued.

Low-income and working-class parents were not the only groups voicing critiques of the organization. In a survey conducted by the MPTO, in interviews, and in meetings where potential changes in the organization's structure were discussed, parents and teachers from across the race and class spectrum raised concerns about MPTO meetings. In an MPTO survey given to parents, one white middle-class parent responded:

I feel the tenor of the MPTO has changed; it seems to be less a place where we all work together for good things for our kids and more about who can plan the most elaborate, biggest fundraiser. . . . I think the "professionaliza-tion" of the volunteerism alienates a lot of the school community; I know it makes me reluctant to continue volunteering.

Ms. Harper echoed these sentiments in her comparison of past and current MPTO meetings:

H: They're a little dry and they're really business-like. And it's a turnoff for a lot of people. I don't mean to negate people's hard work, because all those people, like I said, they do what they're doing and working hard. But it's not attractive. It's a different kind of meeting. It's for people who want to do business meetings. So it's a little bit excruciating for someone like me. Although I'm thankful, but it's just like "uhh, this again."

I: *What was it like—because you were saying before—*

H: Man, it felt like you had gone to one of these ladies' houses and they were having kind of a party. And there's some little business that had to be taken care of, but the rest of it, let's just have a good time together. Like even the way the meetings were run, it was more like you went to someone's house in-stead of going to a business meeting. Really different tone. I think they were gentle, more gentle and conscious about including people in some ways.

The sentiments expressed highlight the key tension between the social and the economic goals of the MPTO: there was a desire to bring a greater number of resources and opportunities to the school, but the focus on get-ting things done and what some long-timers saw as the professionalization of volunteerism negatively impacted the ability of the MPTO to serve as an inclusive organization. Voicing her frustrations with the organization, a member of the school's Diversity Committee stated that "some of the [MPTO] leaders feel that if you slow down, you'll lose the momentum they've built." Many of the parents who felt that the organization should provide more social support and fellowship for families decided not to continue attending MPTO meetings, instead choosing to volunteer in their children's classroom and participate in parental social gatherings organized by the Diversity Committee.

The tension between goals linked to material outcomes (e.g., programs and resources) and those related to social processes (e.g., fostering a more inclusive school community) was ever present throughout the period of research. Parents, working through the MPTO, had volunteered countless hours of their time to build and sustain the numerous programs and re-sources that benefited teachers, staff, and students. With so little support from the district or the state, MPTO parents recognized that in order to sustain things such as the garden and the art and music programs, it was largely up to them to secure the funding. Yet the MPTO's primary focus on bringing more resources to the school often competed with discussions of process, access, and inclusivity within the school community. As the parent-teacher organization grew in size, scope, and affluence, the economic goals of the organization and the need to create and sustain programs and resources overshadowed a focus on social processes and issues of inclusion/exclusion within the demographically shifting school context.

Conclusion

The case of Morningside suggests a shift and a redefinition of the "active parent" in contemporary urban public schooling. In an underresourced urban school district such as Woodbury, schools like Morningside with librarians, art and enrichment programs, and mental-health services for students often depend on the contributions of time and money made by active middle-class parents to ensure that these programs are created and sustained. This is perhaps even more salient today, as the current economic recession and housing crisis have meant drastic budget cuts in districts across the nation, particularly in California (California Department of Education 2010). Many public schools depend greatly on the various forms of capital that parents offer and what one parent described as their "super-human efforts." In a context of rising economic inequality and dramatic cuts in public education spending, middle-class parents are commonly viewed by teachers, administrators, district leaders, and other parents as key components of urban school reform and school success.

The case of Morningside, however, points to the limitations of positioning middle-class parental engagement as a key intervention strategy in urban education. Within the school context, forms of engagement that were made most visible and implicitly (or explicitly) valued by institutional actors were those undertaken by parents with access to dominant social, cultural, and economic capital. Parents like Mariah Brown, who were unable to volunteer long hours or who did not have experience fund-raising and writing grants, ended up feeling "inadequate" despite the various social and cultural resources they employed in support of their children's education. This affected their orientation toward and engagement in the school, as they were less likely to participate in decision-making forums when they felt that their contributions were not needed or valued. The professional-ization of the MPTO intensified racial and class tensions and status posi-tions at the school, and not all resources brought by MPTO parents ben-efited all students.

The findings suggest that the increased economic role played by par-ent-teacher organizations may not only exacerbate status positions and the marginalization of low-income parents within school settings but also have a downside for parents as a collective. Although white middle- and upper-middle-class parents are often better able to conform to the arche-type of the "active parent" because of their social and cultural capital, it is questionable whether a strong reliance on parental contributions in pub-lic education is either realistic or positive. Instead of making changes in state and federal education policy that would reflect a greater commitment to public education, the onus is placed heavily on parents and teachers to provide the educational opportunities and material resources needed to create and sustain high-quality educational experiences for students. This is a dangerous move; it effectively shifts responsibility for the provision of high-quality schooling from the government to individual citizens and the private sector, paving the way for the increased privatization of public edu-cation (see Lipman 2011; Watkins 2012).

As more families struggle to manage the costs of health care, child care, and housing in the context of rising economic inequality (Sawhill and Morton 2008), fewer parents may be able to volunteer long hours at schools and contribute money to fill the resource gaps left by local and state governments. The expectation that parents will support the work of institutional actors through extensive volunteerism places undue pres-sure on single-parent families and those in which both adults are working full-time. Relying on parents to help fund academic programs also raises questions about democratic participation and decision making in public education, as parents who make large financial contributions or help to secure large grants may feel they are entitled to a greater say in matters of curriculum and instruction.

My initial study was conducted during a period of great change at Morningside: it commenced the first year that the school experienced space and enrollment pressures related to the increased number of neighbor-hood families seeking entrance into the school. Although more white and mixed-race middle-class children were enrolling in the lower grades, Afri-can American students still made up the largest racial group at the school, and the school still qualified for Title I money based on the number of students qualifying for free or reduced-price lunches. Morningside's demographics were thus still distinct from those of the public schools in the more affluent western part of the school district. Two years later, I wondered: Had the long-timers' fears that the school would become whiter and more middle and upper-middle class come to fruition? If so, how did parents and teachers understand this change? How might the economic recession and subsequent budget cuts to education affect issues of access, inclusivity, and equity at the school? In the next chapter, I describe my return visit to Morningside and explore the economic, social, and demographic changes that the school community experienced in the two years that I had been away.

SIX

Morningside Revisited

Although I graduated and took a position at a large university in the Midwest, I often thought about the Morningside community, and I remained in contact with several of the people who had participated in the original study. When reading newspaper articles and examining district demographic data about the school, I saw that the student population was continually shifting as more middle-class families enrolled their children there. I also read about the effects of the economic recession on families in Woodbury and the unprecedented budget shortfalls the city, school district, and state were facing.

In light of these changes, I returned to Morningside Elementary in the spring of 2010, three years after completing the period of intensive data collection at the school. I had given my survey results and analysis to the school's principal and members of the Morningside Parent-Teacher Organization (MPTO) after the initial period of data collection. However, I wanted to discuss my overall findings with current and former Morningside parents and teachers, as well as learn more about the changes that had occurred at the school since 2008. I sought to understand how parents and teachers interpreted the more recent changes at Morningside, as well as explore the current school choices and engagement of parents in the original study. Lastly, I wanted to provide an opportunity for parents and teachers to reflect on these changes and give me feedback on my analysis and results.

Much of the literature on school integration has focused on school and district efforts to counter entrenched patterns of residential segregation and resource disparities through explicit policies and practices that promote and ensure school-level diversity (see, e.g., Frankenberg and Debray 2011; Grant 2009; Kahlenberg 2012; Orfield and Eaton 1996; Wells et al. 2009).

This important research has documented the short- and long-term benefits of racial and economic integration in public education as well as promising practices in school districts across the country. The research described in this chapter demonstrates the need to understand the contours and long-term consequences of a different type of integration: one driven in large part by the individual choices and collective engagement of middle-class parents. In the current legal and political climate in which district desegregation policies are under attack, parents' and community members' voluntary efforts to integrate schools may be seen by proponents of choice as a promising and more viable alternative to district mandates and intervention. Through their social networks, marketing, and what some parents describe as "grassroots" organizing, these parents are encouraging other parents like them to invest in underresourced city public schools without threatening a broader system of neighborhood schooling and individual "choice."

The changes at Morningside, as well as parents' and teachers' understandings of these changes, demonstrate the limitations of the "free-market diversity" discussed in chapter 2: diversity resulting from the actions of individual parents and neighborhood demographic shifts rather than explicit desegregation policies. Although parents and teachers voiced concerns about the decline in the number of low-income students and African American students at the school (and several worked to counter this decline through targeted outreach efforts), there was a sense that the demographic shifts at the school were ultimately out of their control, given the composition of the neighborhood and the school district's enrollment policy that privileged neighborhood families. The fact that more families with young children were moving in, staying, and sending their children to Morningside meant that Morningside was no longer an option for most low-income families, who could not afford to live in the school's enrollment zone. Schools such as Morningside that become more socioeconomically and racially diverse through neighborhood demographic shifts and middle-class parent outreach are unlikely to sustain their socioeconomic diversity over time in the absence of dedicated resources and explicit policies to ensure that low-income students have access to them. Yet the choices and engagement of Morningside parents outlined in this chapter suggest that the investments of middle-class parents in urban public schools, *in concert with* school and district integration policies that ensure that these schools remain accessible to low-income students, may help to disrupt entrenched patterns of segregation, resource disparity, and inequity in school districts and public schools.

Following Up

Prior to my return trip, I prepared a report to share with research participants, the school, and the school district. In the report I provided summaries of four main findings that emerged from my research:

1. Parents had a high level of satisfaction with Morningside Elementary.
2. The engagement of middle- and upper-middle-class parents at Morningside attracted other parents of similar class backgrounds to the school and played an influential role in the shifting socioeconomic and racial demographics of the student population.
3. The demographic and material changes that were occurring at the school brought about tensions within the school community related to notions of progress.
4. A reliance on the work of "active" parents put the emphasis on the products of parents' engagement rather than the processes through which this engagement was occurring.

I had a parent (and former participant) provide feedback on an early draft of the report, as I wanted to ensure that it was written in accessible and clear language. I also sent the report to a former MPTO leader to get feedback on its accuracy and tone. Both parents offered helpful suggestions regarding areas that needed clarification, but overall they agreed with the findings. The former MPTO leader, for example, stated in e-mail correspondence that I did a "great job summarizing the facts and assessing the possible solutions or mitigations."

Several weeks before my scheduled trip to Woodbury, I e-mailed the twenty-eight-page report of my findings to the principal and a group of parents and teachers who had participated in the original study. I asked if they would be willing to meet with me for an interview, and I volunteered to discuss my findings with members of the school community. In addition to sending the report to participants who had originally expressed interest in hearing my research results, I asked several MPTO leaders and the principal to distribute the report to other parents or community members who might be interested in the research. One parent, for example, forwarded the report to a school board member representing Morningside's district. In addition to sharing my findings with parents and school staff, I also sent the report to Woodbury Unified's Division of Research (as per their request). One parent did not respond to my requests for an interview, and two parents agreed to be interviewed initially but were ultimately unable to meet during the week I was conducting interviews. One could interpret this as a rejection of the report or my research; or it could simply be an issue of priority, given the multiple demands made on these parents' time.

I returned to Woodbury in February 2010, spending a week meeting with parents and teachers who were part of the original study and who agreed to participate in an interview. Upon the request of a Glenbrook Parents' Group (GPG) member who was active in the MPTO, I also met with and discussed my research report and findings with a small group of current Morningside parents. Most had children in the lower grades at Morningside. With the exception of one Asian American parent, all appeared to be white women. Several of the parents, however, had mixed-race children.

In addition to discussing my findings in this small-group meeting, I interviewed parents who were or had been regularly involved in the MPTO, GPG, or Diversity Committee and who could speak about the changes in these organizations as well as changes at the school more broadly. My interview sample was purposeful, as I sought out parents who were still connected to the school community and yet represented a range in terms of the number of years they had been parents at the school. I interviewed eight parents who had children currently enrolled at the school, and four parents whose children had since graduated from Morningside but who remained in regular contact with the school's families. Seven of the parents were white, two were African American, two were Latino, and one was Asian American. My primary focus on former study participants who were still heavily connected to Morningside meant that my interview sample was (with the exception of one working-class parent) largely middle and upper-middle class. Most of the low-income and working-class parents I had interviewed in the original study now had children who had already graduated from the school, and of those few who were still Morningside parents, only one had participated in a school-wide committee (the Diversity Committee). Thus, the perspectives of parents reflected in this chapter are largely based upon the experiences of parents who had a regular and sustained involvement in the organizational work of the school.

In addition to parents, I also sought out veteran teachers in the lower grades who had participated in the original study and could speak about the demographic changes that were occurring in the kindergarten and first grades. The final group of interviewees included nine parents and three teachers from the lower grades (K–1). In addition to interviewing and meeting with parents and teachers, I interviewed a neighborhood resident who had been active in Morningside's MPTO in the seventies and had lived in the school's neighborhood for close to fifty years. As part of my follow-up research, I analyzed school and district demographic statistics and publicly available district documents for the 2008–10 time period as well.

A Changing Context

When I returned to Morningside in 2010, I found that the school had developed several characteristics similar to those of the more affluent and high-performing "western" schools in the district, yet at the same time, it had retained aspects of its past. In chapter 4, I described the fears of many long-timer parents and teachers about the future of the school: they worried that it would become more like the predominantly middle-class and white schools in the western part of the city, losing its racial and socioeconomic diversity as well as aspects that made it unique. Like the other popular elementary schools in the district, Morningside was indeed experiencing student assignment and enrollment challenges as parents in the neighborhood and across the district sought to enroll their children. There were also fewer students qualifying for free or reduced-price lunches in the lower grades, and white students were now the largest racial group at the school (at 37 percent of the total student population).

Despite the significant demographic and material changes that had occurred at Morningside over the past decade, the school was still in some ways distinct from most of the more affluent and highly sought-out public and private schools in the district. Although the percentage of African American students at the school continued to decline with each passing year, students of color as a whole (Latinos, Asians, African Americans, and mixed-race students) were still in the majority at the school and the school still technically qualified for Title I funds. Test scores had risen at the school—the school's Academic Performance Index scores increased almost 100 points between 2006/7 and 2009/10—yet teachers and parents described Morningside's academic program as similar to what it had been during my initial research, and there had been little turnover among the staff and administration. The school continued to emphasize the arts, the gardens were maintained by parents and staff and were used as teaching tools, and although fewer in number, African American and low-income students continued to have higher test scores than those in most other schools with similar populations in the district and state. These were all aspects of the school that had endured and been built upon, making it stand out among most other elementary schools in Woodbury Unified School District.

The fears that parents voiced in the original study—about the significant demographic and material changes the school was experiencing and the lack of a district policy to ensure that Morningside was accessible to low-income students—were not entirely unfounded. Three major issues were impacting the school: (1) student assignment and enrollment pressures; (2) changing student demographics; and (3) budgetary gaps requiring continual fund-raising.

Student Assignment and Enrollment Pressures

The district as a whole had faced a decline of more than three thousand students since 2005, with declining enrollment projected to continue in the future based upon birthrates, private school enrollment (especially at the middle school level), and a growth in the number of students in charter schools.[1] Several schools had closed or been reconstituted due to declining enrollment, low test scores, or both, and there were a number of contentious community and school board meetings in which parents and community members debated school closures and potential shifts in attendance boundaries.

As was the case in 2006, the district had a "choice" plan that required families to rank district schools in order of preference. Although the new district leadership also sought to improve neighborhood schools so that parents would not "opt out," the goal of the choice plan was to make the cluster of higher-performing schools in the district (most located in upper-middle-class neighborhoods in the western part of the city) accessible to nonneighborhood students. In 2006 neighborhood students received first priority in enrollment in schools where the number of students seeking admittance was greater than the number of available spots. In 2010, however, first preference went to the siblings of students already enrolled in a school, regardless of whether or not they lived within the school enrollment zone. This new policy allowed siblings to attend the same school and also helped to ensure that the high-performing district schools were accessible to at least some nonneighborhood families. Students residing in the neighborhood zone (without siblings at the school) received second preference in the lottery system. By 2010 the number of schools in the west that were at or over capacity had grown, with parent and district speculation that this was due in large part to the economy and a growth in the number of parents selecting public schools rather than paying for private. At several of the top-requested district elementary schools in particular, some neighborhood children were redirected to other schools due to a lack of space to accommodate the growing demand.

Morningside had become one of these coveted schools. Most of the spots for kindergarten were taken by families residing in the school's enrollment zone or by children with siblings already at the school, and there was a waiting list of families from outside the enrollment zone seeking to enroll their children. Between 2008 and 2010, more than ninety families had vied for one of the roughly fifty-five to fifty-nine kindergarten spots.[2] Morningside was now facing many of the same enrollment pressures as schools in the more affluent, western part of the city: the school struggled to meet the growing demand from the neighborhood as well as from outside the enrollment zone.

Historically, Morningside was considered a favorable alternative for parents in enrollment zones with low-performing neighborhood schools; now, parents residing in western neighborhoods with high-performing schools were also seeking out Morningside (either based on preference or the fact that their neighborhood school was oversubscribed and had no more spots for neighborhood children). A number of high-ranking district administrators had also chosen to enroll their children at the school. According to several veteran teachers (and as reflected in parents' descriptions of the school on several parent websites), Morningside was now favorably compared to many of the affluent public and private schools in the area. On regional parent websites, parents lauded Morningside's diversity, integrated arts curriculum, and enrichment programs.

The principal worked to accommodate the increased demand and neighborhood enrollment by raising class sizes in the lower grades, with kindergarten classes expanding beyond the twenty or fewer students they had had in years past. This created challenges for teachers and it threatened Morningside's image as a small school—a feature that had been a point of attraction for many parents. In an interview, Ms. Porter, a kindergarten teacher, explained how the additional students affected her teaching practices:

> So it changed the structure of the class. I mean, you have so many children. Definitely. And so instead of doing all of our [small-group, student-centered] workshops in one day—we did four before in a day—now we break it into two. So we do three one day and then two the next. You know, we mix it up a little. And I actually think it works better for me as a teacher because it's less prep. But it's a disadvantage for the children because academically, they're not going through as—they're not getting as much in each day.

The school remained committed to enriching the district's standards-based curriculum, and it had been granted more flexibility from the district in the area of curriculum and instruction based on a demonstrated record of high test scores. Yet ironically, the fact that the school was now so popular and oversubscribed challenged some of the very features of the school that had attracted middle-class families: the school's small size and the quality of instruction.

Changing Student and Family Demographics

In the two years following the original study, Morningside continued to experience a decline in the number of African American students and an increase in the percentage of white and Hispanic/Latino students.[3] The largest demographic shift occurred among African American students, who comprised just 21 percent of students by the 2009/10 school year, compared with 38 percent two years prior and 78 percent in 2000. In contrast, the proportion of white students rose steadily between 2006/7 and 2009/10, from 18 to 37 percent. Whereas the percentage of Hispanic/Latino students rose to 10 percent of the student population by 2009/10, the percentage of students designated as "multiple/no response" fluctuated. The proportion of Asian students remained relatively stable, showing a slight upward trend (see fig. 1).[4]

Although the proportion of Morningside students enrolled in the free/reduced-price lunch program held relatively stable in the two years following the initial study, the socioeconomic background of the families of students in the lower grades differed from that of families of students in the upper grades. In the 2009/10 school year, for example, only 22 percent

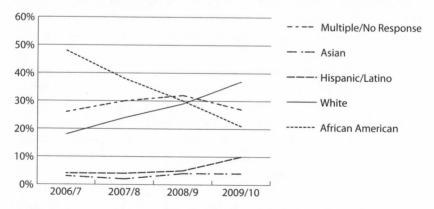

Fig. 1. Student racial/ethnic demographics, 2006–10. American Indian students represented less than 1 percent of the student population.

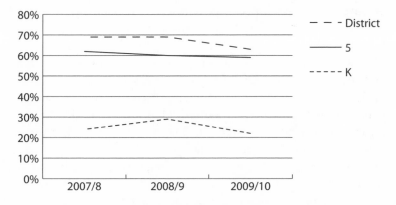

Fig. 2. Socioeconomically disadvantaged students by grade, 2007–10.

of kindergarten students were designated as socioeconomically disadvantaged, compared with 59 percent of fifth-grade students (see fig. 2).[5] Most fourth- and fifth-grade students first enrolled at Morningside prior to the boom in enrollment, a time when the school was an accessible option for families residing outside the largely middle-class neighborhood student assignment zone. Given that the district's student assignment process favored siblings of students already enrolled, and given the demographics of the school's enrollment zone, many, if not most, of those students in the lower grades who qualified as socioeconomically disadvantaged during this period were very likely siblings of students already enrolled at the school. Although Morningside appeared to be an economically integrated school—with approximately 40 percent of its students qualifying for free or reduced-price lunches—the school's socioeconomic mix was not evenly distributed across the grade levels.

While declining in total numbers, African American students continued to be disproportionately represented among students classified as socioeconomically disadvantaged at the school—in 2009/10, for example, 71 percent of all African American kindergartners were socioeconomically disadvantaged, compared with 56 percent of Hispanic/Latinos, 6 percent of whites, and 0 percent of Asians and those students designated as "two or more races."[6] Although the school had experienced increased racial diversity in the lower grades, the majority of students in kindergarten, first, and second grades were not from low-income or socioeconomically disadvantaged families.

This point may be easily missed, because the percentage of students qualifying for free or reduced-price lunches has remained relatively stable despite the demographic shifts. As discussed in chapter 2, lunch program enrollment has limited use for understanding the class backgrounds of students in a school setting. For example, some working-class students may be excluded because their families have incomes that are just above the cutoff for eligibility. Conversely, students whose parents are in graduate school may be eligible for the free/reduced-price lunch program despite the fact that parents' social and cultural capital may afford their children privileges that are not captured by their income alone. Moreover, school and district quantitative data provide only a limited understanding of the socioeconomic changes in Morningside's student population over the last decade, as systems of reporting student demographic data are not always consistent from year to year, and socioeconomic data were not disaggregated by grade level prior to the 2007/8 school year.

The aggregate percentage of students qualifying as socioeconomically disadvantaged has not dramatically shifted since 2000. Archival data and interviews with longtime teachers and parents, however, suggest that the student and family population at the school is more affluent now than in years past. The amount of money that individual families have donated to the school has risen substantially, along with grant money and resources that parents are able to garner for the school. Although household data on the socioeconomic profile of families at Morningside were unavailable, the fact that more families residing in the predominantly middle- and upper-middle-class neighborhoods close to the school are enrolling their children also suggests that most of the newcomer students are of a higher economic status than those in previous years.

On its website in 2010, Morningside continued to be described as a school with a "diverse population" of students. Yet as I discussed in chapter 4, parents and teachers continued to grapple with how to describe the racial and socioeconomic changes at the school. Diversity was commonly discussed in relation to the number of African American students at Morningside, which is not surprising, given that African Americans had historically constituted the largest racial group at the school. By 2010 the school was described by teachers and parents as both "more diverse," given the increased numbers of mixed-race and Asian American students and students from gay and lesbian families, and yet "less diverse" or "not diverse" in relation to the decline in the number of African American students and the growing number of white students at the school.

These demographic shifts were much more clearly evident for some teachers and parents. Indeed, the decline in numbers of African American students was central to their observations. Ms. Porter, a white kindergarten teacher, described the changes she had witnessed during the last six years:

> I would say six years ago I probably had four white students. . . . You know, now I look at my class and I have three African American students. And almost everyone else in the class is white, with a few children who are Latino and white and one child who's Japanese. So it's a totally different demographic.

Ms. Porter went on to say that most of the students in her class— "85 percent"—were now from the neighborhood and that many families walked their children to the school. Most of the few students who lived outside the student assignment zone were enrolled because of an older sibling or because they had a parent who was a staff member at the school.

Erica Zimmerman, a white parent of a second grader and a member of the school's Diversity Committee, also spoke about the shifts she had observed in the kindergarten classes:

> Well, you know, I think if one were to go into a classroom and sort of count the outliers in my son's class or the class that I looked at before we were considering Morningside, you know, you might be able to count the Caucasian children on one hand. And now you go into a kindergarten class and you can count the students of color on one hand. . . . So yeah, it feels different.

Alexis Robinson, an African American upper-middle-class parent, stated that the school's diversity has "gone down" in the three years since she first enrolled her daughter, describing this as a current challenge faced by the school:

I: *And what would you say are some of the challenges that the school is facing?*
A: Certainly diversity. I think that there's, you know, their diversity level's gone down. It's much more homogeneous now. And even though I guess the teacher population's a little bit more diverse now than when we first started, it still seems like it could be a little better. Little more diverse.
I: *When you say the diversity level's gone down, are you speaking racially, socioeconomically?*
A: Mmm, both.
I: *And how is that a challenge? Like in your eyes?*
A: I think my daughter not having as many other children that are the same racial background as her. It puts her at a disadvantage. It forces her to sort of

fit in with a group of children that are not similar, where there's not as many similarities. . . . I think it really has the ability to create some identity challenges for her.

When I asked her to describe the racial demographics of her daughter's class that year, Alexis stated that "there's two other, three other, black girls and just one black boy. There's about five black children out of a class of, I think, twenty-five. Or twenty-two." I followed up by asking her if there were Latinos or Asians in the class, and she said, "Yeah there are a few Asians. Mostly Asian, Asian-Caucasian mixed. But I don't know how many. And there's one Indian boy. One Latina girl. And I think the rest are mostly white." For Alexis, who spoke in our interview about her desire to counter the negative images and representations of blackness found in the media, conceptions of Morningside's diversity were closely tied to the number of other African American students and the opportunities for her daughter to develop a positive identity as a black child within the school setting.

Yet along with the change in African American student representation, some parents and teachers described the school as "more diverse" because of the growing number of mixed-race, white, and Asian American students. Ms. Hawkins and Mr. Foster, two veteran lower-grade teachers at the school, described the school as "more racially diverse" and "international":

H: But I think we're actually more racially diverse. It used to be black-white. Now it's everybody and everything. And there's—I think a large number of families—like when we did the survey for the state or district, and people on their ethnicity and race—we had a huge—like over 30 percent chose "other."
F: We have more biracial.
H: But not just the black-white thing. It's like universal, international.
F: Yeah. More Asian, white. . . . And like, in a way, we've gotten into trouble because of—not in trouble—but there's been a concern that we're losing the black population. But now it's like we're actually more diverse now than we've ever been. It's just socially—economically—we're not.
H: This year we did qualify for Title I, but barely. But I mean, let's face it, we don't look like a Title I school.

Mr. Foster's statement about the concern over the loss of the African American population at the school and Ms. Hawkins's reply that "we don't look like a Title I school" highlight the tensions many teachers and parents grappled with in defining and assigning meaning to the changing student demographics. Although the aggregate percentage of students qualifying for free or reduced-price lunches had not dramatically declined, long-timer teachers and parents described a school that felt and "looked" qualitatively different than it had in the past, because of the demographic changes in the lower grades. As discussed in chapter 2, the "urban" is commonly raced and classed in dominant educational discourse and often serves as a signifier of black and brown low-income students and their families (Leonardo and Hunter 2007; Noguera 2003; Watson 2011). As several scholars have posited, some light-skinned, culturally assimilated, and economically privileged Latinos, Asian subgroups, and multiracial individuals may serve as "honorary whites" within a shifting US racial order, existing as a distinct group between whites and a "collective black" (Bonilla-Silva 2004; Forman, Goar, and Lewis 2002; Rockquemore and Arend 2002). The demographic shifts at Morningside disrupted parents' and teachers' conceptions of a "Title I," urban public school; parents viewed the increase in white, Asian, and mixed-race (Latino-white, Asian-white) students as a different form of "diversity"—one that perhaps did not "count" in the same way.

Budgetary Gaps and the Push to Fund-Raise

The threat of a loss of Title I funds and the pressure to fund-raise were heightened in the year I returned to Morningside. Parents and teachers were concerned about a loss of the Title I funds they received each year based on the percentage of students enrolled in the free/reduced-price lunch program at the school. Although the school had not yet lost its Title I funds, it had lost eligibility for several grants and enrichment programs because of the changing socioeconomic demographics of the student population.

In addition to the impending threat of a loss of Title I funds, Morningside was affected by budget shortfalls at the district and state level. The state of California and the city of Woodbury were hard-hit by the economic recession and housing crisis, with dramatic declines in revenue for public education. The school district's budget was also affected by declining enrollment. Budgets for district central offices were cut by $70 million between 2008 and 2010, and school-site unrestricted budgets were cut by almost 5 percent. The district needed to cut just under $30 million from the 2010/11 unrestricted budget, with roughly $100 million in cuts projected during the next three years.[7] For a state that had per-pupil expenditures that were already well below the national average, and for a district with a majority of low-income students, these cuts meant that schools in the Woodbury Unified School District would be even more dependent upon grants and parent fund-raising.

Morningside thus faced reductions in district and state financial support while also losing eligibility for some of its enrichment programs because of its changing demographics. Those aspects of the school that attracted many parents—namely, the art and music programs and the after-school and enrichment programming—were in danger of being cut. Parents and teachers worked to fill these gaps through grant writing, fund-raising, and volunteerism, resulting in unprecedented amounts of money raised through the MPTO. The school raised more than $30,000 through individual family and employer-matched contributions that helped to fund things like classroom aides to offset increased class sizes, classroom supplies, the art and music programs, science, sports, mental-health services, and gardening at the school. The annual School Auction, traditionally held in the school's multipurpose room/cafeteria, was now scheduled to be held in a local arts space and to have an online bidding component that leaders hoped would help to expand the donations beyond the more than $16,000 they had received from the auctions in the last couple of years. GPG parents continued to support the school through their annual Book Drive, which brought in more than $3,000. According to a member of the Grants Committee, the 2009/10 MPTO budget was now well over $200,000. The MPTO had to hire an accountant to assist with the organization's taxes, and a parent volunteer was responsible for entering all the organization's financial information into a business accounting software program. According to one MPTO parent leader, the organization was trying to "systematize" things in response to the growing budget. Although beyond the scope of my follow-up research, these changes in the work of the MPTO were likely to exacerbate the tensions discussed in chapter 5, as managing the expanded budget required a specialized set of skills and familiarity with financial management systems.

Ms. Porter described some of the changes she saw at the classroom level, including how the kindergarten teachers had "really hit the jackpot" with having the MPTO fund aides for each of the classrooms. In addition, she noted a record number of classroom volunteers; she had handed out an unprecedented forty-six awards for volunteering last year, one for every parent or family member who volunteered in the class at least once. Ms. Porter described how that year's room parents had created a web page where they could send out updates about field trips and classroom events, and "if there's a blank spot on my schedule for volunteers, they'll make sure someone comes." Similarly, she spoke of changes in the type of snacks parents provided for the class:

And, you know, the snack is still happening where I have family members bringing snack once a month, highlighted by their child's name. Moving through alphabetically. And it's just been interesting to see the changes with that. Like the snacks used to be things more like a box of crackers and some purple drink. You know, like really different. Now it's like all organic. Fruits. Vegetables with the dip. Today someone made homemade blueberry muffins wrapped in gourmet wax paper, and they were in a basket with like a white blanket. And they were still hot when we ate them at snack.

Although parents had helped in the classroom and brought snacks in years past, Ms. Porter described parent volunteerism (e.g., creating a classroom web page and bringing organic snacks) that was qualitatively different from what she had experienced in previous years.

It's "Just Not the Same School Anymore"

In their reflections on the material and demographic changes that Morningside had experienced since the early 2000s, many long-timer parents and teachers described a school that was quite different from years past. They talked about a noticeable shift in Morningside's culture, identity, and demographics, as well as a change in the orientation and engagement of the new families in the lower grades. Parents who were newcomers during the time of the original study also reflected on changes they saw at the school. The changes they described, however, were less focused on dramatic shifts in the school culture and instead centered on the increased budget pressures and need for parent volunteerism. Most newcomer parents were aware of the school's history and previous demographics, but they did not have the same institutional memory as long-timer parents and teachers and had not witnessed similar shifts in the school population.

In interviews, long-timers described what they saw as major changes in the school's culture. Similar to my findings in the original study, this was in large part attributed to the actions and orientations of middle- and upper-middle-class parents in the lower grades. Two lower-grade teachers, for example, described the school as more like a "private school," with more parent requests to accommodate their children's individual needs and to keep them "challenged." Several long-timer white parents described themselves as quite different from many of the newcomer parents because of their outlook and experiences. Although most referred to themselves as middle class, they conceptualized their own ways of seeing the world as distinct from those of many of the new parents at the school. A white member of the MPTO whose child was about to graduate from Morningside described this difference:

> But I do think that there is something intangible about the way you interact with people or the way you perceive the world. . . . And it's not like I deny my essentially middle-class posture in the world—it isn't a role that I adopted, but it's just a role that I was always—you know, that I inherited. And I also don't try to—what do you call it—like dispose of it or dispense with it, you know; I accept it.
>
> But by the same token, I just feel like there is something fundamentally different between my approach and outlook than there is about the approach and outlook of the majority of the new incoming families at Morningside. There is less casual acceptance for embracing of socioeconomic and cultural variety than there used to be. And I do think it's mostly socioeconomic. I think that people, for want of a better word, the Glenbrook class, you know, those people are more comfortable with cultural and ethnic diversity than they are with socioeconomic diversity, by far. . . . You know, I always ask myself questions about that, too. . . . What is it that makes me think I'm different from those people, you know, or what is it that—how is it, if at all, that other people perceive me as different from those people? I'm not sure I have the answers to any of those questions, but I feel like I am different.

For this parent, who continued to work on several school committees, Morningside was "just not the same school anymore": it was "just a small group of people who are still interested in those [diversity] issues, trying to do outreach. And the rest of the school community pays lip service to the idea." In this parent's mind, many of the newcomer parents at Morningside emphasized and felt comfortable with Morningside's racial diversity, but they did not place the same value on socioeconomic diversity at the school.

Several long-timers also expressed their displeasure with what they saw as an increased emphasis on fund-raising and the school's budget. Harold White, an African American longtime neighborhood resident and MPTO leader in the early 1970s, described how much they were able to accomplish with so little money when he was active in the organization. Speaking about the importance of creating a strong volunteer base through relationship building, he stated, "Raising money is a good thing, but I like raising people." When I asked how the current MPTO compared with the organization when he was involved, he said, "Now you have a different group of people. . . . They like to spend money to get things done; we had volunteers."

Indeed, other long-timer parents supported this notion. For example, when describing one of the school's major fund-raisers, Molly Clausen stated that "it just keeps getting more and more outrageous. . . . It's just turned into a whole new level of fund-raising." Similarly, Suzie Miller, by then a parent of Morningside alumni, described what she saw as a shift in the priorities and focus of the MPTO:

> I came to Morningside because it was a small school, and I don't know. It became much more of a business; the raising of money, the big budgets, the constant harassment to give money I found incredibly tiresome. There's a big economic difference between me and our family and what people seem to be able to bring to the table and were expected to bring to the table, so I started to get very tired of that part of it, and then it became a life of its own. The whole budget then became a huge focus . . . and the parents become more of the focus than the staff, like what they wanted to do with this money and the committees.

Because of the changes at the school, Suzie said, "I'm not sure I'd pick Morningside [again]."

Although all the long-timer parents described a shift in both the demographics and the culture of engagement at the school, some pointed out that certain aspects of the "old Morningside" had been passed down and were reflected among some of the newcomer families. In an interview, Hannah Sorenson (who was by then a parent of Morningside alumni) told me that she had met Morningside's current MPTO chair at an event for parent leaders that was hosted by a school board member. She said, "She's carrying on the tradition; she gets the history. It's just so nice to see that the culture continues." Later in the interview, when I asked her about what this meant, she said, "The current MPTO president has the same philosophy that I have. . . . We expect everybody to participate, and if not, it's our job to find a way to have them do that." For Hannah, the demographics of the school may have shifted, but there still were newcomers who shared the same "philosophy" as long-timer parents. According to Hannah, this philosophy was based on the belief that all parents have something to contribute to the school and can play a role in its success.

Newcomer parents, however, were operating within a different context—they were confronted with a different set of issues than what long-timer parents had faced. Although Morningside's parent leaders included newcomers who shared long-timers' ideals about parent engagement and diversity, the demographic and material shifts that had occurred at the school created a context that made these ideals difficult to achieve.

Changes in Marketing and Outreach

By 2010 the historic efforts of parents and teachers to boost student enrollment and build neighborhood support for the school were no longer needed. The GPG continued to exist as a neighborhood organization but placed less emphasis on building neighborhood support for Morningside now that the neighborhood-school relationship was firmly cemented. Middle-class neighborhood children enrolled in Morningside were no longer an exception to the rule, as students living in the surrounding area were strongly represented in the kindergarten and first-grade classes. Judy Chu, an early member of the GPG who was still a part of the group, described the changes in the organization:

> The school's reputation is pretty firm right now. And people are coming to the neighborhood, as you know, for the school and wanting to come to the school. So it's not like we need to attract more attention and recruit or anything like that. And then in terms of getting to know each other, for those of us who have the school-age kids, we know each other because we have kids in school together. So we don't need to necessarily meet more neighbors.

In the past the GPG was the common point of connection for neighborhood parents; now, many parents' social networks and activities were built around Morningside.

The school continued to offer parent-led tours and open houses for prospective parents, but MPTO parents' marketing and outreach efforts had changed. Concerned with the declining numbers of low-income students in the lower grades, a group of parents in Morningside's newly created Kindergarten Outreach Committee sought to target child care centers that served a predominantly low-income population. Parents sent flyers about the school to Head Starts in the area and made several presentations about the school at local child care centers and family centers. In interviews, parents shared that they were also talking about the possibility of holding special school tours for parents at these centers and providing them with information about the enrollment process. The school's website was also changed to emphasize the high achievement of African American students at Morningside and the award the school had recently received for being a high-achieving, successful Title I school.

MPTO parents were also exploring opportunities to share resources and information across schools. Several parents, for example, had participated in a forum organized by a school board member on the creation of a city-wide network of parents in support of public schools. MPTO parents had also met with and shared their experiences and best practices with other parents seeking to support and improve their own local public school. Members of the Diversity Committee and Kindergarten Outreach Committee had met with the principal of Harambee, a neighboring school that had a predominantly low-income African American population, to talk about information sharing and collaboration between the two schools.

In discussing the report of my findings, several parents who were active in the MPTO mentioned the challenges they faced in trying to promote a racially and socioeconomically diverse student body at Morningside. In my meeting with a small group of MPTO parents, for example, one white parent from the neighborhood talked about not wanting to "tokenize" parents of color or low-income parents in the outreach efforts. She explained that once, at a prospective parent event, she had an African American parent question why they were highlighting African American achievement specifically at Morningside. The prospective parent had asked her why it needed to be singled out, which made her reflect on whether and how they should highlight difference at the school. Similarly, a member of the MPTO's leadership team commented on the difficulty of reaching out to low-income families, stating, "It sounds sort of crass, but how do you go befriend poor people?" Like this parent leader, many of the current MPTO parents desired a racially and socioeconomically mixed school community and yet did not have a clear sense of how best to go about fostering diversity at the school. And, as I discuss in a later section, there was no general agreement among parents and staff about what specifically constituted a "diverse" school, highlighting the flexibility of the term.

Parents' comments suggest that parent leaders faced challenges in their efforts to promote and foster diversity within the current school context. As discussed in chapters 4 and 5, most long-timer white parents were used to being racial minorities in the school, and many lived in predominantly black or racially and socioeconomically mixed neighborhoods in the city of Woodbury. Fostering parent participation at the school necessitated reaching out to parents of a different racial and class background than themselves. Many of these new white MPTO parents, in contrast, could easily see families of their own race and class background reflected in Morningside's student and family population and in the neighborhoods in which they resided. Because of the changing demographics at the school, white families in the lower grades were not forced to interact across lines of race and class to the same extent as white long-timer families had been.

In my report to teachers and parents, I outlined two major recommendations for future policy and practice (for more details, see chapter 7): (1) changes in student assignment, data collection, and resource allocation; and (2) parent and community organizing for educational transformation. I drew attention to the limits of individual solutions and proposed that the district "adopt an assignment policy that leaves a percentage of spots at schools open for incoming kindergartners who are eligible for free or reduced-price lunch." I noted that the information passed along through parent social networks and through their outreach had played a significant role in the changes at Morningside; however, "further developing and sustaining parents' targeted outreach efforts to those low-income and working-class families in Morningside's enrollment zone and in the broader district can also play an important role in promoting the socioeconomic diversity of incoming kindergarten classes at the school." I argued, "Processes of gentrification are never uniform or guaranteed, and thus efforts can be taken before the school reaches a 'tipping point' to ensure that the growing interest and investments in Morningside contribute to an integrated and inclusive school community."

Several parents who read the report expressed a feeling of inevitability related to the demographic changes, given patterns of residential segregation in the city of Woodbury and current school district policies that gave priority in enrollment to neighborhood families. When describing the school's efforts to reach out to more low-income families, a white middle-class member of the MPTO's leadership team stated that they were "stuck in some ways," given that the school is located in a predominantly white, middle-class neighborhood. Similarly, responding to the report of my findings, an MPTO parent commented:

> There are concerted efforts being made [to reach out to a working-class and low-income population], now more than ever. However, the effort seems increasingly Sisyphean in the face of the increasing gentrification. I don't see how we will *ever*, now that we have reached what you call the "tipping point," be able to tip it back.

This parent and several others expressed the sentiment that the school's demographics were out of their hands, given the demographics of the neighborhood and Woodbury Unified's student assignment policies.

Some of these same parents, however, also doubted that changes in district student assignment policies would be a politically viable solution to their current issues. In his response to the recommendations listed in my report, one white middle-class parent asked: "Would revising the district enrollment priorities district-wide really solve this issue? What other issues would it create, and could they be overcome?" Another white middle-class parent, speaking in the small-group discussion, shared that her friend had a child in a school that was experiencing similar issues, despite the fact that the school was in a district with an economic integration plan. These parents wanted a racially and socioeconomically diverse school for their children, but they did not see clear and viable solutions for how to ensure this at Morningside, given broader demographic and political contexts and the district's assignment plan.

Yet according to Jessica Rodriguez, a working-class Morningside parent who was very involved at her older daughter's district middle school, said there *were* ways to ensure that low-income students had a place at the school. She felt that part of the problem was that the school and broader district had not anticipated the demographic shifts:

> I think what's happening with Morningside is just what's happening with . . . gentrification and that kind of thing. . . . We don't plan ahead. We don't see it coming. We don't acknowledge that it's happening and then try to plan around that, or try to make sure we can maintain the same things or just— it's just happening. Then we're just dealing with it as it happens.

Comparing the recent changes at Morningside to gentrification in the city, Jessica argued that instead of simply reacting to changes as they occur, it is necessary for communities to plan ahead.

During my original period of research, MPTO members were actually attempting to "plan ahead" for the demographic shifts—but in different ways perhaps than those conceived of by Jessica. As discussed in the previous chapter, MPTO parents regularly talked about and planned for a potential loss of Title I funds based on the demographic shifts. The focus of their planning efforts was largely on the financial and programmatic future of the school, however, rather than on the social and political dynamics that the changes had engendered within the school community.

In contrast, Jessica, a former leader of the Diversity Committee, had sought to put social issues related to the changing demographics on the MPTO's radar. Both she and her cochair organized a workshop and discussion about white privilege, for example, seeking to expand the Diversity Committee's scope beyond the annual dinner and to have dialogues about the changes students and families were experiencing at the school. As was discussed in the previous chapter, however, many of the issues that were talked about in Diversity Committee meetings—issues like privilege, students' racial experiences at the school, and tensions between families linked to race and class—were not focused on or addressed in regular MPTO meetings. Although many MPTO members attended the annual Diversity Dinner and several attended the workshop on white privilege, Diversity Committee events and meetings were separate from the parent-teacher organization. Thus, although both groups were seeking to "plan ahead," the issues that they sought to address were distinct.

Building Advocates for Public Education: Life after Morningside

Many Morningside parents went on to hold leadership positions in their children's public middle and high schools. Some were also active at the district and state level, helping to shape policy and maintain resources for public education in a context of shrinking state and local budgets. Several stayed connected to the Morningside community by attending a few school events or sharing their experiences with new parents in the MPTO when asked to do so.

When first interviewed, many of these long-timer parents spoke of their support for public education. Yet these same parents mentioned the challenges they faced in maintaining this commitment when deciding upon middle and high schools for their children, describing few high-quality schooling options in the district. Of those parents who had children graduating or children who were now Morningside alumni, one enrolled her child in a charter school, one was considering enrolling his child in that same charter school, and three had sent their children to both public and private middle and high schools. Morningside's feeder middle school was in Program Improvement status under No Child Left Behind because of its low test scores, and although there was new leadership at the school and neighborhood parents were working to bring about improvements, many long-timer Morningside parents I interviewed felt that their children would not flourish within this school. These parents were reluctantly considering private or charter schools on the basis of their children's own preferences.

These parents were not alone; a local newspaper article in 2010 reported that one in four students in Woodbury left the district's traditional public schools in favor of private, suburban, or charter schools.

When describing their decision-making process in choosing middle and high schools for their children, all the long-timer parents expressed a desire to support public schools. When asked if she had considered private schools when her child was assigned to the feeder middle school, Hannah mentioned her misgivings about the private middle schools in the area:

> I definitely considered it, and I visited private schools. . . . The thing that was just hard for me, besides the money issue, which was certainly an issue, but the overwhelming feeling I got from parents in the private middle schools that I visited was they could not imagine their children in public middle school. It was just so scary to them, and I just could not imagine being in a community of parents that felt that way. I had been really active at Morningside, and I just felt like they were too—I mean, I guess "elitist" would be the word because the sense of—they hadn't visited public schools. They just couldn't think about public school, and yeah, at that point I felt like I was still pretty committed to public.

For Hannah, who had been an MPTO leader at Morningside, the community of parents at these schools was a big factor in her decision not to enroll her child. Hannah's oldest child ultimately went to her local public middle school, and Hannah got involved in the school's parent leadership team meetings. When I interviewed her, however, she said that she and her husband were considering a private high school for their daughter. Although her older child had gone to a public high school in the area, Hannah lamented that her younger child did not feel academically challenged at her middle school. Hannah said that her daughter had asked her if she could go to a private high school so that she could "be where there's more of a sense of a community of learners."

Those parents such as Hannah who ultimately decided to send one or more of their children to a private school discussed how difficult this decision had been but said they made it on the basis of the specific academic needs of their children. These parents had explored their public school options first; they decided to enroll their children in private schools when they did not get their top choices of district public schools. Several long-timer parents made different choices for each child, however, enrolling one in private and one in public, or choosing a private middle school and then a public high school for the same child.

As the examples above indicate, many long-timer parents who had been active during their children's years at Morningside continued to support public education at the school, district, and, in some cases, state level. Their commitment to a public education for their children was more difficult to maintain for middle and high school; parents expressed concern about the academic challenge and preparation their children would receive in the local public schools. In the original study, when parents described their decision to enroll their children at Morningside, most of the long-timer parents had expressed the sentiment that their children would "do well anywhere" and that the social education at a school like Morningside was more important to them than test scores. In the follow-up interviews, however, it was clear that the level of academics and the specific needs and interests of students played a much larger role in parents' school choices than when their children were in elementary school. Most parents ultimately considered charter and private schools because of what they perceived as a limited number of viable public options in the district.

Conclusion: (Re)Defining "Diversity" in the Context of Urban School Change

Many of the challenges associated with the demographic and material shifts at Morningside illustrate the tensions associated with diversity and urban change. Most parents and teachers at Morningside wanted the school to remain "diverse," yet this meant different things to different people and was used to signify a range of social groups at the school. Although the Kindergarten Outreach Committee and members of the Diversity Committee had begun to target low-income families in activities for prospective parents, their use of the word "diversity" made it difficult to ascertain the priorities and values underlying their actions. As Berrey (2005, citing Goode 2001) argues, "diversity" is now a popular and unthreatening word in everyday discourse, especially for white middle-class people. It may be a vehicle through which activists can address social problems or a tool used by elites to obscure inequalities. Berrey (2005, 164) posits that diversity can become "an elusive, moving quota," and therefore, a focus on rights is more politically strategic for marginalized groups. Discussions of rights and justice necessitate a focus on power, privilege, and (dis)advantage in school contexts, whereas more general diversity discourses can obfuscate power relations and inequalities within school settings. For parents seeking to ensure that Morningside remains an accessible and viable option for low-income and working-class families, explicit discussions about entitlement and rights may be in order. Who has the right, for example, to attend "good" schools like Morningside? Are neighborhood children entitled to a spot in the school and, if so, with what consequences? In the absence of a clearer discourse and strategic plan, MPTO parents' efforts to promote Morningside's image as a "diverse" public school may simply attract more white middle- and upper-middle-class parents in the district who want their children exposed to children of other races and class backgrounds, rather than address school inequalities and the rights of low-income parents of color who are seeking high-quality school options for their children.

My research findings suggest tensions among parents related to issues of entitlement, responsibility, and rights. Middle-class newcomer parents wanted Morningside to continue to be a "diverse" public school, but there was no clarity about the definition of "diversity" or the ideal demographics of the student population. Nor was there clarity or agreement related to who was responsible for ensuring that the student body remained diverse. Some parents, working through the Diversity Committee and MPTO, targeted prospective low-income families of color in their outreach efforts. Yet for some of these parents the idea of instituting specific policies to ensure socioeconomic diversity did not seem politically viable, as it potentially conflicted with parents' desires to send their children to their neighborhood school. I found that there were even parents outside the school's enrollment zone who stated that neighborhood parents should have priority in assignment. When I asked James Hall, an African American parent residing in a predominantly black and Latino working-class neighborhood, what he thought of the preference in enrollment given to neighborhood families, he stated:

> I see nothing wrong with it. I have no problem. I mean, every neighborhood kid has—should have—the opportunity to go to their neighborhood school if they choose to. I think anything . . . outside of that would have to be considered secondary. Siblings, out of district. But I think the options should be there for those neighborhood kids. I'm not against that at all.

James went on to acknowledge that the priority given to neighborhood families didn't really affect him because he had been able to get his child into the school three years ago. James expressed views similar to those he voiced in the original study (see chapter 4) when he stated that he valued Morningside's diversity because of the exposure it gave his child to different types of families and that he also appreciated the educational opportunities and resources that middle- and upper-middle-class parents helped bring to the school (e.g., the salad bar, the music program). James's neighborhood school and most of the public elementary schools in the area where he lived did not have these same resources and educational op-portunities. Reflecting other research showing parents' desire for diversity and yet preference for neighborhood schooling and "choice," James and other parents interviewed wanted "diverse schools" for their children with-out district intervention.[8]

Based on the composition of Morningside's neighborhood and the priority given to families in the enrollment zone, the school is no longer accessible to most students who live in neighborhoods like James's that lack the resources and opportunities that Morningside offers its students. Although some low-income and working-class families may seek out the school as a result of the outreach efforts of Morningside parents, the fact remains that, because of limited space, parents who live outside the pre-dominantly middle- and upper-middle-class neighborhood and do not al-ready have children at the school currently have little chance of getting a spot for their children.

Many of Morningside's long-timer white families were forced to interact and work with low-income and working-class families of color in shared neighborhood and classroom contexts; now, most newcomer parents can interact almost solely with parents of similar class backgrounds because of the large number of middle-class parents at the school. Several white parent leaders with stated commitments to socioeconomic diversity encountered difficulties in reaching out to low-income families because of their limited organizing and outreach experience and because of their discomfort in do-ing so. Thus, it seems unlikely that a primary reliance on the initiative and outreach efforts of MPTO parents will be an effective and sustainable strat-egy for ensuring that the school is accessible to low-income students.

As argued in the report I gave to teachers and parents, Morningside's future is undecided; much can change in a matter of years in the realm of public education. As Mr. Foster stated in his description of the changes at Morningside: "I think everybody thinks of schools—like, whoever they are—their identity is static. I think it's really a living, breathing thing. And all of it's fragile. I think it can change radically." As illustrated in this chap-ter, public schools like Morningside are in a state of flux because of broader social, political, and economic shifts. Budget cuts, a shift in parent or school leadership, and neighborhood demographic shifts can all effect school change. A change in Morningside's administrative leadership, for example, could result in significant declines in enrollment as families with other options pull out their children. At the same time, the current economic recession may prompt greater numbers of college-educated, middle-class parents to consider public schools like Morningside. Rather than investing thousands of dollars in private schooling, many parents at Morningside, for example, chose instead to invest in their local public school.

To ensure that schools like Morningside remain accessible to low-income students—in effect to ensure equitable development—resources and policies devoted to making this happen are needed. In their absence, schools like Morningside that are affected by demographic change are likely to be "laissez-faire" diverse communities (Nyden, Maly, and Lukehart 1997), or "diverse by default," with few policies or resources devoted to promoting and sustaining this diversity over time (Berrey 2005). Becoming a "self-consciously diverse" community (Nyden, Maly, and Lukehart 1997) would mean dedicating resources and advocating for school and district policies to ensure that low-income families benefit from the educational opportunities Morningside provides its students. This requires difficult conversations—forcing parents, educators, and district personnel to move beyond the discourse of diversity and talk about issues of entitlement, privilege, rights, and responsibility in public schooling.

Although patterns of public school enrollment are subject to factors such as birthrates, neighborhood demographics, and the "buzz" about schools passed along via parental social networks, education policy *can* play a major role in guiding the direction of urban school change. School demographic change such as that occurring at Morningside is not inevitable, nor is it part of a "natural" progression. Rather, it is linked to policies and practices occurring at multiple levels.

SEVEN

Maintaining a "Commitment to Everyone": Toward a Vision of Equitable Development in Urban Public Schooling

Even actions which are not driven by struggle for advantage over others, indeed, even those that have egalitarian motives, are likely to be twisted by the field of class forces in ways which reproduce class hierarchy.

—Sayer 2005, 169

In this book, I have tried to show the limitations of relying upon parents— and middle-class parents in particular—to drive or sustain high-quality, "diverse," and integrated urban public schools. I have shown that the choices and engagement of even the most well-meaning parents can con- tribute to inequality in public schooling because of their positions within broader systems of advantage and disadvantage. I hope to have provided a more nuanced account of middle-class parental engagement in public edu- cation than that reflected in the media or popular discourse, showing that these parents are neither saviors nor villains but are social actors within a broader educational terrain marked by public disinvestment, segregation, limited choices, and neoliberal restructuring. I have illustrated the need for the state, and not simply parents, to ensure that changes to urban public schools are equitable and reflect a "commitment to everyone" rather than further advantaging the middle and upper-middle class. The case of Morn- ingside demonstrates that parents—whose primary interest is the educa- tional success of their own children—cannot be the main drivers of school improvement and integration. Nor should we expect them to be.

In this concluding chapter, I suggest new ways to conceptualize and re- search contemporary school transformation processes, focusing in particu- lar on middle-class investments in urban schooling. I highlight the need for critical and nuanced studies of urban school change, as well as evaluations of "progress" and "reform" in urban education that extend beyond such commonly used markers as rising test scores and greater material resources. I also offer several recommendations for policy makers, district and school staff, and parents based upon the findings of this study.

A Recap: The Limits of the Middle Class as Drivers of Urban School Change

At Morningside, middle- and upper-middle-class parents brought resources to the school and volunteered in ways that served not only their own children but also the broader school community. Implementing a salad bar and fresh-produce stand, hiring a school mental-health counselor, helping to fund the Spanish teacher and librarian through their fund-raising and financial contributions, and advocating on behalf of the school in relations with the school district benefited the entire Morningside student body. Parents' marketing and outreach efforts helped not only to increase the support of neighborhood families but also to attract other families from across the city. For a school that had once faced the threat of closure due to low enrollment, the boost in student enrollment and neighborhood support brought Morningside a degree of stability.

Yet the case of Morningside highlights the limits of positioning middle-class parents—even those committed to diversity, integration, and public education—as major drivers of urban public school reform. Most middle-class parents desired a racially and socioeconomically diverse school for their children, favorably comparing Morningside's demographics and culture to those of the more affluent and predominantly white schools in the district. Indeed, it was common to hear stories of parents who had chosen Morningside over public and private schools in the area with higher test scores and more material resources. As discussed in chapter 3, however, the enrollment and investments of middle-class parents ultimately shifted the demographics of the student and family population. By the end of the decade, as described in chapter 6, the school was a highly sought-out option for parents in the district and was increasingly likened to the more affluent public and private schools in the area. Although the school in 2009/10 still had just over 40 percent of students qualifying for free or reduced-price lunch—due in large part to the district's and school's efforts to accommodate siblings of older children in the school—the grade-level demographic trends outlined suggest that this mix is unlikely to be sustained in the absence of explicit programs and policies. Indeed, the most recent numbers (the 2012/13 school year) indicate that the percentage of students qualifying for the free/reduced-price lunch program has dropped well below

40 percent, largely due to shifts in the socioeconomic status of students in the lower grades. The racial shifts have also continued, with white students now making up just over half of the student population at the school (disproportionately much higher than the 11 percent of white students in the district as a whole).[1]

In addition, as explored in chapters 4 and 5, the demographic, sociocultural, and material changes occurring at Morningside created new tensions within the school community. Many of the resources that had attracted middle-class parents—the school sports program, the additional staff support in classrooms, the enrichment programs—were in danger of being cut because of a decline in low-income students and the impending loss of Title I funds. As a result, the school was more dependent on parental fundraising and donations to sustain these programs and resources. Norms for engagement were redefined, with a greater MPTO emphasis on fund-raising and more volunteer positions requiring specialized skills. Although MPTO leaders saw themselves as working on behalf of all students, the increased professionalism of the organization and the visibility given to MPTO parents exacerbated race and class tensions and status positions among adults in the school community. Morningside's historic status as a small school was changing as well; class sizes swelled in the lower grades and portable classrooms were added to accommodate the growing student enrollment.

The case of Morningside illustrates the limitations and fragility of free-market diversity, or a voluntary integration driven in large part by middle-class parent choices and engagement. By supporting and investing in an underresourced and increasingly "diverse" city public school for their children, middle-class parents may threaten the very demographic mix and school organizational features that many of them desire—often despite their best intentions. One could argue that Morningside represents a "best-case" scenario for racial and economic integration, as many long-timers and newcomers across the race and class spectrum spoke of racial and socioeconomic diversity as an asset and something to be preserved. The school had a history of parent activism, with a core group of parent leaders who had worked to bring in resources that would benefit the entire school community. Yet, given the absence of specific school and district policies to ensure that Morningside remained accessible to low-income and working-class students of color, the population served by the school dramatically shifted. Fewer low-income students were ultimately able to benefit from the resources and opportunities flowing into the school. Although aspects of the "old" Morningside were still present, elements of the school's culture and organizational context had changed.

I have argued that a reliance on middle-class parental engagement unfairly positions parents, rather than government, as the primary drivers of school improvement. The onus is placed largely on parents and teachers, instead of on state and federal education policy makers, to provide the educational opportunities and material resources necessary to create and sustain high-quality urban public schools. In the context of rising economic inequality, fewer parents may be able to devote their time to fundraise or to contribute their own money to support things like art, sports, foreign-language, and music programs in the public schools. Indeed, these programs—once core elements of the school day—are now largely supplemental programs in a growing number of districts, available only to those with private resources (see, e.g., Armario 2012; Bryant 2011; England-Nelson 2013; Koskey 2011). This has huge equity implications, as access to a well-rounded education—one that includes content and experiences beyond those reflected on state standardized tests—is increasingly tied to students' socioeconomic background and the level of parental fund-raising. Although resource disparities linked to race and class are not new in public education, recent budget cuts have exacerbated historic inequities in funding within and across districts.

In Pursuit of Equitable Development in Urban Education

When sharing my research in academic and community settings, I am commonly asked, "What can be done?" Like the parents involved in my follow-up research at Morningside, many middle- and upper-middle-class parents with whom I speak are concerned about the role that they or others like them play in processes of educational inequality, but they are unsure how to address it. Questions of responsibility for change are central to these discussions. Every parent wants the best for his or her children. So whose responsibility is it to ensure that changes in the local schools are equitable? What is and should be the role of parents? How can educational policies and contextual factors support or constrain parental efforts to foster more equitable outcomes in urban schooling? Now, as a stepparent of a child in a public elementary school, I find myself grappling with these questions on both a personal and an academic level.

The concept of equitable development provides a useful lens through which to analyze material and demographic shifts in city public schools. PolicyLink, a national institute devoted to advancing economic and social equity, states:

Equitable development is an approach to creating healthy, vibrant, communities of opportunity. Equitable outcomes come about when smart, intentional strategies are put in place to ensure that low-income communities and communities of color participate in and benefit from decisions that shape their neighborhoods and regions.[2]

In contrast to gentrification through direct or "exclusionary displacement" (Marcuse 1986), where demographic and material changes render a community inaccessible to low-income and working-class individuals, equitable developments in public schooling would allow for both material improvements *and* the social, political, and numerical inclusion of low-income and working-class families in a particular school context. In historically underresourced city public schools that receive an infusion of resources due to individual parental contributions, grants, or government funding, equitable developments would mean that any demographic and material changes associated with these increased resources would not result in the exclusion of current (or prospective) low-income and working-class families. Although the exact socioeconomic mix of students would need to be determined on the basis of the particular historical, geographic, and demographic context of the school and its broader region, the point here is that the school and the increased resources would be accessible not just to more affluent newcomer families but to low-income and working-class families as well (I explore this further below in a section on student assignment).

Pursuing equitable developments would also mean careful attention to and a diligent monitoring of issues of power, privilege, and inequality in processes of school change. It would mean identifying who is least served by particular reform initiatives and engaging in organizing and leadership development to ensure that the perspectives and needs of these families are represented in school transformation efforts. Discussions of demographic and material shifts in schools would focus not simply upon diversity or desegregation but on opportunities for social inclusion and participation. As Carter (2009, 295) states in making a distinction between desegregation and integration in public schooling: "we cannot fully rectify the systematic racial and ethnic inequalities affronting our nation and our schools without paying attention to both equity in resources and heightened consciousness and care for one another across myriad social lines." Equitable development would thus entail democratic deliberation over the future of public school communities, with the recognition that what constitutes "progress" is socially constructed and politically contested. Implementing and sustaining equitable developments in urban schooling would require changes in policy and practice at multiple levels—in and across schools and on the level of districts, states, and the federal government.

I know there are no "quick fixes" or easy solutions to the challenges I have outlined in this book. The issues are not unique to Morningside Elementary; parents, administrators, and educators in cities across the nation are faced with similar challenges (Cucchiara 2013b; Grim 2006; Jan 2006; Smith 2009; Stillman 2012). Actions taken in the following areas, however, may prove fruitful in efforts to both create and sustain racially and socioeconomically diverse, high-quality, *and* equitable school communities.

Understanding School Social and Historical Contexts and Processes of Change

As discussed in chapter 4, parents are commonly framed in our current era of accountability as "consumers" in an educational marketplace characterized by competition and "choice" (Apple 2006; Schneider, Teske, and Marschall 2002). Those schools with the highest test scores and greatest consumer demand are the ones commonly recognized as successful in the current system. Yet the case of Morningside demonstrates the importance of paying attention to the *processes* through which school change is occurring, as well as the social, political, and historical *contexts* in which schools are situated. A sole focus on common markers of progress in public education such as rising test scores and increased material resources may obscure other, more negative consequences of school change such as increased exclusion linked to class, race, and residence. A rise in test scores in demographically shifting schools, for example, may simply be attributable to a change in student population rather than an improvement in instruction or school quality.

Evaluations of progress must account for processes of inclusion or exclusion in school change efforts, as well as alternative visions of "good schools" that are not represented in dominant educational-reform discourses. To do so would require understanding the history and social contexts of school communities, as well as the lived experiences and perspectives of parents, teachers, and students within these changing settings. Whereas the perspectives and school choices of highly educated, white professionals in urban districts have received more scholarly and media attention in recent years, few studies have examined how school change is experienced by "long-timers" within these settings.[3] Qualitative studies of school change—studies that include the stories and everyday experiences of parents and teachers in these settings—are thus needed to uncover potential opportunities for and obstacles to achieving full integration.

Use of Transparent Language and Disaggregated Data

Recent demographic, economic, and political shifts in metropolitan regions have prompted the need for new ways of conceptualizing and researching urban school change. As discussed in chapter 2, "urban" is commonly used to signify low-income populations of color, underresourced public institutions, and, in education, "underperforming" schools. Yet my own research and that of others has identified constituencies and processes of change in urban institutions that are not easily explained by these dominant framings. Do increasingly affluent city schools like Morningside still qualify as "urban" schools, and, if so, by what measures and with what consequences?

The urban context still matters for schools like Morningside that are situated in large urban school districts because the cities within which they are embedded are marked by historical legacies of racial and economic inequality that continue to shape present-day economic, political, and social contexts. Although Morningside has been increasingly likened to the private schools in the area, it cannot fully shed its connection to "urban" education given that it's irrevocably tied to and influenced by the issues facing the district as a whole. However, there is a need for a precise and contextually based investigation of demographic, social, and material changes in urban spaces and institutions. Scholars, policy makers, and educators need to substitute more precise and transparent language for the terms commonly used in urban discourses; in other words, general terms such as "urban" need to be replaced by more specific references to the racial, socioeconomic, and geographic demographics of the institutions and populations studied.

There is a need for a more detailed tracking of student demographics—at the level of individuals and grades rather than simply by school. Most district and school profiles of student demographics, as well as those found on most websites for parents (e.g., the popular greatschools.net), list the racial and socioeconomic composition of a school's aggregate student population rather than statistics by grade. As the case of Morningside highlights, however, the demographics of students in the upper grades can significantly differ from those in the lower grades. A Latino parent seeking a school in which his or her child will not be "the only one" of his or her race, for example, may be surprised to find that the child's class or grade does not reflect the demographics of the aggregate student population. Similarly, a funding source specifically designed to support the educational experiences of low-income students may grant money to a school on the basis of the aggregate number of students qualifying for free or reduced-price lunches, but the money or resources from this grant (if distributed evenly across grade levels) may ultimately benefit a large number of middle-class students if there is an uneven distribution of low-income students across the grades. In 2006/7 fewer kindergartners than fifth graders qualified for the free/reduced-price lunch program; yet all students at Morningside benefited from the in-school sports program designed to support schools with low-income student populations in the district. One might argue that all students should have access to resources such as this and that by distributing them evenly across students and grades, there is no stigma attached to their use. My point here is simply that a more precise and disaggregated tracking and reporting of student demographics would provide important information to guide the decision making of those individuals and organizations wanting to invest in reforms that benefit low-income students and that address inequalities in public education. Having the information allows for challenging, but necessary, discussions about the distribution of resources within and across district schools.

Not only would tracking and public reporting of student socioeconomic and racial demographics by grade provide valuable information to parents, funders, and the broader community, but it would also illuminate emerging demographic trends for the district. In addition to tracking and analyzing neighborhood birthrates in an effort to predict future enrollment numbers, the district should also track subtle changes in the racial and socioeconomic demographics of neighborhoods and their local schools. This would require the collaboration of city and school district demographers, who would share data to identify how neighborhood demographic change may affect the demographics of local schools and vice versa. In doing so, both the district and school sites would be better positioned to proactively address changes.[4]

In addition to guiding education policy and practice, the tracking and public reporting of disaggregated data would allow for a more precise discourse of urban change. In cities like Philadelphia and Chicago that have been affected by neighborhood gentrification, there are often wide variations in the socioeconomic backgrounds of residents not just by neighborhood but by street or even house. As illustrated in this book, school populations may not mirror that of neighborhoods because of nonneighborhood-based enrollment policies or the disinvestment of neighborhood families in their local schools. Despite these nuances, discourses of the "urban" are still commonly used in reference not simply to geographic location but to neighborhoods and schools with large numbers of students of color and low-income students. In fact, the urban discourse has extended beyond city limits and is now used by some in reference to inner-ring suburban schools as well (DeWitt 2012). Shifting dominant conceptualizations and discourses in the public imagination is no easy task; however, having more precise data can help counter the conflation of race and class and the use of euphemisms that often occur in discussions of "urban" schools and families. The use of specific labels (e.g., "low-income African American students" or "low-income Southeast Asian students" versus "urban students") would lead to greater transparency in decision-making processes, particularly when allocating resources. This transparency is also needed in scholarly and media accounts of the school choices and experiences of middle-class parents in urban districts, as "middle and upper-middle class" are often conflated with "white" in descriptions of middle-class parents in urban public schools.

Changes in Student Assignment

Within the context of ongoing patterns of residential segregation in most cities, policies that support neighborhood schooling often exacerbate broader inequalities linked to race, class, and residence. Given this, there is a need for a student assignment policy that disrupts current patterns of enrollment in the district. As described in chapters 2 and 6, most elementary schools in the western part of the district are challenged to accommodate the large number of neighborhood families who seek to enroll their children. In these schools there are few or no spots open for students who reside outside the predominantly middle- and upper-middle-class neighborhoods and who do not have siblings already enrolled in the school. During my follow-up research, I found that Morningside was confronted with similar issues because of changes in both the neighborhood and the school. Those parents who had insider, or "hot," knowledge (Ball and Vincent 1998) about enrollment strategies and particular schools (due in large part to their social networks) were better positioned to succeed in enrolling their children in one of the more academically successful public schools in the district.

Since the time of my original research, the new district leadership has developed an extensive plan to improve the quality of education offered in all Woodbury schools, and it is worth noting that there are already several academically successful elementary schools in the district that serve predominantly low-income families. However, with few exceptions, great differences exist between the educational resources and opportunities available at those schools in the west serving predominantly middle-and upper-middle-class students and those in the eastern part of the district serving predominantly low-income and working-class students of color. The district student assignment plan now gives first preference to siblings in student assignment, which ensures that some students who reside outside the school's enrollment zone can enroll. The number of neighborhood students at these highly sought-out schools will continue to grow, however, as nonneighborhood children and their siblings graduate.

To counter the disparities linked to race, class, and residence, the district should adopt a "controlled-choice" student assignment policy. Ideally, such a policy would take *both* race and class into consideration, as economic integration programs alone do not ensure racial desegregation in schools (Reardon and Rhodes 2011). However, an assignment policy that takes into account a student's socioeconomic status rather than race is more likely to be viable in the present political and legal climate. Such a policy would ensure that a percentage of spots (e.g., 20–40 percent) at highly sought-out schools are open for incoming kindergartners who are eligible for the free/reduced-price lunch program.[5] A controlled-choice plan would help to accommodate many neighborhood families who wish to enroll their children in their local school while also facilitating a more balanced distribution of educational resources and opportunities across district schools.

Adoption of these plans is often met with resistance from those parents and community members who seek to preserve a system of neighborhood schooling or unrestricted choice, yet there are numerous examples of communities across the United States that have fought to implement and sustain these plans. At the time of this writing, over eighty districts have implemented economic integration plans as a way to promote and ensure a more equitable distribution of educational resources. There is also evidence that white middle- and upper-middle-class parents—those most likely to benefit from market-based school choice policies—want diverse and more equitable educational settings for their children. In their study of the school choices of white, high–socioeconomic status parents in New York City, for example, Roda and Wells (2013) found that these parents were troubled by the segregation within and across public schools in the city and wanted more diverse learning environments for their children. Yet most ended up choosing predominantly white schools, given the lack of options for high-quality, racially diverse district schools. The research on the school choices of white middle- and upper-middle-class parents speaks to the need for district policies to create racially and socioeconomically balanced schools, policies that would meet parents' demand for diverse schools while ensuring that schools like Morningside maintain their racial and socioeconomic mix over time.

The specific elements of controlled-choice plans often vary according to the unique demographics and contexts of districts, but in cities like Woodbury—cities that are in aggregate racially and socioeconomically mixed—the integrative potential of these plans is great. In cities with less socioeconomic diversity, metropolitan solutions that involve the outlying suburbs may be necessary. Although parents' primary motivations for enrolling their children in "diverse" schools may not always overlap (see, e.g., chapter 4), their desire for a diverse public school for their children is common and can be built upon through controlled choice. Policies to promote and ensure integrated schooling are never perfect and are often contested, but they are, nevertheless, necessary, given broader patterns of residential segregation and resource disparities in most cities and districts.

Targeted Outreach and Partnerships

Parent leaders and school staff can engage in targeted and sustained outreach to prospective low-income and working-class families in the neighborhood or across the district. Although district assignment policies play a dominant role in school demographics, my interviews, observations, and surveys of parents confirm previous studies demonstrating the strong influence that parents' social networks and social class have on school choice and information about schools (Holme 2002; Schneider, Teske, and Marschall 2002). Schools like Morningside can develop partnerships with child care centers and organizations serving predominantly low-income families, sharing information and resources. Although several parents at Morningside had sent flyers to local child care centers and met with their staff, more effort could be made to create long-lasting and mutually beneficial partnerships between the school and organizations serving low-income children and their families. School events and fund-raisers, for example, could be jointly sponsored by not just neighborhood parent groups and schools but also a local Head Start program and a nonprofit organization for youth. Proceeds from these events could be shared across the organizations. The social and familial connections possessed by many long-timer parents, teachers, and support staff may prove fruitful in these relationship-building efforts. Targeted outreach to low-income and working-class families, *combined* with changes in student assignment policies, can play an important role in sustaining socioeconomic diversity in schools impacted by demographic shifts.

Supporting Families through City-School
Collaboration and Resource Allocation

Changes in district policy and parent outreach are not enough, however, because larger structural issues impede Woodbury Unified's ability to provide high-quality schooling options for all students. Changes in the district's student assignment policy can help mitigate inequalities linked to residential segregation; but there is a need for public policies and partnerships that provide low-income and working-class families with greater access to community resources and opportunities. Educational and civic leaders should work hand in hand in this effort to develop more collaborative and coordinated policies and practices that promote racial and socioeconomic diversity, high-quality schools, safe and affordable housing, and healthy neighborhoods. Some of these efforts are already under way in the city of Woodbury, as the district has worked to develop partnerships with community organizations and city agencies. There are also a number of promising examples of city-school collaboration in areas across the country, with city planners, civic leaders, and nonprofit organization staff working with educational leaders to address many of the issues facing metropolitan regions (see, e.g., McKoy, Vincent, and Bierbaum 2011).

In addition to city-school collaboration, efforts to counter racial and economic disparities in public education require financial resources. Districts and schools in California have faced dramatic cuts to public education since 2008, resulting in teacher and staff layoffs and the elimination or massive reduction of academic and extracurricular programs in many schools. The financial crisis of 2007 and 2008 exacerbated an already-inadequate system of funding, and the onus is increasingly on teachers and parents to provide resources for public schools. To ensure that all children have access to a high-quality education, the state and the federal government need to make public education a priority in their resource allocation.[6]

Districts can also implement policies that ensure a more even distribution of funds raised by parent-teacher and school-based nonprofit organizations. A cap can be placed on the private fund-raising dollars each school can receive, for example, with a district-wide fund used to ensure that less-affluent schools that may not have parents with the social, cultural, and economic capital to raise large sums of money have access to resources. Rather than leaving it up to individual school communities to fund instructional aides and art teachers, a district-wide foundation could be responsible for managing instructional funds to ensure that students' access to programs such as art and music does not solely depend on the size of their school's parent-teacher organization or educational foundation budget. The Portland Public School District, for example, has a policy in which one-third of funds (beyond $10,000) raised through local school foundations must be given to a citywide foundation, which in turn makes allocation decisions based on the goal of closing achievement and opportunity gaps in the district.[7] Although low-income schools in all districts receive Title I funding, these funds are earmarked for specific programs and are often insufficient to close the opportunity gaps between rich and poor schools in districts.

Parent and Community Organizing for Educational Transformation

Bringing about changes in district, state, and federal policy requires advocacy and organizing across a diverse group of constituents. Information campaigns and organizing are often needed to ensure that broad-scale, redistributive policies such as those outlined above are enacted and sustained, since those schools and groups currently benefiting from disparities in and between district schools may resist the proposed changes. As other research has shown, it is common for parents with the social, cultural, and economic capital to do so to "game the system" in ways that advantage their own children, often at the expense of others (Brantlinger 2003; McGrath and Kuriloff 1999). The current culture of competition and emphasis on individual achievement in education supports these efforts to "get ahead" despite the social, emotional, and political costs to students (Demerath 2009; Pope 2003). The organizing and activism of parents, teachers, and other public education supporters are thus necessary to facilitate changes in policy and practice that ensure educational equity.

Moving beyond their own children's school, parents can organize across school and district lines to advocate for changes that would improve the quality of public education for all children.[8] Public school parents in Woodbury, for example, created a listserv to share information and encourage action among parents and public school supporters in the city. Several Morningside parents were active at the district, city, and state level, pushing elected officials to provide greater support and funding for public education. As with most organizing efforts, the challenge lies in bringing individuals together across lines of race, class, and residence in collective action to achieve shared goals. There is a need to ensure that parental organizing efforts are led by a racially, ethnically, and socioeconomically diverse membership that reflects and is responsive to the needs of all parents—particularly low-income and working-class parents, who are often least served by educational-reform efforts. Relationship building and outreach (within and across schools) are key to the organizing and mobilization efforts of parents.

Building Relationships Across and Within

Within racially and socioeconomically diverse school communities, parent social networks and organizations tend to be segregated by race and class. As Cashin (2004, 73) writes in her discussion of the challenges faced by integrated communities: "It takes care and daily effort to make an institution truly inclusive and truly integrated. Recognizing that such work and sensitivity is required may be half the battle in striving toward successful diversity." Thus, in addition to building coalitions of parents across school and district lines, efforts to promote greater inclusiveness and equity within school communities are needed. Constant and vigilant efforts to build relationships across the fault lines of race and class are key. As demonstrated in my research, parents were more likely to participate in meetings, committees, and events when they were personally invited or had a relationship with the person who was asking. To their credit, several parent and school leaders at Morningside recognized this need for relationship building and sought to counter historic patterns of segregation in engagement and organizational work at the school. Of the few low-income and working-class parents of color who were in leadership roles at the school, almost all stated that an MPTO parent had gotten to know them and personally encouraged them to get involved in a specific task or activity that drew from their strengths and matched their interests. However, many middle-class parents in the lower grades socialized with other middle-class families and had few meaningful or sustained interactions with low-income families. Building these relationships—and often confronting and addressing hard issues related to race and class—takes time, commitment, and intentionality.

Diversifying the membership of parent-teacher organizations and the student body is only one step in promoting greater equity and inclusion. Structures that create regular opportunities to reflect on, discuss, and address hard issues related to race and class in school communities need to be established. This is perhaps even more salient in schools like Morningside that are experiencing demographic shifts in their student and family populations. Morningside did have a Diversity Committee, but during the period of research, the committee was disconnected from the larger MPTO and had little influence on issues of governance and resource allocation. Many of the issues discussed in Diversity Committee meetings—racially segregated social groupings, the developing racial identities of students, the politics of neighborhood schooling—were never focused on or addressed in the MPTO, the major decision-making body of the school. Parents may want to keep committees such as these as separate and "safe spaces" to discuss issues of inequality, with the purpose and structure of these committees or groups purposefully distinct from those of parent-teacher organizations. If these groups are given little advisory or decision-making power, however, the issues and needs discussed in their meetings and events are unlikely to translate into concrete changes in policy or practice in schools.

To ensure that the issues and perspectives of parents of color and low-income and working-class parents are represented in school improvement initiatives, parents of similar racial, socioeconomic, ethnic, or cultural backgrounds could come together around common issues of concern in organizations that are not tied to one school or school district. Madres Unidas in Oakland, California (Dyrness 2011), and Parent U-Turn in the Los Angeles metropolitan area (Oakes and Rogers 2006) are examples of groups in which parents, supported by university or community organization staff and resources, become informed and involved leaders in their local schools and the broader community. As organizations that are separate from traditional parent-teacher organizations, parent groups such as these illustrate the influential role that parents can play in school improvement efforts without having to fit traditional, school-based models of parental engagement.

Bringing about inclusive and equitable reform in urban education requires building relationships within and across school walls and expanding our notions of community. It requires a shift from individualistic notions of progress to a focus on the collective good and shared interests. In their book on community organizing as a catalyst for school reform, Warren and Mapp (2011, 234) argue that "strong forms of organizing all find an authentic means to engage communities around a sense of shared history, tradition, and narrative. Meanwhile, they work to reshape and expand those ties to create a broader understanding of shared fate and a new history through concerted action." Recent budget cuts and changes in the economy may prompt this understanding of a shared fate, as more and more families are asked to give and do more in an era of economic uncertainty. Economic and political changes in metropolitan regions may indeed serve as a catalyst for organizing across a broad range of constituencies in education, or they may simply exacerbate competition for resources across groups and individual schools. There is thus a need for changes in ideology and the public will as well as changes in policy—and community organizing can help to bring about both.

Concluding Remarks

My focus in this book is on middle-class parents and the ways in which their engagement and investments in urban public schooling both exacerbate and mitigate educational inequalities. Rather than blaming individual parents, I have sought to portray how their engagement is shaped by the broader political, economic, and social contexts in which they operate. All parents want the best education possible for their children, yet in a larger system marked by racial stratification and economic inequality, some parents have access to more resources than others in achieving this goal. Individual actions and choices do matter, and as outlined earlier, members of school communities like Morningside can take steps to mitigate the reproduction of inequality. However, it is my hope that in this book I have also demonstrated the need for structural, rather than simply individual, solutions.

Changes such as those occurring at Morningside present both opportunities and challenges regarding racial and socioeconomic diversity and equity. As greater numbers of middle- and upper-middle-class families invest in the "urban" through their housing and school choices, new opportunities arise for social mixing and material improvements in local public schools. This is particularly true at the elementary level, as primary and elementary schools tend to be smaller, systems of tracking and stratification are often not as pronounced, and parents tend to have more of a visible and regular presence than at other levels of K–12 education. As Lewis (2003, 190) writes, "Schools remain places of hope—they offer the possibility for new realities." Public schools, as shared institutions, have the potential to bring a wide array of constituencies together through a shared interest in the education of children and youth.

Given patterns of social reproduction and broader systems of inequality, however, ensuring that urban change is equitable requires the constant monitoring of demographic shifts, as well as organizing and policies to ensure that low-income individuals and families benefit. As the research findings suggest, creating and maintaining racially and socioeconomically diverse *and* equitable public institutions—fully integrated institutions—is no simple task. It is easy for even the most well-meaning attempts at school improvement to have unintended consequences, given a broader system of social inequality. As "urban" and "suburban" areas change in new and complex ways, educational and civic leaders, parents, and community members must pursue equitable development in public education by engaging in open, critical dialogues about both the processes and the products of change, working to ensure that *all* children and families have access to high-quality, well-resourced neighborhoods and schools.

Social Class Categories

The following categories of classification are context specific; that is, they are based in large part on the sample of study participants as well as the particular geographic region in which the study was conducted. Although scholars such as Oliver and Shapiro (1995) have pointed out that individuals can be low income or working class and own their own home, none of the study participants qualifying as low income or working class based on education or occupation were homeowners. With a median home value of close to $600,000 in 2006 in the city of Woodbury, homeownership was not a viable option for many families.

Upper-middle class: An individual, his or her partner, or both have a graduate or professional degree; are employed in a position that requires highly complex, educationally certified skills; own their home; make over $100,000 (above the area median income for 2006).

Middle class: An individual, his or her partner, or both have a college degree (BA, BS, or higher); are employed in a position that requires educationally certified skills; may or may not own their own home; child does not qualify for free/reduced-price lunch program based on income.[1]

Working class: An individual, his or her partner, or both have a high school diploma or some college; are employed in steady clerical or service work ("blue-collar"); do not own their own home; child does not qualify for free/reduced-price lunch program based on income and family size.[2]

Low income: An individual, his or her partner, or both have no high school diploma or have a high school diploma/GED; do not own their own home; child qualifies for free/reduced-price lunch program based on income and family size.

Methodological Approach

Entering graduate school after working as a fourth-grade teacher in a large urban district, I sought to better understand and address the relationship between race, class, space, and educational equity. I had originally thought that my research would focus on the experiences of students and families in a district with an explicit desegregation policy. This changed, however, when I read an article about the Glenbrook Parents' Group (GPG) and their efforts to increase neighborhood support for and enrollment in their local public school. Their efforts and engagement ran contrary to many of the studies of urban schooling that I had read and also to my experiences as an educator, as the predominantly white and middle-class group sought to support and invest in their predominantly African American neighborhood school. Instead of a district policy to promote and ensure racial and economic integration, it was largely *parents* who were working to bring about demographic change at the school. Through their efforts to increase the enrollment of neighborhood families they were key actors in processes of school change. I sought to better understand the goals, strategies, and actions of the GPG, as well as how their actions were received by the school community.

To gain a better familiarity with the school community and its members, I volunteered in a fifth-grade classroom from February until June 2006.[1] As I learned more about the history, culture, and changing demographics at the school, I began to refine my research interests and eventually designed a qualitative study that would enable me to answer the following overarching research question:

In what ways does middle-class parental engagement in urban public schooling mitigate and/or exacerbate existing inequalities linked to race, class, and residence in public education?

I also developed three specific subquestions for the study: What motivates middle- and upper-middle-class parents to consider the school? How do parents and teachers in the school community understand and respond to these parents' engagement? What are the equity implications of middle-class parents' efforts to support and invest in urban schooling?

Qualitative methods were particularly well suited to help me understand these questions, as the aim of qualitative research is to understand social phenomena and meaning-making in "real-life" settings. The emphasis is on how particular aspects of the social world are "experienced, interpreted, and understood in a particular context and at a particular point in time" (Bloomberg and Volpe 2008, 80). Rather than seeking to prove or disprove a preliminary hypothesis, I sought to understand the context, processes, and meaning-making associated with the enrollment and engagement of middle- and upper-middle-class families in a city public school.

To answer my specific research questions it was necessary for me to utilize a range of qualitative methods. My project thus included interviews, participant observation, surveys, and document analysis. In particular, my qualitative approach drew upon the in-depth engagement that comes from ethnographic methods. Ethnographic methods, in particular, involve the researcher's long-term participation in people's lives and within the particular contexts studied, watching, listening, and asking questions (Hammersley and Atkinson 1986, 1). Throughout the 2006/7 school year, I was a participant observer at Morningside Elementary and was very much immersed within the school community. I spent more than six hundred hours at Morningside—in classrooms, on the school yard, in school meetings, and at events—observing social interactions and talking to parents, teachers, and school staff. I saw and interacted with participants in multiple settings over an extended period of time, and many parents, teachers, and students (particularly those students in the kindergarten and fifth-grade classes) knew me by name. I was invited to parents' houses for interviews and parent meetings and developed close relationships with many teachers and staff. Although the period of intensive data collection ended in June 2007, I conducted follow-up interviews and observations up until the spring of 2008. I also returned to Woodbury in the spring of 2010 and conducted follow-up interviews with former participants (see chapter 6).

The research upon which this book is based was guided by an ethnographic case study methodology. Although case studies and ethnography are sometimes described as one and the same (Taft 1997), given common methods of data collection, the difference between the two methods lies in the intention of the study. As Cohen and Court (2003, abstract) argue,

"Ethnography is inward looking, aiming to uncover the tacit knowledge of culture participants. Case study is outward looking, aiming to delineate the nature of phenomena through detailed investigation of individual cases and their contexts." I employed ethnographic methods of data collection to understand the sociocultural context of the school and the meaning-making of participants, but my aim was to examine the politics of change at Morningside as a case study of middle-class parental engagement in urban public schooling. In the sections that follow, I discuss my methods of data collection, analysis of data and issues of validity, and the limitations of the study. I conclude with a description of my subjectivity as a researcher.

Data Collection Procedures for the Original Study

To gain an in-depth understanding of the phenomenon under study, the use of multiple methods of data collection is critical. As Bloomberg and Volpe (2008) argue, compiling data from multiple sources and using multiple methods add breadth and depth to the research and provide corroborative evidence. I thus used a variety of methods in my data collection; I explain each of these methods below.

Participant Observation and Field Notes

During the course of the study, I spent approximately 640 hours observing participants at the school and during school-related events. During the 2006/7 academic year, I worked as a volunteer teacher's aide in a kindergarten class for two hours each day and a tutor in a fifth-grade class twice each week for an hour. As a result of my volunteer commitments in the classroom and participant observation during out-of-classroom activities, meetings, and events, I spent between two and five hours a day at the school. Although my research did not include observations of students and classroom dynamics, these regular volunteer commitments provided me with the opportunity to have a regular presence at the school and to interact with many members of the school community. During recess and before and after school, I engaged in conversations with parents and teachers and observed social interactions.

In addition to these daily interactions and observations, I engaged in participant observation at school meetings, events, and activities in which parents took part. At meetings and during my observations of participants, I took extensive field notes in a small notebook I carried with me at all times. At meetings and in conversations with participants, field notes were directly written in the notebook. When taking notes I used quotation marks to designate which phrases or sections were direct quotes.

As a participant observer, there were times when it was not possible to directly record my notes. Talking with parents while we were working in the garden or with teachers while I was helping move classroom supplies, for example, did not afford me this opportunity. In these instances I would write up my notes from the conversation or observations as soon as I had a free moment, usually within the hour. At the end of each day or period of observation at the school, I would type up all handwritten field notes.

Interviews

Data sources include transcriptions from semistructured interviews with parents, teachers, and community members—seventy-one individuals in total (see table 3).[2] Although parents were the primary focus of my study and constitute the majority of my interviews, I interviewed seven teachers and eight staff members as well to learn more about the school's history and their experiences with and views toward the parent community. Seven community members were also interviewed to provide information about the school's neighborhood, to contextualize the issues at Morningside in relation to changes in the district and broader region, or both.

In selecting interviewees I used "purposeful sampling" (Maxwell 1996). I sought to capture the range of perspectives and experiences within the school community, as well as gain a better understanding of school and neighborhood history. Parents were selected based upon the number of years they had been connected to the school as well as their race, class, area of residence, and scope of involvement. Given my focus on middle- and upper-middle-class parents in school change processes, this social group is overrepresented in my sample (see table 4). Teachers and staff members were also selected in order to get a range of perspectives by number of years at the school, position, and grades of students with whom they primarily worked. I sought out community members who had a historical connection to the school (e.g., neighborhood residents and parents of Morningside alumni) or who could provide information about other neighborhood or citywide parent groups in Woodbury or the broader region. In many instances, individuals fell in more than one category of interviewees: three of the staff members interviewed and one teacher, for example, had children or other family members who had attended Morningside in the past. Similarly, five of the staff members and one teacher interviewed had lived or continue to reside in the neighborhoods included in Morningside's

Table 3 Characteristics of the full participant sample

Data sources	Number
Interviews	
Glenbrook Parents' Group (GPG) parents	10 (9 separate families)
Non-GPG Morningside parents	34 (30 separate families)
Non-GPG prospective parents	5
Teachers, staff, and administrators[a]	15
Community members and parents of alumni[b]	7
Total number of interviewees	**71**
Race/ethnicity of parent sample ($n = 49$)	
White	20
African American	19
Asian American	4
Hispanic/Latino	1
Mixed race	5
Class status of parent sample	
Upper-middle class	15
Middle class	22
Working class or low income	12
Race/ethnicity of teachers, staff, administrators	
White	8
African American	5
Hispanic/Latino	1
Mixed race	1

[a]Three of the staff members and one teacher interviewed had children or other family members who had attended Morningside in the past.
[b]Individuals included in this category are a local realtor, a school district administrator, a director of a regional parent organization, two parents of Morningside alumni, and two longtime neighborhood residents.

Table 4 Profile of parent interview participants

	Upper-middle class	Middle class	Working class or low income	Total
White	8	12	0	20
African American	3	8	8	19
Asian American	2	1	1	4
Mixed race	2	1	2	5
Hispanic/Latino	0	0	1	1
Total	15	22	12	49

enrollment zone and were able to provide their views of neighborhood history and change. In most cases participants were selected for interviews because I had met them and interacted with them at the school or community events; in some cases, I selected other participants on the basis of interviewee suggestions.

Interviews lasted between one and two hours, and all but one of the interviews were audio-recorded. Parent and community member interviews were held at a café close to the school or at individual houses depending upon the preference of the interviewee(s). Interviews with teachers were conducted at the school or in a local café, according to their preference. Both parents, when applicable, were invited to participate in the interview, but the majority of interviews were conducted with one parent (usually the mother).

In interviews, I asked parents about their experiences with the school enrollment process, their experiences as Morningside parents, and their views of the school's major strengths and challenges. I asked teachers about what brought them to Morningside and their experiences with and views toward the parent community. Interviews with community members (e.g., parents of Morningside alumni, neighborhood residents, a realtor) included questions related to the history of the school and neighborhood as well as their experiences in relation to the school. Instead of asking interviewees directly about their views of the demographic changes at the school in the beginning of the interview, I intentionally asked a more general question about the school's strengths and challenges. I did this in order to both gauge the extent to which they felt the changes were a key issue and allow them the opportunity to describe the changes in their own words. In most cases participants brought up the demographic changes occurring at Morningside without prompting; however, for those who did not, I asked a more direct question about their views of the changes at the end of the interview. Parents were asked to complete a demographic data sheet at the conclusion of the interview, in which they listed the race/ethnicity, occupation, total household income, and highest level of education of both themselves and their child's other parent.

Surveys

I designed and conducted two surveys during the course of my research to collect demographic data on parents and to explore their experiences with and perceptions of the school. My intention in conducting these surveys was to get responses from as wide a pool of respondents as possible, complementing my other data collection methods.

Prospective-Parent Survey

In January 2007 I conducted an anonymous survey of parents attending the school's Open House for families with an incoming kindergartner. I made an announcement at the beginning of the event in which I described myself as a graduate student researcher and expressed my interest in learning more about what they were looking for in a school for their child and what led them to consider Morningside in particular. Surveys were distributed to all attendees (one per family), and parents who chose to participate completed and handed in the survey at the end of the event ($n = 29$).[3] I also had parents who were interested in being interviewed about their experiences in the school enrollment process fill out a separate, detached sheet with their contact information.

Morningside Parent/Caregiver Survey

As a complement to the interviews and observations I had done throughout the year, I designed a parent/caregiver survey that would enable me to collect information about the engagement and experiences of parents from a larger sample of the school population. I both designed and distributed the survey at the end of the school year (May 2007) in order to build upon the information I obtained in interviews and observations, as well as to enable respondents to base their responses on their experiences over the course of the year. In addition to providing me with pertinent information for my study, the survey was also intended to solicit data that were of particular use to the school community. Thus, in designing my survey I asked several members of Morningside's Diversity Committee and the Morningside Parent-Teacher Organization (MPTO), as well as the principal, for suggestions on types of questions they would like to be included. I added such questions to the survey, and the survey was pilot-tested with several parents first before I sent it out to all parents/caregivers (survey questions are available from author upon request).

The anonymous parent/caregiver survey was sent home with each child. Both an English and a Spanish version of the survey were created, and Spanish-speaking families were given the choice of completing either version.[4] Both parents (when applicable) were given the option of either completing the survey and having their child return it in the envelope provided or dropping it off in a box in the front office of the school. Parents were also given the option of completing the survey online through www.surveymonkey.com, with a link to the website provided. Parents who completed the survey were instructed to fill out a raffle ticket for a prize drawing, and three winners were ultimately selected and received gift certificates to local businesses. A total of 111 parents completed the survey, representing 89 different families (39 percent participation rate of separate family units). Twenty-five of the surveys were completed online, and 86 paper copies were completed. I entered the parent responses that were on paper copies into the online survey, and results were compiled, tabulated, and disaggregated using the online survey tool (www.surveymonkey. com). I made the decision to use the online survey tool (rather than more specialized, statistical software) because of my primary interest in obtaining descriptive statistics (e.g., number of parents who selected Morningside as their first choice in the enrollment process).[5] In addition, the MPTO had used this tool to conduct a parent survey earlier in the year, and thus, many parents were already familiar with the format and process of survey completion.

Archival Data and Document Analysis

In addition to the methods outlined above, I utilized secondary sources to contextualize my study in relation to broader trends and issues as well as to provide descriptive and historical information related to parental engagement at Morningside.

Parent Listservs and Websites

During the course of the research I read and analyzed postings from several online listservs for parents and community members. Parents at Morningside, particularly those who were active in the MPTO, regularly posted information about school-related issues and events on the school's listserv. Several MPTO leaders posted information about the district enrollment process, providing reminders about deadlines and suggestions on how to navigate the district bureaucracy to parents with younger children and to prospective parents. Parents also posted information about community events such as rallies to protest cuts to public education.

The online listserv, subscribed to by parents, teachers, prospective parents, alumni, and community members, was also a major avenue of parent communication and dialogue about issues affecting the school community. Issues discussed ranged from an outbreak of lice at the school to the MPTO budget and fund-raising. On particularly contentious issues within the school community or in relation to the district, numerous e-mails were sent by parents about a particular topic. I read each posting on the listserv and took notes on themes and issues that related to my specific research questions. To protect the anonymity of participants, information obtained from the listservs was de-identified, and no direct quotes were used.

I also checked a publicly accessible regional parent website and a publicly accessible national parent website (www.greatschools.net) one or two times each month for postings related to Woodbury's student enrollment process and for postings about Morningside in particular. The postings on these websites enabled me to examine how Morningside was being represented in the broader community and provided me with a deeper understanding of the desires, frustrations, and experiences of prospective parents and, more generally, of elementary school parents in the district and surrounding region.

School and Community Documents

As a means of triangulation to enhance the validity of my conclusions and the accuracy of information recorded in my field notes (Maxwell 1996), I collected various documents during the duration of the research. These documents included school newsletters, MPTO agendas and handouts, and brochures and other documents created for prospective parents. I also collected handouts and agendas from neighborhood meetings and school board meetings, as well as the Glenbrook neighborhood newsletter.

Background and Demographic Data

During the course of the research I read and collected online newspaper articles and blogs about educational issues in Woodbury and the surrounding region. This helped me situate my study of Morningside in relation to broader district trends and issues. I also read and collected articles about demographic changes occurring in the city and broader region to better contextualize my study in relation to regional trends.

My Role

My own subjectivity was key in the research process: it shaped the questions I asked, the way I designed my study, my relationships with participants, and my analysis of the data. I had volunteered at the school in the spring prior to the start of my data collection, so I had met many Morningside teachers and staff. Although I worked primarily with students in a fifth-grade classroom, I had a regular presence at the school and attended several school events. When I decided to conduct a research project on parental engagement at Morningside, my presence was well received by the principal and staff because of the relationship I had established with the school community. In addition, my prior experience as an elementary school teacher and the fact that I was willing to help out regularly in classrooms meant that I would be able to "give back" to the school in an immediate and tangible way.

During the year of intensive data collection at Morningside, I juggled multiple roles in multiple contexts and social groupings. Working as a teacher's aide each day enabled me to build relationships with teachers and staff and have many conversations over an extended period of time about the school's history and culture, as well as the staff's perspectives on parental engagement at the school. My relationships with teachers and staff and my work in the classroom, however, may have affected the extent to which some parents felt comfortable sharing their experiences and views with me. To account for this, I emphasized my role as a volunteer rather than as a member of the staff. At an event for prospective parents, for example, I declined when a teacher asked me if I'd like to wear an "I'm proud to be a Morningside teacher" sticker. Similarly, despite the fact that I had previous experience as a classroom teacher, I made a concerted effort to avoid situations involving the discipline of students that might negatively affect my relationship with parents. I was never "in charge" of classes, and I engaged in the types of activities that were common to the work of parent helpers.

In my interactions with and observations of parents, I worked to avoid affiliating myself with one particular social group or perspective on a school-related issue. In my field notes, I recorded where and with whom I sat at school events or meetings, and I tried not to establish a particular pattern of interaction or sit by the same person or group (e.g., teachers, parents of a particular grade of students) each time. I also attended a range of meetings and events to get to know a variety of families. Despite these efforts, however, my regular attendance at MPTO meetings and the decision I made to regularly attend Diversity Committee meetings (rather than other event-planning committees, for example) may have shaped how others saw me at the school, as parents may have affiliated me with the leaders and members of these groups.

Intersecting with my participation at the school, my status as a youngish, African American and white, middle-class woman with no children (at the time) undoubtedly influenced the research process. Not only did my subjectivity influence my research questions and design, but it also shaped my interactions with participants. As a mixed-race woman who people often assume to be white, my perceived racial identity gave me access to conversations about race with white parents who might not have been as candid with me had I been more racially identifiable as an African American. I did not intentionally conceal my racial background, however, and shared it openly in many instances, such as in Diversity Committee meetings when group members were asked their racial backgrounds. I believe that several mixed-race parents and African American parents and staff members who knew my racial background were more forthcoming in conversations with me than they might have been otherwise. When I first e-mailed a middle-class African American prospective parent and asked if he'd be willing to be interviewed, for example, he declined, saying that he didn't like my university and felt that it wasn't "oriented to issues that are important to the black community." When I responded to his e-mail by telling him that I was a mixed-race, black and white graduate student and was interested in the experiences of black families seeking out the school for their children, however, he agreed to be interviewed, writing, "Okay, sister, I'll do what I can to help you." My race and the ways in which participants perceived me shaped our interactions and played a role in the types of information they divulged.

My position as a middle-class woman and as a graduate student also affected my interactions with participants. With many middle- and upper-middle-class parents, my status as a doctoral student was a source of connection, as parents shared about their own experiences in getting a master's degree or a doctorate. My class and educational background also undoubtedly played a role in my conversations and interviews with low-income and working-class parents, yet I sought to "de-professionalize" our interactions as much as possible by interviewing parents in their homes or other places of their choosing and by conducting interviews that were semistructured rather than extremely formal.

Throughout the research process and in writing this book, I faced the challenge of how best to both understand and convey the politics of middle-class parental engagement in urban public schooling. During the course of my study, I both identified with and was critical of middle-class parents. As a middle-class "newcomer" living in a demographically shifting neighborhood similar to that of Frazier Park, I was in many ways a part of the urban change processes that I was examining, as the presence of people like me contributed to rising property values and rents. I also empathized with those middle- and upper-middle-class parents who sought to support and strengthen public schools like Morningside through their fund-raising and volunteerism, hoping to benefit the collective student body while also ensuring that their children received the best education possible. At the same time, I was concerned about issues of equity and how the changes at Morningside and in the surrounding area might affect low-income students and their families. I recognized that my seemingly benign or well-intentioned choices—of where to live and where to educate my future children, for example—could contribute to a larger system of inequality.

The tensions I felt throughout the research process and my own subjectivity as a researcher complicated an already-complex study. The different roles I had at the school and the multiple social groups I interacted with—as well as the different ways people may have perceived me—did not make anything simple or straightforward. Yet I believe that these circumstances were also assets with respect both to the types of data I was able to collect and to my analysis of these data. Ultimately, this flexibility enabled me to conduct a study of parental engagement and the politics of change that I hope highlights the tensions, challenges, and possibilities that the movement of the middle class into urban public schools engenders.

Data Analysis

Although a large portion of my analysis occurred once data collection was completed, I began data analysis in the data collection stage of the research and it was ongoing throughout the project. I began my analysis with inductive coding using a grounded-theory strategy, later recoding as clear categories emerged. As my analysis progressed, I moved from descriptive to analytical categories (Miles and Huberman 1994), coding both for emic concepts and categories (e.g., a "critical mass" of parents) and for those concepts that derived from my theoretical framework (e.g., social and cultural capital). Secondary sources (e.g., listserv postings and school documents) were coded by hand, whereas interviews and field notes were coded using qualitative data software (Hyperresearch). Prospective-parent survey results were compiled and tabulated by hand, and responses were not disaggregated, given the small sample size ($n = 29$) and relative racial and socioeconomic homogeneity of the population. The Morningside parent/caregiver surveys were compiled and tabulated using an online survey tool (www.survey monkey.com), with results disaggregated by parents' race, grade of oldest child, and total household income in order to look for potential patterns based on these groupings. Throughout the stages of data analysis I wrote analytical memos to explore the themes, "puzzles," or trends that emerged, which helped me to critically reflect on and conceptually organize the data. During both the year of data collection and the year following, I also met regularly with my academic adviser and participated in a monthly research group with several of my colleagues, enabling me to receive feedback on my emerging hypotheses and interpretation of the data.

To address issues of validity, interviews were recorded and transcribed, and field notes were typed up the day they were taken. I also used triangulation in my interpretation and analysis of the data, comparing multiple sources of data (e.g., interviews, field notes, archival documents) related to the same phenomenon (Hammersley and Atkinson 1986). In interviews and in my frequent interactions with participants over the course of the school year, I was able to explore how different members of the school community interpreted the same event or phenomenon. I was able to compare these interpretations with my field notes and any written materials I collected. In analyzing MPTO meetings focused on the budget or changes in the leadership structure, for example, I was able to compare multiple sources of data—my field notes, interviews with parents and teachers who attended the meeting, and written materials collected from the meeting. Because my research was conducted over an extended period of time, I was able to use subsequent interviews and observations to further explore the themes that were emerging in initial coding.

Limitations

As with any research project, my study included several limitations. First, the views and engagement of parents who had a regular presence at the school are overrepresented in my study. During data collection I intentionally sought to solicit the perspectives of parents whom I did not see regularly in MPTO meetings or on school grounds. I stayed after school and met parents who picked their children up from the after-school program several hours after school let out, for example, and I distributed a parent/caregiver survey to all Morningside families. I had conversations with parents in the neighborhood, and I used purposeful sampling to identify additional parents to interview on the recommendation of some of my participants. Although the views of parents who were not "regulars" at the school are represented in some of my interviews, field notes, and survey responses, my observations and interviews are largely focused on the engagement of parents who had a regular or semiregular physical presence at the school. This makes sense, given my focus on the ways in which middle- and upper-middle-class parental engagement mitigates or exacerbates race and class inequalities in education. Members of the MPTO and other parents who had a regular presence at the school played an influential role in shaping school practices, policies, and opportunities affecting all students; thus, my study is largely focused on the actions and implications of these individuals. In understanding parents' views of the demographic changes at the school, however, my study would have benefited from a greater representation of the perspectives of parents who did not have a regular physical presence at the school. Similarly, statistics on and interviews with parents who were not able to enroll their child at Morningside would have strengthened my ability to assess the implications of the demographic changes in regards to educational equity. Although I attempted to get statistics on the racial and socioeconomic profile of families who were not assigned to Morningside despite their preference for the school, this information was unavailable from the district. My data include anecdotal accounts from several Morningside staff members and parents about families who did not get in, but this is an area for future research.

Second, although I sought to solicit participation from as many parents as possible, Morningside parent/caregiver survey results were ultimately based upon a limited sample (39 percent participation rate) and did not fully reflect the demographics of the student population. Thus, my ability to draw conclusions about differences due to parents' race, socioeconomic status, and oldest grade of child was limited.

And lastly, the findings of any qualitative research project using ethnographic methods are ultimately an interpretation of the views and actions of participants, filtered through the lens of the researcher's understanding (Merriam 1998). My beliefs, previous experiences, and positionality as a researcher influenced each stage of the research process and the interpretation and presentation of my data. Throughout the research process, however, I sought to be better aware of and account for my own subjectivity through (a) regular written reflections, (b) notes in my field notes and at the end of interview transcripts describing my role within a particular setting and how I may have shaped participants' actions and responses, and (c) the sharing of several pieces of raw data and my preliminary analyses of these data with advisers and colleagues to obtain alternative explanations and further explore the ways in which my own subjectivity may have influenced my interpretation of the data. As Lewis (2003, 9) points out, however, the subjectivity of a researcher can have positive implications for a study as well. I believe that my experiences as a public school teacher, a scholar of urban education, and a mixed-race woman provided me with both access to and insight into the research process that someone differently situated might not have had.

NOTES

1. I use pseudonyms for all people and places throughout the book. Some identifying characteristics may have also been slightly changed or omitted in order to protect the anonymity of individuals and specific locations. When doing so, however, I did not significantly change the subjectivity of individuals or the major characteristics of a particular location or place.

2. Title I of the Elementary and Secondary Education Act of 1965 provides financial assistance to schools serving low-income student populations. Schools are eligible for federal Title I Schoolwide Program funding when at least 40 percent of the students in the school (or attendance area) are designated as low income on the basis of free or reduced-price lunch counts or census, Temporary Assistance for Needy Families, or Medicaid data.

3. Throughout I use "parent" in reference to biological and nonbiological caregivers and guardians.

4. Parental engagement here refers to a dynamic and interactive process that is defined not simply by what parents *do* to support the educational experiences of their children but includes their relationships within the context in which engagement takes place (Calabrese Barton et al. 2004). My focus on parental engagement thus explores the intersections of parents' practices and actions to influence their children's education, the relationships that parents have with other members of the school community, and the particular contexts in which the parents operate.

5. I use "urban schools" throughout the book in reference to public schools that are a part of large districts located in densely populated cities or districts that span a metropolitan area.

6. In a 2012 national opinion poll conducted by the Pew Research Center, for example, 46 percent of American adults making more than $100,000 defined themselves as middle class, yet their income puts them in the top 20 percent of earners. The poll also found that similar percentages of whites (51 percent), blacks (48 percent), and Hispanics (47 percent) say they are middle class, despite census data showing that whites as a group have a higher median income and greater amounts of wealth than blacks or Hispanics (see www.pewsocialtrends.org/2012/08/22/the-lost-decade-of -the-middle-class/1/).

7. This is with the recognition that the socioeconomic position of families is not fixed,

particularly given rising economic inequality and economic shifts. Toward the end of the research period (2008), for example, housing prices began to steadily decline in many of the neighborhoods surrounding Morningside as the nation experienced an economic downturn. My classification of families is thus based on one snapshot of their economic situation. Parents' income and material wealth were not my sole concern in examining social class, however, as I was also interested in the ways in which parents used their social and cultural capital to benefit their children and the broader school community. Thus, although professional parents' income may drop because of a recent job loss, their status, social networks, and practices may nevertheless place them in an elevated social position compared with that of other parents within the school community.

8. For research on race and racial inequality in US public education, see, e.g., Howard 2010; Lareau and Horvat 1999; Lee 2005; Lewis 2003; Pollack 2005.

9. See, e.g., Billingham and Kimelberg 2013; Butler, Hamnett, and Ramsden 2013; Butler and Robson 2003; Cucchiara 2013b; Cucchiara and Horvat 2009; Hankins 2007; Karsten 2003; Posey 2012; Raveaud and van Zanten 2007; Reay et al. 2008; Stillman 2012; van Zanten 2003.

10. Butler, Hamnett, and Ramsden 2013 is an exception here, as the authors show how neighborhood gentrification can also result in exclusionary practices in schooling. In their study of white middle-class parents in a recently gentrified neighborhood in East London, the authors found that the new middle-class parents displaced poor students as well as less-affluent middle-class children from the popular schools in the area. This was based upon parents' ability to make strategic residential and school choice decisions that gave them preference in enrollment on the basis of "distance to school" criteria. My research builds upon this work by demonstrating how processes of exclusion may occur *within* school settings and how middle-class parents—through both their individual choices *and* collective engagement and volunteerism—may contribute to exclusionary displacement in city public schooling. Whereas Butler, Hamnett, and Ramsden (2013) treat exclusionary displacement in education as an extension of neighborhood gentrification, I posit that although "school gentrification" is related to neighborhood gentrification, it is a unique process.

11. Cucchiara 2013b is an exception here.

CHAPTER TWO

1. Despite the increase in the number of students of color in suburban districts overall, there has been only a modest increase in the racial and ethnic diversity of student populations at the level of individual suburban schools (Fry 2009), pointing to new patterns of segregation developing in suburban areas.

2. These views were reflected by the plaintiffs in the *Parents Involved in Community Schools v. Seattle School District* and *Meredith v. Jefferson County Board of Education* Supreme Court cases, which focused on the use of race in K–12 student assignment. They were also reflected in *Fisher v. The University of Texas*, a Supreme Court case focused on the use of race in college and university admissions.

3. Some studies have shown that not all forms of middle-class parental engagement are viewed as desirable by teachers and staff, however, as teachers prefer supportive (rather than confrontational or "helicopter") parents (Lareau 2000; Lewis and Forman 2002; McGrath and Kuriloff 1999).

4. American Indian and Alaska Native students represented less than 1 percent of the district population.

5. The demographic data included in this chapter are taken from the California Department of Education's Educational Demographics Unit / DataQuest (data1.cde .ca.gov/Dataquest). The statistics reported on DataQuest are close but not identical to those reported by the Common Core of Data (CCD) Program of the US Department of Education's National Center for Education Statistics. The CCD makes a distinction between the number of students eligible for free lunches and those eligible for reduced-price lunches, for example, whereas DataQuest groups these together under a "socioeconomically disadvantaged" category. Despite the different labels used, the total number of students qualifying either for free or reduced-price lunches or as socioeconomically disadvantaged was the same across the two data sets, as were student racial/ethnic demographics. I draw from data reported by the California Department of Education, given the general consistency across the CCD and California Department of Education data sets and the fact that DataQuest is commonly used by principals and administrators in Woodbury Unified School District.

6. In their study of the effects of interdistrict choice, Richards, Stroub, and Holme (2012) found that "students in 94.5 percent of failing schools have no meaningful access to higher-performing schools, because other schools in the district either don't perform better or have no capacity for transfers" (Kahlenberg 2012, 15).

7. District committee meeting minutes, February 1, 2008.

8. ZIP code data are from city-data.com. Information on Glenbrook housing was obtained from flyers and electronic real estate listings that I collected from properties for sale in 2006 and 2007.

9. Information on median incomes and college attainment is based on the 1990 and 2000 censuses. Home value statistics were taken from www.dataquick.com.

10. Statistics provided by the school district.

CHAPTER THREE

1. Between 2001 and 2006, Morningside maintained a Similar Schools Rank of 10, meaning that its Academic Performance Index scores were in the highest 10 percent of all schools in the state with similar demographics (from School Accountability Report Card data collected from the California Department of Education). Its African American students have consistently exceeded the minimum requirements for subgroup performance under No Child Left Behind. The percentage of students qualifying for free or reduced-price lunches ranged from 40 to 60 percent in the period from 2000 to 2006.

2. This is based on observations at events for prospective parents, as well as an anonymous survey of parents attending Morningside's Open House for prospective parents (see appendix B). Of the twenty-nine parents who completed the survey, twenty-two were white, two were African American, two were Asian American, one was Hispanic/Latino, and two were Hispanic/Latino and white. Twenty-seven of the twenty-nine respondents stated that they had a bachelor's degree or higher, with twelve holding a master's or professional degree. The total annual family income of the majority of respondents was over $100,000 (with eighteen out of twenty-nine respondents, or 62 percent, selecting $100,001 or above). Although statistics on every parent seeking to enroll his or her child in the school were unavailable, the de-

mographics of the parents who participated in this survey, as well as my interviews and observations at events, confirm what many Morningside teachers and parents described as a growing number of middle- and upper middle-class parents showing interest in the school.

3. This information was provided by the Woodbury Unified School District's Research and Assessment Office. According to district and school staff, however, several spots for nonneighborhood families commonly became available before the start of the school year because some neighborhood parents chose other schooling options (e.g., private and charter schools) for their children.

4. This is a somewhat amorphous category, but according to my own observations as a kindergarten volunteer and my conversations with teachers, there were a number of children from mixed-race families (mostly Asian-white or Latino-white) in kindergarten as well as a greater number of white students than that reflected in the California Department of Education numbers (only one white student out of fifty-five kindergartners was reported).

5. The use of free and reduced-price lunch counts as a proxy for the number of socioeconomically disadvantaged students in a school has several limitations. First, the measure does not take into account the significant variation in economic circumstances of children who participate in this program (e.g., homeless students, multigenerational poverty versus recent economic hardship, parents' education level). Second, the measure does not take into account regional variations in the cost of living, which may have a major impact on the well-being and economic situation of families. Third, research has shown that as many as 20 percent of students may be incorrectly certified as eligible or ineligible. See Harwell and LeBeau 2010 for a more extensive discussion of the limitations of using participation in the free/reduced-price lunch program as a measure of socioeconomic status in educational research.

CHAPTER FOUR

1. For United States–based research, see, e.g., Billingham and Kimelberg 2013; Cucchiara 2013b; Cucchiara and Horvat 2009; Edelberg and Kurland 2011; Hankins 2007; Petrilli 2012; Stillman 2012; Roda and Wells 2013. For research on white middle-class parents and urban public schooling in Europe, see Butler, Hamnett, and Ramsden 2013; Butler and Robson 2003; Karsten 2003; Raveaud and van Zanten 2007; Reay et al. 2008, 2007; van Zanten 2003. This emergent research is almost entirely focused on the perspectives and choices of the white middle class, leaving gaps in our understanding of how school staff and working-class families understand, experience, and evaluate their own school communities. Cucchiara 2013b and Reay 2004 are exceptions.

2. California Department of Education, DataQuest.

3. Respondents were instructed to fill out one survey per household.

4. This information was obtained from my prospective-parent survey and from the demographic sheets that parents completed in interviews (see appendix B). Survey questions are available upon request.

5. South Woodbury is a predominantly African American, low-income area of the city.

CHAPTER FIVE

1. Proposition 13, passed in 1978, capped, with a few exceptions, property tax rates at 1 percent of full cash value at the time of acquisition. Prior to Proposition 13, local jurisdictions in California established their own tax rates, and the total property tax

rate was the composite of the individual rates, with few limitations (www.california taxdata.com/pdf/Prop13.pdf).

2. Sociological literature on work and occupations associates professionalization with characteristics such as rigorous training, participation in a professional organization, authority, compensation, and prestige (see Ingersoll and Merrill 2011 for a discussion of these concepts in relation to teaching as a profession). Although a great deal of research and popular debate over the last two decades has focused on issues related to the professionalization of teaching, few studies have explored this concept in relation to parent-teacher organizations or parent volunteerism in public schooling more broadly. In this chapter I focus on the professionalization of a parent-teacher organization, describing a phenomenon characterized by shifts in the structure and routines of the organization, the funds parents raised, and the status associated with parents' collective engagement at the school.

3. Those parents who volunteered at the school may have been more inclined to take the survey. The survey had a 39 percent response rate, with 111 parents completing the survey (see appendix B).

4. Field notes, August 29, 2007.

CHAPTER SIX

1. Information obtained from the 2009 budget report of the Woodbury Unified School District.

2. Information obtained from e-mail correspondence with the District Student Assignment Office administrator.

3. The manner in which race and ethnicity data were collected in California public schools changed in 2009/10 to be consistent with federal reporting requirements. Whereas previously Hispanic/Latino was listed as a racial category, in 2009/10 it was collected as a question about a student's ethnicity, separate from race. This may account for the increase in the Hispanic/Latino category, as it now includes students of any race. Similarly, some parents who may have classified their child's race as Hispanic/Latino in the past may have marked their child's race as white under the new reporting system, thus contributing to the higher percentage of white students as a whole.

4. Although no quantitative data were available on the racial backgrounds of students marking "multiple/no response," interviews with teachers and parents suggest that Asian-white and Latino-white students compose the majority of mixed-race students in this category. My interview data with teachers and parents and observations of the school population also suggest that there may be a number of white students who fall into the "no response" category. For the 2009/10 school year, the category was disaggregated and reported in the California Department of Education database (DataQuest) as "two or more races, not Hispanic" and "not reported." To retain comparability across all years, I have grouped the two categories together for the 2009/10 school year.

5. California Department of Education data on students classified as socioeconomically disadvantaged were not disaggregated by grade level prior to the 2007/8 school year, thus making it difficult to quantitatively compare differences in grade level before 2007.

6. I excluded the "not reported" category because there was only one student in this category.

7. Information obtained from a handout distributed at a 2010 public meeting on the district's budget shortfall.

8. A 2011 study of 1,800 Jefferson County (Kentucky) parents, for example, revealed that while 91 percent of parents said their children benefit from diverse schools, 79 percent said their children should be able to attend the nearest school, even if it increases segregation (see gseis.ucla.edu/news-events/press-releases/press-clips/90 -percent-of-jcps-parents-favor-diverse-schools-survey-says).

CHAPTER SEVEN

1. Information obtained from DataQuest, California Department of Education.
2. See www.policylink.org/site/pp.aspx?section=Overview&c=lkIXLbMNJrE&b=5136575 for more details and information about PolicyLink's Equitable Development Toolkit.
3. Cucchiara 2013b and Sieber 1982 are exceptions here.
4. The School Attendance Boundary Information System (SABINS), housed at the Minnesota Population Center, is an example of efforts to map the demographic data of neighborhoods with school attendance boundary information.
5. "Controlled-choice" plans generally require the percentage of students eligible for free or reduced-price lunches in each school to fall within a small range of the district average. These plans are intended to accommodate parents' school preferences while also taking into account factors such as students' socioeconomic status, English-language learner status, special-education status, gender, siblings, and residence when assigning students to district schools (see, e.g., Grant 2009; Kahlenberg 2006, 2012). Although proponents of racial integration programs rightly point out that student assignment based on socioeconomic status alone does not ensure racial diversity (Orfield and Frankenberg 2013), the 2007 Supreme Court ruling that race-conscious student assignment plans are unconstitutional significantly constrains the ability of districts to promote and maintain racially integrated schools. For a discussion of the implications of the Court's ruling, see Wells and Frankenberg 2007.
6. The state of California has devoted billions of dollars to massively expand its prison system, despite a steady decline in crime rates (Gilmore 2007). A greater investment in public education, rather than the criminal justice system, would be a proactive measure to improve the lives of millions of children in the state.
7. See the Portland Schools Foundation, http://www.thinkschools.org/local-school -foundations/faq/.
8. To be clear, the type of parent organizing I'm describing here is distinct from the efforts of some educational-reform organizations to mobilize parents in efforts to widely expand charter school options in districts and weaken the power of teacher unions (Hess and Lautzenheiser 2012; McGuinn and Kelly 2012). While there are many traditional public schools that need improvement, I am not convinced that market-based solutions and punitive accountability measures are a panacea for the issues plaguing our public education system. Despite their faults, our public schools remain the only institutions of learning required to serve *all* children regardless of their social class, race, and academic abilities. Rather, the mobilization of "parent power" that I'm advocating aims to support and improve, rather than dismantle, traditional public schools.

APPENDIX A

1. I made two exceptions regarding inclusion in this category. One exception was a parent who had an associate's degree and her partner had some college, but they had a total household income of $75,000–$100,000 for a family of three. Given

the managerial authority she had in her job and the fact that the area median income for a family of her size was $75,400 in 2006, I classified her as middle class. Similarly, one parent was a small-business owner and a homeowner in the school's enrollment zone (where the median home value for 2006 was $600,000), and thus I classified him as middle class despite the fact that he had not completed college coursework for a degree.

2. To qualify for the free/reduced-price lunch program in the 2006/7 school year, parents' income had to be below 185 percent of the federal poverty level, which translated to $37,000 for a family of four according to the US Department of Agriculture.

APPENDIX B

1. Although I was regularly engaged with the school community during this time, data collection did not begin until the beginning of the 2006/7 school year.
2. Six of the interviews included two parents.
3. The exact number of attendees was not recorded by the school, but I observed approximately forty to forty-five parents in attendance.
4. Classroom teachers identified Spanish-speaking families.
5. The types of information I was interested in obtaining from the survey did not require multivariate analyses or modeling and thus did not necessitate use of a more specialized program such as SPSS.

REFERENCES

Anderson, Elizabeth. 2010. *The Imperative of Integration*. Princeton, NJ: Princeton University Press.

"Annual Report of the White House Task Force on the Middle Class." 2010. www.whitehouse.gov/sites/default/files/microsites/100226-annual-report-middle-class.pdf.

Anyon, Jean. 1997. *Ghetto Schooling: A Political Economy of Urban Educational Reform*. New York: Teachers College Press.

———. 2005. *Radical Possibilities: Public Policy, Urban Education, and a New Social Movement*. New York: Routledge.

APA and AICP. 2000. *The Millennium Survey: A National Poll of American Voters' Views on Land Use*. Washington, DC: American Planning Association and American Institute of Certified Planners.

Apple, Michael W. 2006. *Educating the "Right" Way: Markets, Standards, God, and Inequality*. 2nd ed. New York: Routledge.

Armario, Christine. 2012. "Elementary School Arts Classes Reduced, Report Says." *Huffington Post*, April 2. www.huffingtonpost.com/2012/04/02/report-arts-classes-at-el_n_1398550.html.

Aron-Dine, Aviva, and Arloc Sherman. 1997. "New CBO Data Show Income Inequality Continues to Widen." Center on Budget and Policy Priorities. www.cbpp.org/cms/?fa=view&id=957.

Ball, Stephen J. 2004. "Performativities and Fabrications in the Education Economy: Towards the Performative Society." In *The RoutledgeFalmer Reader in Sociology of Education*, edited by Stephen J. Ball, 143–55. London: RoutledgeFalmer.

Ball, Stephen, and Carol Vincent. 1998. "'I Heard It on the Grapevine': 'Hot' Knowledge and School Choice." *British Journal of Sociology of Education* 19, no. 3: 377–400.

Barlow, Andrew. 2003. *Between Fear and Hope: Globalization and Race in the United States*. Lanham, MD: Rowman and Littlefield.

Bernstein, Jared, and Karen Kornbluh. 2005. "Running Faster to Stay in Place: The Growth of Family Work Hours and Incomes." *New America Foundation*. newamerica.net/publications/policy/running_faster_to_stay_in_place.

Berrey, Ellen C. 2005. "Divided over Diversity: Political Discourse in a Chicago Neighborhood." *City and Community* 4, no. 2: 143–70.

Bertrand, Marianne, and Sendhil Mullainathan. 2004. "Are Emily and Greg More Employable than Lakisha and Jamal? A Field Experiment on Labor Market Discrimination." NBER Working Paper Series, no. 9873. Cambridge, MA: National Bureau of Economic Research.

Bierbaum, Ariel, Jeffrey Vincent, and Deborah McKoy. 2010. "Linking Transit-Oriented Development, Families, and Schools." *Community Investments* 22, no. 2: 18–45.

Billingham, Chase, and Shelley Kimelberg. 2013. "Middle-Class Parents, Urban Schooling, and the Shift from Consumption to Production of Urban Space." *Sociological Forum* 28, no. 1: 85–108.

Bloomberg, Linda, and Marie Volpe. 2008. *Completing Your Qualitative Dissertation*. Los Angeles: Sage Publications.

Bonilla-Silva, Eduardo. 2004. "From Bi-racial to Tri-racial: Towards a New System of Racial Stratification in the USA." *Ethnic and Racial Studies* 27, no. 6: 931–50.

———. 2006. *Racism without Racists: Color-Blind Racism and the Persistence of Racial Inequality in the United States*. Lanham, MD: Rowman and Littlefield.

Bonilla-Silva, Eduardo, and David Dietrich. 2011. "The Sweet Enchantment of Color-Blind Racism in Obamerica." *Annals of the American Academy of Political and Social Science* 634, no. 1: 190–206.

Bourdieu, Pierre. 1977a. "Cultural Reproduction and Social Reproduction." In *Power and Ideology in Education*, edited by Jerome Karabel and A. H. Halsey, 56–68. New York: Oxford University Press.

———. 1977b. *Outline of a Theory of Practice*. New York: Cambridge University Press.

———. 1984. *Distinction: A Social Critique of the Judgment of Taste*. Cambridge, MA: Harvard University Press.

———. 1985. "The Forms of Capital." In *Handbook of Theory and Research for the Sociology of Education*, edited by J. G. Richardson, 241–58. New York: Greenwood.

———. 1990. *In Other Words: Essays towards a Reflexive Sociology*. Cambridge: Polity Press.

Bourdieu, Pierre, and John C. Passeron. 1977. *Reproduction in Education, Society, and Culture*. Thousand Oaks, CA: Sage Publications.

Boyd, Michelle. 2005. "The Downside of Racial Uplift: The Meaning of Gentrification in an African American Neighborhood." *City and Society* 17, no. 2: 265–88.

Brantlinger, Ellen. 2003. *Dividing Classes: How the Middle Class Negotiates and Rationalizes School Advantage*. New York: RoutledgeFalmer.

Briggs, Xavier De Souza, ed. 2005. *The Geography of Opportunity: Race and Housing Choice in Metropolitan America*. Washington, DC: Brookings Institution Press.

Brown-Saracino, Japonica, ed. 2010. *The Gentrification Debates*. New York: Routledge.

Bryant, Jeff. 2011. "Starving America's Public Schools: How Budget Cuts and Policy Mandates Are Hurting Our Nation's Students." Campaign for America's Future and National Education Association. www.ourfuture.org/report/2011104111/starving-americas-public-schools.

Buckley, Jack, and Mark Schneider. 2009. *Charter Schools: Hope or Hype?* Princeton, NJ: Princeton University Press.

Burke, Lindsey. 2009. "School Choice in America 2009: What It Means for Children's Futures." *Heritage Foundation*, no. 2332: 1–22.

Butler, Tim, Chris Hamnett, and Mark Ramsden. 2013. "Gentrification, Education, and Exclusionary Displacement in East London." *International Journal of Urban and Regional Research* 37, no. 2: 556–75.

Butler, Tim, and Garry Robson. 2003. "Plotting the Middle-Classes: Gentrification and Circuits of Education in London." *Housing Studies* 18:5–28.

Calabrese Barton, Angela, Corey Drake, Jose Gustavo Perez, Kathleen St. Louis, and

Magnia George. 2004. "Ecologies of Parental Engagement in Urban Education." *Educational Researcher* 33, no. 4: 3–12.

Caldas, Stephen, and Carl Bankston. 2005. *Forced to Fail: The Paradox of School Desegregation*. Westport, CT: Praeger.

California Budget Project. 2011. "California's Public Schools Have Experienced Deep Cuts in Funding since 2007–08." June 7. www.cbp.org/pdfs/2011/110607_K12_Cuts_by_District.pdf.

California Department of Education. 2010. "State Schools Chief Jack O'Connell Releases School District Budget Cuts Survey Results." California Department of Education, Sacramento. www.cde.ca.gov/nr/ne/yr10/yr10rel71.asp.

Calvert, Kyla. 2011. "Parents Try to Fill Funding Void at Some San Diego Schools." September 29. www.kpbs.org/news/2011/sep/29/parents-try-fill-funding-void-some-san-diego-school/.

Campbell, Leslie K. 2008. "Planning to Leave Town Because of the Schools? This Parent Didn't, and Couldn't Be Happier." *San Francisco Chronicle*, September 5. www.sfgate.com/cgi-bin/article.cgi?file=/g/a/2008/09/05/lessonplan.DTL.

Carter, Prudence. 2009. "Equity and Empathy: Toward Racial and Educational Achievement in the Obama Era." *Harvard Educational Review* 70, no. 2: 287–97.

Cashin, Sheryll. 2004. *The Failures of Integration: How Race and Class Are Undermining the American Dream*. New York: Public Affairs.

CEOs for Cities. n.d. "City Talent: Keeping Young Professionals (and Their Kids) in Cities." Chicago. Accessed June 18, 2013. http://miplace.org/sites/default/files/CEOsFor Cities_KidsInCities.pdf.

Charles, Camille Zubrinsky. 2005. "Can We Live Together? Racial Preferences and Neighborhood Outcomes." In *The Geography of Opportunity: Race and Housing Choice in Metropolitan America*, edited by X. Briggs, 45–80. Washington, DC: Brookings Institution Press.

Chubb, John, and Terry Moe. 1990. *Politics, Markets, and America's Schools*. Washington, DC: Brookings Institution Press.

Cohen, Arie, and Deborah Court. 2003. "Ethnography and Case Study: A Comparative Analysis." *Academic Exchange Quarterly*. goliath.ecnext.com/coms2/gi_0199-1241785/ Ethnography-and-case-study-a.html.

Conley, Dalton. 2009. *Being Black, Living in the Red: Race, Wealth, and Social Policy in America*. 2nd ed. Berkeley and Los Angeles: University of California Press.

Cooper, Camille Wilson. 2009. "Parent Involvement, African American Mothers, and the Politics of Educational Care." *Equity and Excellence in Education* 42, no. 4: 379–94.

Cucchiara, Maia B. 2013a. "'Are We Doing Damage?' Choosing an Urban Public School in an Era of Parental Anxiety." *Anthropology and Education Quarterly* 44, no. 1: 75–93.

———. 2013b. *Marketing Schools, Marketing Cities: Who Wins and Who Loses When Schools Become Urban Amenities*. Chicago: University of Chicago Press.

Cucchiara, Maia B., and Erin M. Horvat. 2009. "Perils and Promises: Middle-Class Parental Involvement in Urban Schools." *American Educational Research Journal* 46, no. 4: 974–1004.

Darling-Hammond, Linda. 2010. *The Flat World and Education: How America's Commitment to Equity Will Determine Our Future*. New York: Teachers College Press.

de la Torre, Marisa, and Julia Gwynne. 2009. "When Schools Close: Effects on Displaced Students in Chicago Public Schools." *Consortium on Chicago School Research, Urban Education Institute*, 1–48.

Deluca, Stephanie, and Peter Rosenblatt. 2010. "Does Moving to Better Neighborhoods Lead to Better Schooling Options? Parental School Choice in an Experimental Housing Voucher Program." *Teachers College Record* 112, no. 5: 1443–91.

Demerath, Peter. 2009. *Producing Success: The Culture of Personal Advancement in an American High School.* Chicago: University of Chicago Press.

DeWitt, Peter. 2012. "Suburban Schools Are Getting the Urban Experience." *Education Week,* January 31. blogs.edweek.org/edweek/finding_common_ground/2012/01/suburban_schools_are_getting_the_urban_experience.html.

Dougherty, Jack, Jeffrey Harrelson, Laura Maloney, Drew Murphy, Russell Smith, Michael Snow, and Diane Zannoni. 2009. "School Choice in Suburbia: Test Scores, Race, and Housing Markets." *American Journal of Education* 115, no. 4: 523–48.

Dyrness, Andrea. 2011. *Mothers United: An Immigrant Struggle for Socially Just Education.* Minneapolis: University of Minnesota Press.

Edelberg, Jacqueline, and Susan Kurland. 2011. *How to Walk to School: Blueprint for a Neighborhood Renaissance.* Lanham, MD: Rowman and Littlefield.

Ehrenhalt, Alan. 2012. *The Great Inversion and the Future of the American City.* New York: Knopf.

Emirbayer, Mustafa, and Victoria Johnson. 2008. "Bourdieu and Organizational Analysis." *Theory and Society* 37:1–44.

England-Nelson, Jordan. 2013. "Budget Cuts Threaten Viability of Top-Notch Music Programs." *Orange County Register,* February 21. www.ocregister.com/articles/school-496787-music-elementary.html.

Fabricant, Michael, and Michelle Fine. 2012. *Charter Schools and the Corporate Makeover of Public Education: What's At Stake?* New York: Teachers College Press.

Feagin, Joe R. 2010. *Racist America: Roots, Current Realities, and Future Reparations.* 2nd ed. New York: Routledge.

Florida, Richard. 2005. *Cities and the Creative Class.* New York: Routledge.

Forman, Tyrone A., Carla Goar, and Amanda E. Lewis. 2002. "Neither Black nor White? An Empirical Test of the Latin Americanization Thesis." *Race and Society* 5, no. 1: 65–85.

Frankenberg, Erica, and Elizabeth Debray. 2011. *Integrating Schools in a Changing Society: New Policies and Legal Options in a Multiracial Generation.* Chapel Hill: University of North Carolina Press.

Frankenberg, Erica, and Gary Orfield, eds. 2012. *The Resegregation of Suburban Schools: A Hidden Crisis in American Education.* Cambridge, MA: Harvard Education Press.

Frey, William. 2004. *The New Great Migration: Black Americans' Return to the South, 1965–2000.* Washington, DC: Brookings Institution Press.

———. 2006. *Diversity Spreads Out: Metropolitan Shifts in Hispanic, Asian, and Black Populations since 2000.* Washington, DC: Brookings Institution Press.

———. 2011. "The New Metro Minority Map: Regional Shifts in Hispanics, Asians, and Blacks from Census 2010." Brookings Institution. August 31. www.brookings.edu/papers/2011/0831_census_race_frey.aspx.

Fry, Richard. 2009. "The Rapid Growth and Changing Complexion of Suburban Public Schools." Pew Research Hispanic Center. March 31. pewhispanic.org/files/reports/105.pdf.

Fuller, Bruce, Richard Elmore, and Gary Orfield. 1996. *Who Chooses? Who Loses? Culture, Institutions, and the Unequal Effects of School Choice.* New York: Teachers College Press.

Gilbert, Dennis. 2008. *The American Class Structure in an Age of Growing Inequality.* Thousand Oaks, CA: Pine Forge Press.

Gilmore, Ruth. 2007. *Golden Gulag: Prisons, Surplus, Crisis, and Opposition in Globalizing California*. Berkeley and Los Angeles: University of California Press.

Goode, Judith. 2001. "'Let's Get Our Act Together'": How Racial Discourses Disrupt Neighborhood Activism." In *The New Poverty Studies: The Ethnography of Power, Politics, and Poverty in the United States*, edited by Judith Goode and Jeff Maskovsky, 364–98. New York: New York University Press.

Graham, Kristen A. 2010. "Parents Work to Rejuvenate a Public School." *Philadelphia Inquirer*, April 14.

Grant, Gerald. 2009. *Hope and Despair in the American City: Why There Are No Bad Schools in Raleigh*. Cambridge, MA: Harvard University Press.

Graue, Elizabeth, and Denise Oen. 2009. "You Just Feed Them with a Long-Handled Spoon: Families Evaluate Their Experiences in a Class Size Reduction Reform." *Educational Policy* 23, no. 5: 1–29.

Grim, Ryan. 2006. "A Line in the Sandbox." *Washington City Paper*, June 16. www.washingtoncitypaper.com/cover/2006/cover0616.html.

Gulson, Kalervo N. 2011. *Education Policy, Space, and the City: Markets and the (In)visibility of Race*. New York: Routledge.

Hackworth, Jason. 2007. *The Neoliberal City: Governance, Ideology, and Development in American Urbanism*. Ithaca, NY: Cornell University Press.

Hammersley, Martyn, and Paul Atkinson. 1986. *Ethnography: Principles in Practice*. New York: Routledge.

Hankins, Katherine B. 2007. "The Final Frontier: Charter Schools as New Community Institutions of Gentrification." *Urban Geography* 28, no. 2: 113–28.

Hartigan, John. 1999. *Racial Situations: Class Predicaments of Whiteness in Detroit*. Princeton, NJ: Princeton University Press.

Harvey, David. 2005. *A Brief History of Neoliberalism*. Oxford: Oxford University Press.

Harwell, Michael, and Brandon LeBeau. 2010. "Student Eligibility for Free Lunch as an SES Measure in Educational Research." *Educational Researcher* 39, no. 2: 120–31.

Hess, Frederick, and Daniel Lautzenheiser. 2012. "Putting the Punch in Parent Power." *American Enterprise Institute for Public Policy Research*, no. 5: 1–7.

Holme, Jennifer. 2002. "Buying Homes, Buying Schools: School Choice and the Social Construction of School Quality." *Harvard Educational Review* 72, no. 2: 177–205.

Horvat, Erin M. 2003. "The Interactive Effects of Race and Class in Educational Research: Theoretical Insights from the Work of Pierre Bourdieu." *Penn GSE Perspectives on Urban Education* 2, no. 1: 1–25.

Horvat, Erin M., Elliot Weininger, and Annette Lareau. 2003. "From Social Ties to Social Capital: Class Differences in the Relations between Schools and Parent Networks." *American Educational Research Journal* 40, no. 2: 319–51.

Howard, Tyrone. 2010. *Why Race and Culture Matter in Schools: Closing the Achievement Gap in America's Classrooms*. New York: Teachers College Press.

Hursh, David. 2007. "Assessing No Child Left Behind and the Rise of Neoliberal Education Policies." *American Educational Research Journal* 44, no. 3: 493–518.

Hyra, Derek. 2008. *The New Urban Renewal: The Economic Transformation of Harlem and Bronzeville*. Chicago: University of Chicago Press.

Ingersoll, Richard M., and Elizabeth Merrill. 2011. "The Status of Teaching as a Profession." In *Schools and Society: A Sociological Approach to Education*, edited by J. Ballantine and J. Spade, 185–89. 4th ed. Thousand Oaks, CA: Pine Forge Press / Sage Publications.

Jan, Tracy. 2006. "School Makeovers, Fueled by the Middle-Class: As Parents Raise Funds, Standards, Some Fear Impact on Diversity." *Boston Globe*, November 26. www.boston

.com/news/education/k_12/articles/2006/11/26/school_makeovers_fueled_by_the _middle_class?mode=PF.

Johnson, Dirk. 1993. "The Middle Class Goes Public." *New York Times*, January 10. query. nytimes.com/gst/fullpage.html?res=9F0CEED71F3CF933A25752C0A965958260.

Johnson, Heather B., and Thomas M. Shapiro. 2003. "Good Neighborhoods, Good Schools: Race and the 'Good Choices' of White Families." In *White Out: The Continuing Significance of Racism*, edited by A. W. Doane and E. Bonilla-Silva, 173–88. New York: Routledge.

Johnson, Nicolas, Phil Oliff, and Erica Williams. 2010. "An Update on State Budget Cuts." Center on Budget and Policy Priorities. August 3. www.cbpp.org/cms/index .cfm?fa=viewandid=1214.

Kahlenberg, Richard. 2001a. *All Together Now: The Case for Economic Integration of the Public Schools*. Washington, DC: Brookings Institution Press.

———. 2001b. "Socioeconomic School Integration." *Poverty and Race* (Poverty and Race Research Action Council) 10, no. 5: 1–4.

———. 2006. "The New Integration." *Educational Leadership* 63, no. 8: 22–26.

———. 2012. *The Future of School Integration: Socioeconomic Diversity as an Education Reform Strategy*. New York: Century Foundation Press.

Karsten, Lia. 2003. "Family Gentrifiers: Challenging the City as a Place Simultaneously to Build a Career and to Raise Children." *Urban Studies* 40, no. 12: 2573–84.

Kennedy, Maureen, and Paul Leonard. 2001. *Dealing with Neighborhood Change: A Primer on Gentrification and Policy Choices*. Washington, DC: Brookings Institution Press.

Kimelberg, Shelley, and Chase Billingham. 2013. "Attitudes towards Diversity and the School Choice Process: Middle-Class Parents in a Segregated Urban Public School District." *Urban Education* 48, no. 2: 198–231.

Kirshner, B., M. Gaertner, and K. Pozzoboni. 2010. "Tracing Transitions: Understanding the Impact of a School Closure on Displaced Students." *Educational Evaluation and Policy Analysis* 32, no. 3: 407–29.

Kirshner, Ben, and Kristen Pozzoboni. 2011. "Student Interpretations of a School Closure: Implications for Student Voice in Equity-Based School Reform." *Teachers College Record* 113, no. 8: 1633–67.

Koskey, Andrea. 2011. "Art Programs in San Francisco Schools Silenced by Budget Trouble." *San Francisco Examiner*, May 13. www.sfexaminer.com/local/2011/05/arts -programs-san-francisco-schools-silenced-budget-trouble.

Koumpilova, Mila. 2011. "Parents Footing Bill for Teachers." *Pioneer Press*, April 15. www .twincities.com/ci_16948492.

Kozol, Jonathan. 1991. *Savage Inequalities*. New York: Crown.

Lacireno-Pacquet, Natalie, Thomas Holyoke, Michele Moser, and Jeffrey Henig. 2002. "Creaming versus Cropping: Charter School Enrollment Practices in Response to Market Incentives." *Education Evaluation and Policy Analysis* 24, no. 2: 145–58.

Lacy, Karyn. 2007. *Blue-Chip Black: Race, Class, and Status in the New Black Middle-Class*. Berkeley and Los Angeles: University of California Press.

Ladson-Billings, Gloria. 2004. "Landing on the Wrong Note: The Price We Paid for *Brown*." *Educational Researcher* 33, no. 7: 3–13.

Lareau, Annette. 1987. "Social Class Differences in Family-School Relationships: The Importance of Cultural Capital." *Sociology of Education* 60:73–85.

———. 2000. *Home Advantage: Social Class and Parental Intervention in Elementary Education*. Lanham, MD: Rowman and Littlefield.

———. 2003. *Unequal Childhoods: Class, Race, and Family Life*. Berkeley and Los Angeles: University of California Press.

Lareau, Annette, and Erin M. Horvat. 1999. "Moments of Social Inclusion and Exclusion: Race, Class, and Cultural Capital in Family-School Relationships." *Sociology of Education* 72:37–53.

Lareau, Annette, and Vanessa Muñoz. 2012. "'You're Not Going to Call the Shots': Structural Conflicts between the Principal and the PTO at a Suburban Public Elementary School." *Sociology of Education* 85, no. 3: 201–18.

Lareau, Annette, and Elliott Weininger. 2003. "Cultural Capital in Educational Research: A Critical Assessment." *Theory and Society* 32, nos. 5–6: 567–606.

Lee, Stacey J. 2005. *Up against Whiteness: Race, School, and Immigrant Youth*. New York: Teachers College Press.

———. 2008. "The Ideological Blackening of Hmong American Youth." In *The Way Class Works: Readings on School, Family, and the Economy*, edited by W. Lois, 305–15. New York: Routledge.

Lees, Loretta, Tom Slater, and Elvin Wyly. 2008. *Gentrification*. New York: Routledge.

Leonardo, Zeus. 2009. *Race, Whiteness, and Education*. New York: Routledge.

Leonardo, Zeus, and Margaret Hunter. 2007. "Imagining the Urban: The Politics of Race, Class, and Schooling." In *International Handbook of Urban Education*, edited by W. T. Pink and G. W. Noblit, 779–802. New York: Springer.

Lewis, Amanda E. 2003. *Race in the Schoolyard: Negotiating the Color Line in Classrooms and Communities*. New Brunswick, NJ: Rutgers University Press.

Lewis, Amanda E., and Tyrone A. Forman. 2002. "Contestation or Collaboration? A Comparative Study of Home-School Relations." *Anthropology and Education Quarterly* 33, no. 1: 60–89.

Lipman, Pauline. 2008. "Mixed-Income Schools and Housing: Advancing the Neoliberal Urban Agenda." *Journal of Education Policy* 23, no. 2: 119–34.

———. 2011. *The New Political Economy of Urban Education: Neoliberalism, Race, and the Right to the City*. New York: Routledge.

Marcuse, Peter. 1986. "Abandonment, Gentrification and Displacement: The Linkages in New York City." In *Gentrification of the City*, edited by N. Smith and P. Williams, 153–77. London: Unwin Hyman.

Maxwell, Joseph. 1996. *Qualitative Research Design: An Interactive Approach*. Thousand Oaks, CA: Sage Publications.

McGhee Hassrick, Elizabeth, and Barbara Schneider. 2009. "Parent Surveillance in Schools: A Question of Social Class." *American Journal of Education* 115:195–225.

McGrath, Daniel, and Peter J. Kuriloff. 1999. "'They're Going to Tear the Doors Off This Place': Upper Middle-Class Parent School Involvement and the Educational Opportunities of Other People's Children." *Educational Policy* 13:603–29.

McGuinn, Patrick J., and Andrew P. Kelly. 2012. "Parent Power: Grass-Roots Activism and K–12 Education Reform." American Enterprise Institute. July 31. www.aei.org/files/2012/07/31/-parent-power-grassroots-activism-and-k12-education-reform_134233335113.pdf.

McKoy, Deborah, Jeffrey Vincent, and Ariel Bierbaum. 2011. "Opportunity-Rich Schools and Sustainable Communities: Seven Steps to Align High-Quality Education with Innovations in City and Metropolitan Planning and Development." Center for Cities and Schools, University of California, Berkeley. http://citiesandschools.berkeley.edu/reports/ccs_wwc_%20report.pdf.

Merriam, Sharan B. 1998. *Qualitative Research and Case Study Application in Education*. San Francisco: Jossey-Bass.

Miles, Matthew, and A. Michael Huberman. 1994. *Qualitative Data Analysis*. Thousand Oaks, CA: Sage Publications.

Noguera, Pedro. 2003. *City Schools and the American Dream: Reclaiming the Promise of Public Education*. New York: Teachers College Press.

———. 2008. *The Trouble with Black Boys . . . and Other Reflections on Race, Equity, and the Future of Public Education*. San Francisco: Jossey-Bass.

Nyden, Phillip W., Michael T. Maly, and John Lukehart. 1997. "The Emergence of Stable, Racially and Ethnically Diverse Urban Communities: A Case Study of Nine U.S. Cities." *Journal of Housing Policy Debate* 8, no. 2: 491–534.

Oakes, Jeannie, and John Rogers. 2006. *Learning Power: Organizing for Education and Justice*. New York: Teachers College Press.

Oliver, Melvin, and Thomas Shapiro. 1995. *Black Wealth / White Wealth: A New Perspective on Racial Inequality*. New York: Routledge.

Olsen, Laurie. 1997. *Made in America: Immigrant Students in Our Public Schools*. New York: New Press.

Orfield, Gary, and Susan Eaton. 1996. *Dismantling Desegregation: The Quiet Reversal of Brown v. Board of Education*. New York: New Press.

Orfield, Gary, and Erica Frankenberg. 2013. *Educational Delusions? Why Choice Can Deepen Inequality and How to Make Schools Fair*. Berkeley and Los Angeles: University of California Press.

Orfield, Gary, Erica Frankenberg, and Liliana Garces. 2008. "Statement of American Social Scientists of Research on School Desegregation to the U.S. Supreme Court in *Parents v. Seattle School District* and *Meredith v. Jefferson County*." *Urban Review* 40:96–136.

Orfield, Gary, John Kucsera, and Genevieve Siegel-Hawley. 2012. "E Pluribus . . . Separation: Deepening Double Segregation for More Students." Civil Rights Project, University of California, Los Angeles. http://civilrightsproject.ucla.edu/research/k-12-education/integration-and-diversity/mlk-national/e-pluribus . . . separation-deepening-double-segregation-for-more-students.pdf.

Orfield, Gary, and Chungmei Lee. 2005. "Why Segregation Matters: Poverty and Educational Inequality." Civil Rights Project, Los Angeles, CA. www.civilrightsproject.ucla.edu/research/deseg/Why_Segreg_Matters.pdf.

Pattillo, Mary E. 2008. "Race, Class, and Neighborhoods." In *Social Class: How Does It Work?*, edited by A. Lareau and D. Conley, 264–93. New York: Russell Sage Foundation.

Pedroni, Thomas C. 2007. *Market Movements: African American Involvement in School Voucher Reform*. New York: Routledge.

Perez Carreon, Gustavo, Corey Drake, and Angela Calabrese Barton. 2005. "The Importance of Presence: Immigrant Parents' School Engagement Experiences." *American Educational Research Journal* 42, no. 3: 465–98.

Petrilli, Michael. 2012. *The Diverse Schools Dilemma: A Parents' Guide to Socioeconomically Mixed Public Schools*. Washington, DC: Thomas B. Fordham Institute.

Piketty, Thomas, and Emmanuel Saez. 2003. "Income Inequality in the United States: 1913–98." *Quarterly Journal of Economics* 118, no. 1: 1–39.

Pollack, Mica. 2005. *Colormute: Race Talk Dilemmas in an American School*. Princeton, NJ: Princeton University Press.

Pope, Denise 2003. *Doing School: How We Are Creating a Generation of Stressed-Out, Materialistic, and Miseducated Students*. New Haven, CT: Yale University Press.

Posey, Linn. 2012. "Middle- and Upper Middle-Class Parent Action for Urban Public Schools: Promise or Paradox?" *Teachers College Record* 114, no. 1: 122–64.

Posey-Maddox, Linn. 2013. "Professionalizing the PTO: Race, Class, and Shifting Norms of Parent Engagement in a City Public School. *American Journal of Education* 119, no. 2: 235–60.

Posey-Maddox, Linn, Shelley Kimelberg, and Maia Cucchiara. 2012. "Gentrification Goes to School: A Three-City Examination of Middle-Class Investment in Urban Public Schools." Paper presented at the American Sociological Association Annual Meeting, Denver, Colorado, August 17–20.

Raveaud, Maroussia, and Agnes van Zanten. 2007. "Choosing the Local School: Middle Class Parents' Values and Social and Ethnic Mix in London and Paris." *Journal of Education Policy* 22, no. 1: 107–24.

Reardon, Sean F., and Lori Rhodes. 2011. "The Effects of Socioeconomic School Integration Policies on Racial School Desegregation." In *Integrating Schools in a Changing Society: New Policies and Legal Options for a Multiracial Generation*, edited by Erica Frankenberg and Elizabeth Debray, 187–207. Chapel Hill: University of North Carolina Press.

Reay, Diane. 2004. "'Mostly Roughs and Toughs': Social Class, Race, and Representation in Inner City Schooling." *Sociology* 38, no. 5: 1005–23.

———. 2007. "Unruly Places: Inner-City Comprehensives, Middle-Class Imaginaries and Working-Class Children." *Urban Studies* 44, no. 7: 1191–201.

Reay, Diane, Gill Crozier, David James, Sumi Hollingsworth, Katya Williams, Fiona Jamieson, and Phoebe Beedell. 2008. "Re-invigorating Democracy? White Middle Class Identities and Comprehensive Schooling." *Sociological Review* 56, no. 2: 238–55.

Reay, Diane, Sumi Hollingsworth, Gill Crozier, Fiona Jamieson, David James, and Phoebe Beedell. 2007. "'A Darker Shade of Pale?' Whiteness, the Middle Classes and Multiethnic Inner City Schooling." *Sociology* 41, no. 6: 1041–60.

Richards, Meredith, Kori Stroub, and Jennifer Jellison Holme. 2012. "Can NCLB Choice Work? Modeling the Effects of Interdistrict Choice on Student Access to Higher-Performing Schools." In *The Future of School Integration: Socioeconomic Diversity as an Education Reform Strategy*, edited by Richard Kahlenberg, 223–57. New York: Century Foundation Press.

Rizvi, Fazal, and Bob Lingard. 2009. *Globalizing Education Policy*. New York: Routledge.

Rockquemore, Kerry Ann, and Patricia Arend. 2002. "Opting for White: Choice, Fluidity and Racial Identity Construction in Post Civil-Rights America." *Race and Society* 5:49–64.

Roda, Allison, and Amy Stuart Wells. 2013. "School Choice Policies and Racial Segregation: Where White Parents' Good Intentions, Anxiety, and Privilege Collide." *American Journal of Education* 119, no. 2: 261–93.

Rogers, Teri K. 2009. "The Sudden Charm of Public School." *New York Times*, April 3. www.nytimes.com/2009/04/05/realestate/05Cov.html.

Ross, Wayne, and Rich Gibson. 2007. *Neoliberalism and Education Reform*. Creskill, NJ: Hampton Press.

Saporito, Salvatore. 2003. "Private Choices, Public Consequences: Magnet School Choice and Segregation by Race and Poverty." *Social Problems* 50, no. 2: 181–203.

Saporito, Salvatore, and Annette Lareau. 1999. "School Selection as a Process: The Multiple Dimensions of Race in Framing Educational Choice." *Social Problems* 46, no. 3: 418–39.

Sassen, Saskia. 2001. *The Global City*. Princeton, NJ: Princeton University Press.

Sawhill, Isabel, and John E. Morton. 2008. "Economic Mobility: Is the American Dream Alive and Well?" Economic Mobility Project. www.economicmobility.org/assets/pdfs/EMP%20American%20Dream%20Report.pdf.

Sayer, Andrew. 2005. *The Moral Significance of Class*. Cambridge: Cambridge University Press.

Schneider, Mark, Paul Teske, and Melissa Marschall. 2002. *Choosing Schools: Consumer Choice and the Quality of American Schools*. Princeton, NJ: Princeton University Press.

Shujaa, Mwalimu. 1992. "Afrocentric Transformation and Parental Choice in African American Independent Schools." *Journal of Negro Education* 61, no. 2: 148–59.

Siddle Walker, Vanessa. 2009. "Second-Class Integration: A Historical Perspective for a Contemporary Agenda." *Harvard Educational Review* 70, no. 2: 269–84.

Sieber, R. Timothy. 1982. "The Politics of Middle-Class Success in an Inner-City Public School." *Journal of Education* 164:30–47.

Smith, Janet L., and David Stovall. 2008. "'Coming Home' to New Homes and New Schools: Critical Race Theory and the New Politics of Containment." *Journal of Education Policy* 23, no. 2: 135–52.

Smith, Russell S. 2009. "Affluent Parents Return to Inner-City Schools for Educational Opportunities." *Edutopia*, August 26. www.edutopia.org/parents-activism-urban-public-schools.

Spencer, Kyle. 2012. "At the PTA, Clashes over Cupcakes and Culture." *New York Times*, March 16. www.nytimes.com/2012/03/18/education/at-the-pta-clashes-over-cupcakes-and-culture.html?_r=1&partner=rss&emc=rss.

Stillman, Jennifer B. 2012. *Gentrification and Schools: The Process of Integration When Whites Reverse Flight*. New York: Palgrave Macmillan.

Swartz, David. 1997. *Culture and Power: The Sociology of Pierre Bourdieu*. Chicago: University of Chicago Press.

Taft, R. 1997. "Ethnographic Research Methods." In *Educational Research, Methodology and Measurement: An International Handbook*, edited by J. P. Keeves, 59–63. 2nd ed. Oxford: Pergamon Press.

Tefera, Adai, Genevieve Siegel-Hawley, and Erica Frankenberg. 2010. "School Integration Efforts Three Years after *Parents Involved*." Civil Rights Project, University of California, Los Angeles. www.civilrightsproject.ucla.edu/legal-developments/court-decisions/school-integration-efforts-three-years-after-parents-involved.

Thernstrom, Abigail, and Stephan Thernstrom. 2003. *No Excuses: Closing the Racial Gap in Learning*. New York: Simon and Schuster.

Thompson, William, and Joseph Hickey. 2005. *Society in Focus*. Boston: Pearson.

Toppo, Greg. 2012. "Urban Middle Class Boosts School Diversity." *USA Today*, November 6. www.usatoday.com/story/news/nation/2012/10/28/schools-seeking-diversity-get-boost-from-urban-middle-class/1661557/.

Turner, M. A., R. Struyk, and J. Yinger. 1991. *The Housing Discrimination Study*. Washington, DC: Urban Institute.

Tyack, David. 1976. "Ways of Seeing: An Essay on the History of Compulsory Schooling." *Harvard Educational Review* 46, no. 3: 355–89.

Tyson, Karolyn. 2011. *Integration Interrupted: Tracking, Black Students, and Acting White after Brown*. New York: Oxford University Press.

Valdes, Guadalupe. 1996. *Con Respeto: Bridging the Distances between Culturally Diverse Families and Schools*. New York: Teachers College Press.

van Zanten, Agnes. 2003. "Middle-Class Parents and Social Mix in Urban Schools: Reproduction and Transformation of Class Relations in Education." *International Studies in Sociology of Education* 13, no. 2: 107–23.

Varady, David P., and Jeffrey A. Raffel. 1995. *Selling Cities: Attracting Homebuyers through Schools and Housing Programs*. Albany: State University of New York Press.

Warren, Mark R., and Karen Mapp. 2011. *A Match on Dry Grass: Community Organizing as a Catalyst for School Reform*. Oxford: Oxford University Press.

Watkins, William H. 2012. *The Assault on Public Education: Confronting the Politics of Corporate School Reform*. New York: Teachers College Press.

Wells, Amy, Jacquelyn Duran, and Terrenda White. 2008. "Refusing to Leave Desegregation Behind: From Graduates of Racially Diverse Schools to the Supreme Court." *Teachers College Record* 110, no. 12: 2532–70.

Wells, Amy Stuart, and Erica Frankenberg. 2007. "The Public Schools and the Challenge of the Supreme Court's Integration Decision." *Phi Delta Kappan* 89, no. 3: 178–88.

Wells, Amy Stuart, Jennifer Jellison Holme, Anita Tijerina Revilla, and Awo Korantemaa Atanda. 2009. *Both Sides Now: The Story of School Desegregation's Graduates*. Berkeley and Los Angeles: University of California Press.

Wells, Amy Stuart, and Irene Serna. 1996. "The Politics of Culture: Understanding Local Political Resistance to Detracking in Racially Mixed Schools." *Harvard Educational Review* 66, no. 1: 93–119.

Wells, Amy Stuart, Julie Slayton, and Janelle Scott. 2002. "Defining Democracy in the Neoliberal Age: Charter School Reform and Educational Consumption." *American Educational Research Journal* 39, no. 2: 337–61.

Welner, Kevin, and Kenneth Howe. 2005. "Steering toward Separation: The Policy and Legal Implications of 'Counseling' Special Education Students Away from Charter Schools." In *School Choice and Diversity: What the Evidence Says*, edited by J. Scott, 93–111. New York: Teachers College Press.

Williams, Joan C., and Heather Boushey. 2010. "The Three Faces of Work-Family Conflict: The Poor, the Professionals, and the Missing Middle." Center for American Progress. January. www.americanprogress.org/issues/2010/01/three_faces_report.html.

Wise, Tim. 2010. *Color-Blind: The Rise of Post-racial Politics and the Retreat from Racial Equity*. San Francisco: City Light Books.

Yin, Robert K. 2009. *Case Study Research: Design and Methods*. 4th ed. Thousand Oaks, CA: Sage Publications.

INDEX